WITHDRAWN

MORE STATELY MANSIONS

Eugene O'Neill

MORE
STATELY
MANSIONS

THE UNEXPURGATED EDITION

———

EDITED BY

Martha Gilman Bower

NEW YORK   OXFORD
OXFORD UNIVERSITY PRESS
1988

Oxford University Press

Oxford   New York   Toronto
Delhi   Bombay   Calcutta   Madras   Karachi
Petaling Jaya   Singapore   Hong Kong   Tokyo
Nairobi   Dar es Salaam   Cape Town
Melbourne   Auckland

and associated companies in
Berlin   Ibadan

Published by Oxford University Press, Inc.,
200 Madison Avenue, New York, New York 10016

Oxford is a registered trademark of Oxford University Press

Library of Congress Cataloging-in-Publication Data
O'Neill, Eugene, 1888–1953.
More stately mansions.
1. Bower, Martha Gilman. II. Title.
PS3529.N5M736   1988   812'.52   88–1467
ISBN 0–19–505364–8

Previously unpublished writings by Eugene O'Neill © 1988,
Collection of American Literature,
Beinecke Rare Book and Manuscript Library,
Yale University.

2 4 6 8 9 7 5 3 1

Printed in the United States of America
on acid-free paper

For Paul

EDITORIAL NOTE

This complete edition of *More Stately Mansions* is based on the typed version of Eugene O'Neill's third longhand draft, finished, according to his *Work Diary,* on January 20, 1939. The latest date typed on the manuscript, however, is December 30, 1938, and there are several earlier dates typed on the script. It appears that Carlotta, his wife, typed material and revisions as O'Neill completed them and dated only certain sections, namely, the ones finished before January 1939. I have included these dates in the text. The typescript is also laced with O'Neill's handwritten revisions in blue ink and deletions made with a blue crayon. Some of these alterations were made after January 1939, at least as late as the fall of 1942. O'Neill made it very clear, as he edited his script, what he wanted added or omitted, and thus it was O'Neill's hand that directed me as I prepared this edition of the play. There were, however, editorial judgments that had to be made en route. I corrected all spelling and punctuation errors and obvious typographical slips. I retained O'Neill's idiosyncratic use of adverbs in stage directions and his unusual use of capital letters, hyphens, and commas except when they were inconsistent and/or blatantly incorrect. When other such inconsistencies occurred, I entered the "correct" choice. For instance, "summerhouse" is spelled both with and without a hyphen and even as two words, so I chose the one-word spelling, which is the correct one for the gazebo-like house in Deborah Hartford's garden. In at least one instance I emended O'Neill's use of archaic spellings ("courtesy" for "curtsy") and retained others (as "wile" and "smoulder"). In a few places I have bracketed words that I had to supply when they were missing from a sentence— words Carlotta failed to type in as she transcribed O'Neill's tiny handwriting. When there was no clue as to the word(s) left out, I suggested probable substitutes and referred to the text in question in a note. In some instances I used "[*sic*]" where O'Neill's syntax seemed unclear, and in one place in act 4, scene 2 I inserted a bracketed space for words left out because the confusion of the syntax did not allow for an editorial suggestion.

There is one page missing from the typescript, which was missing when Carlotta gave it to Yale University. The page is from act 1, scene 1, and contains dialogue that breaks the continuity in the conversation between Nora and Sara. Rather than inventing dialogue to close this gap, I have inserted a note that provides the probable content of the missing lines.

I have kept my annotations of the text to a minimum, for I did not want to disturb the dramatic flow of the dialogue and thereby lessen the reader's enjoyment or understanding of the play. The notes I have included provide an index of historical and cultural references to the period—especially those pertinent to the action of the play—as they occur in the dialogue. Other notes point out similarities in dialogue or circumstance that occur between *More Stately Mansions* and O'Neill's late plays, while still others refer the reader to sources of quotations and factual data referred to in my introduction. I have also provided the meanings of Irish words used by the characters. Employing the aforementioned editorial apparatus, I strove to make this edition as faithful a reproduction of the original typescript as possible. All the transcriptions of O'Neill's handwritten insertions are a reflection of my own best reading of the playwright's words.

Contoocook, N.H.   M.G.B.
January 1988

ACKNOWLEDGMENTS

During the long process of preparing this edition of *More Stately Mansions,* there were many who assisted me along the way. I would like to extend my gratitude to the staff of the Beinecke Rare Book and Manuscript Library at Yale University, especially Rick Hart, and to Patricia Willis and Donald Gallup, the present and past curators, respectively, of the Collection of American Literature. I am deeply grateful to David Schoonover, who was curator of the Collection of American Literature when I was engaged in research on the cycle plays and *More Stately Mansions.* He was extremely cooperative and helpful throughout and assisted me in the logistics of obtaining permission to prepare this edition. I would like to extend my gratitude to the Yale Committee on Literary Property, Office of the General Counsel, and William Stempel, Associate General Counsel, for their part in obtaining permission to publish the original typescript of the play; and to Henry Krawitz, my editor at Oxford Universi y Press. Finally, I am indebted to David Watters for his continued support of me and my work, to Philip Nicoloff for his editorial expertise, and to Robert Hapgood, who has been an ongoing source of encouragement and sound advice during the course of my research on the cycle plays and the preparation of this edition.

Contents

———

MORE STATELY MANSIONS

Introduction

Although Eugene O'Neill's *More Stately Mansions* takes place between 1832 and 1842, there is little doubt that the characters and the action speak to contemporary audiences. It is a play that recalls our industrial past and catches up with our present by depicting America's unique and contradictory personality—a duality that merges innocence with evil, opportunity with greed. Central to the lasting value of *More Stately Mansions* is the American history O'Neill envisioned as drama: real people, living in small towns, neurotic, ambitious, jealous, grasping, accumulating possessions, and playing by the rules of survival. With this play O'Neill pointed the way to a contemporary materialism that both defines our strengths and exposes our weaknesses as a nation. Although composed by O'Neill in the late 1930s, the play strikes at the heart of the competitive and psychological pressures of the 1980s. O'Neill's plot is classic and powerful in its depiction of a bizarre love triangle consisting of mother, son, and wife. He was far ahead of his time in creating two female characters whose heroic stature remains unique in the history of American theater.

Sara Melody Harford is feminine but self-sufficient, strong, aggressive, and ambitious. In his initial description O'Neill gives her "a curious blending . . . of aristocratic and peasant characteristics" and she becomes at once emblematic of a major theme in the play and the embodiment of America's pioneer past and technological present, a woman who has "brains for more than just sleepin' with the man I love an' havin' his children an' keepin' his house." She represents those traits in the Harfords that O'Neill outlined in an interview with journalist Elizabeth Shepley Sergeant: "The family are people with guts. When they feel negative, they burn the building. They are the kind of people who go after success and succeed and fail but never stay fallen."[1] The

---

1. Donald Gallup showed me his copy of the interview and told me it probably took place in August 1945.

most contemporary of O'Neill's women, Sara is an androgynous character who typifies the best and the worst in Americans, men and women who will "never stay fallen" and will continue to build ever more stately mansions.

In his characterization of Deborah Harford, O'Neill had the courage to explore the forbidden regions of an implicit—if not explicit—incestuous mother/son bond, one that reduces Simon Harford to a fawning suppliant who, in the play's final scene, admits to his mother: "I am your Simon and my one longing is to forget she [Sara] is alive." And in the same scene Deborah passionately declares to her son: "Our love can make a heaven, even in hell if we are together—if we are one again!" At the core of the psychological intricacies of this mother/son entanglement are hints of O'Neill's unresolved feelings toward his own mother, Ella O'Neill. Deborah, another O'Neill New Woman, goes beyond *Strange Interlude*'s Nina Leeds in her ability to control and seduce, and she matches Sara's canny materialism with her eloquence and intellect, her astute commentaries on the meaning of life, love, and death.

This complete edition of *More Stately Mansions,* prepared from the original typescript, follows two other versions of the play. The first was the "performing" script shortened by Karl Ragnar Geirow from the same typescript. Directed by Geirow, the play was performed in Stockholm at the Swedish Royal Dramatic Theater in 1962. The other version was edited by Donald Gallup, former curator of the American collection at the Beinecke Library at Yale University. Gallup's "reading" version, published by Yale University Press in 1964, was prepared in accordance with Geirow's abbreviated acting version.[2] According to Gallup's prefatory note to the earlier edition, the script "represents less than half of O'Neill's complete typed script." Both Geirow's and Gal-

---

2. The Geirow version was based on the only extant script of the play, typed by Carlotta from O'Neill's handwritten third longhand draft and revisions of that draft, and completed on January 20, 1939. Jose Quintero directed *More Stately Mansions* (hereafter referred to in the notes as *MSM*) in Los Angeles. The play opened on September 12, 1967, and again in New York on November 11. Quintero retained the first scene of act 1 and the epilogue but shortened the original version to three hours' playing time. Ingrid Bergman and Colleen Dewhurst played the roles of Deborah and Sara, respectively. This version of the play is available on a recording of the New York production (New York: Caedmon Records TRS 331).

lup's shortened editions of the play were welcomed at a time when Carlotta O'Neill was protective of her late husband's unpublished manuscripts and allowed only trusted friends to work with the material. But now, thirty-five years after O'Neill's death and almost a quarter of a century after the 1964 edition, Yale has wisely deemed it appropriate to make the play available in its complete form.

Included in this unabridged version of *More Stately Mansions* are act 1, scene 1, the beginning of act 3, scene 2, and the epilogue. These sections of the play provide not only continuity but also elements that are essential to the development of character, theme, and plot. In addition to the large sections just mentioned, there are hundreds of words, lines, and phrases from other scenes—now included in this edition— that retain O'Neill's poetic diction and his intended dramatic impact, pointing up the nuances of character and scene.

For example, without act 1, scene 1, transitional material that links *A Touch of the Poet* with *More Stately Mansions* and motivates the three main characters in the remainder of the play is lost. As in *A Touch of the Poet,* Maloy and Cregan open the play and once again are the expositional characters who close the four-year gap between the two plays. Cornelius Melody lies dead in an upstairs room as barkeep and barfly rehearse his exploits and his career as an officer in Wellington's army—some of the same history that they relate in *A Touch of the Poet.* It is important to O'Neill that this be repeated, not only because it joins the later play with the previous one but also because it enables audiences to read and view the two plays separately. O'Neill was aware that he might not live to finish the entire cycle.

No less important are Sara's scenes with Cregan and Nora. In her scene with Cregan she reviews Con's nonfunctional retreat from life, and the debts he has amassed. In her scene with Nora we learn that Sara and Simon are going to buy out their partner's share of the mill business and that they are happy, if not rich—a fact that intensifies the effects of the destruction that ensues after they move in with Deborah. Sara also articulates her disappointment in her father, her bitterness over his treatment of her mother, and Con's loss of pride in himself and the vestiges of his patrician past. More important, Sara, although pregnant and the mother of three other children, reaffirms her determination to "rise to the top." Another key element that only becomes evident in the complete version is the renewal of the mother/daughter bond that was apparent at the end of *A Touch of the Poet,* a bond that is placed in sharp contrast to Sara and Deborah's intense rivalry.

In this first scene there is also the reiteration of the theme of acquisition expressed by Deborah in act 2 of *A Touch of the Poet,* when she refers to Sara's kinship to the three Harford sisters: "They would approve of you, I think. They would see that you were strong and ambitious and determined to take what you want." Sara confirms Deborah's observations in the earlier play when she tells Nora that Simon must not sell the land the cabin is on, "for this is America not poverty-stricken Ireland where you're a slave! Here you're free to take what you want, if you have the power in yourself." It is an essential theme, a form of the O'Neillean choric device, that is used to illuminate Sara's ruthless ambitious side—a metaphor for American greed.

In an effort to emphasize the importance of the tension that underlies much of the action, O'Neill highlights the contradictions in Sara's personality that inform her scenes with Cregan and Nora. In an argument with Cregan over her reluctance to pay her father's debts Sara "lapses unconsciously into peasant brogue." Later she reprimands Nora for allowing the women to "keen"[3] at the wake: "It's old ignorant superstition. It belongs back in Ireland, not here!" This speech, like the one cited earlier, is significant in that it shows Sara's determination to free herself from her innate Irishness and to merge with mainstream American culture and society. She is perhaps the only O'Neill character to break through the isolation barrier and diligently compete for the American Dream.[4]

One of the most compelling arguments for the retention of scene 1 again relates to O'Neill's penchant for opposites and contrasts. Act 1, scene 1, provides the only Irish setting and introduces the pervasive

3. The word "keen" comes from the Gaelic *caoinim.* It is an Irish lament for the dead, a dirge with a wailing sound produced by bagpipes.
4. John Raleigh discusses the alienation of the Tyrones and the Irish in general—their inability to meld with mainstream American society—in his essay "O'Neill's *Long Day's Journey into Night* and New England Irish-Catholicism," in *O'Neill: A Collection of Critical Essays,* ed. John Gassner (Englewood Cliffs, N.J.: Prentice-Hall, 1964), pp. 124–41.

theme of aristocrat versus peasant. It is the last time we see the Melodys interacting on their own turf and speaking their native brogue. At the end of the scene O'Neill has Cato, Deborah's black servant, enter with a message for Simon that he meet her alone at the cabin. It is a dramatic moment, one that prepares the audience for the conflicts to come, but it also signals the end of Con Melody's generation of Irish immigrants and the beginning of Sara's peasant intrusion upon Harford patrician territory. Although absent from the scene, the Melody Inn is suffused by Deborah Harford's presence; from now on all contests involving her will take place on Harford ground.

Among hundreds of restored phrases that modify character and add to the impact of O'Neill's poetic language is Deborah's speech in act 1, scene 2, in which she tells Simon that she is the victim of time. The entire speech that begins "While you are still beautiful and life woos you" is now included, together with lines that bring out Deborah's satanic side, the "morbid and diseased" influence described by O'Neill in early notes to the play, lines that provide motivation for her subsequent behavior in the garden. "Time," Deborah says, "lashes your face with wrinkles, or stamps your body into shapelessness or smears it with tallow-fat with malicious fingers. . . ." These lines are representative of many more now included in the script that underline Deborah's twisted imagination and obsession with growing old.

At the heart of this first scene between mother and son is their past life together, their intimacy, their fairy-tale world of kings and queens. But also added to this scene are lines that depict Deborah as more than a dreamer and an obsessed mother. She reads and she thinks. She has taught Simon much of what he knows about love, death, history, philosophy, and life. Deborah tells Simon how she lost her faith in the "Sacred Books," and how Brahma became "nothing at all but a foreign name for Death." Choosing words that Mary Tyrone or O'Neill himself might have used, she explains that her digression into oriental thought was like "the flight of one who, bored at home, blames the surroundings, and sails for far lands, only to find a welcoming figure there to greet one—oneself! . . . And straightaway the exotic palms turn into old familiar elms or maples, the houses are the same old houses, the gardens the same gardens. . . ." And in another burst of poeticism in act 2, scene 1, she explains her existential views to Gadsby by claiming that life is "like an aimless improvisation on a far-off, out of tune piano that tinkles into silence." The omission of these lines and others not only deprives the audience of O'Neill's poetry but erodes the complex structure of character that O'Neill has carefully erected.

In this same scene lines have been restored which show Deborah as being less than patriotic: "I would like to have lived there [in France] when life was free and charming and fastidious, not vulgar and ignoble and greedy as it is in this country today." And, again, in the speech the following significant line has been retained: "I must find someone outside myself in whom I can confide and so escape myself. If I only had a close woman friend. . . ."; this line mimics Mary Tyrone in *Long Day's Journey* and provides another link to O'Neill's past.[5] Also restored are three pages of dialogue that help to explain Deborah's abnormal personality, as well as recollections about her past with her father. Whereas Mary Tyrone loses touch with reality as a result of a morphine addiction, Deborah Harford's madness is innate and complicated. Her long monologues (e.g., the ones in act 2, scene 1) are Shakespearean in their perceptions and demonstrate O'Neill's genius for realizing the delicate balance between madness and brilliance. To omit a word is to upset that balance.

Act 3 of the play has been expanded from nineteen to thirty-two pages. At the beginning of the act, after Joel's exit, Simon has a monologue that is equal in significance and impact to Hickey's long sermons in *The Iceman Cometh,* reflecting a blend of truth and madness. The sixty-one lines deleted from Simon's speech in the Yale edition have been restored. Although laden with typical O'Neill-like repetition, Simon's monologue depicts more graphically and sensationally the full range of his split personality. When he says of Sara that "it has been a long time since I have slept with her—but at home her body has become repugnant, her beauty ugly," and expresses his desire to revenge

---

5. In *Long Day's Journey* (hereafter referred to in the notes as *LDJ*) Mary says, "If there was only some place I could go to get away for a day, or even an afternoon, some woman friend I could talk to—not about anything serious, simply laugh and gossip and forget for a while—someone besides the servants—that stupid Cathleen!" (Eugene O'Neill, *Long Day's Journey into Night* [New Haven: Yale Univ. Press, 1956], p. 46).

the wounds inflicted by both wife and mother, his ambivalent sexuality is fused with O'Neill's own. In fact, the whole monologue appears revelatory of much of O'Neill's most painful private experience.

The second scene of act 3, in which the Harford sons now appear with their grandmother, has been enlarged by approximately two thirds. Several lines are now included that are crucial to an accurate description of the garden—lines that exaggerate the monotonous green of the setting. The presence of the Harford sons allows Deborah to expose her grandmotherly side and adds an extra dimension to her character, injecting a note of sympathy. As she reads Byron to the boys, Deborah asserts her intellectual influence and identifies herself as the major opponent to the peasant Melody strain.

The introduction of the Harford sons in act 3 not only provides a transition between *More Stately Mansions* and subsequent cycle plays, in which each son will play a major role, but also supplies clues to their future behavior inherent in their dialogue and character descriptions. Wolfe doesn't "care what I grow up to be," and Honey wants "to be a gentleman and 'lected President of America." The aristocracy/peasant theme appears again in O'Neill's description of the boys: Jonathan bears a "striking" resemblance to his father, but Honey "takes after his mother's side of the family." The inclusion of their games and optimism temporarily softens the geometric, sterile, monochromatic garden setting. O'Neill interjects a bit of comic relief as the boys color the atmosphere with their laughter and light banter prior to the next scene, in which Deborah, Simon, and Sara engage in a grim confrontation.

In act 4, scene 1, this edition restores many lines that portray Sara as an object of sexual desire. Sara's portrait now includes a description in which she wears clothes that are "designed with the purpose of accentuating her large breasts, her slender waist, her heavy rounded thighs and buttocks, and revealing them as nakedly as the fashion will permit."

Again in act 4, scene 1, there are lines of dialogue which give definition to Sara's role as Simon's "mistress," such as her monologue to the mirror following Joel's exit. The complete monologue, increased by fifty-one lines, reveals the extent to which Sara believes herself a whore and sheds added light on her divided self and the ensuing conflicts contingent upon this split. Her hatred of Deborah is never more apparent, and the speech exposes her as a woman of reason as well as stealth. Not to include the complete monologue is to lose essential clues to her character and drastically distort the tone of the scene. It is here that Sara shows not only her anger at Simon but her own guilt and self-flagellation. The sexual overtures she directs toward Joel are given more play in this complete version, and when she repeats her yearnings for wealth and power we hear reverberations of a theme that serves as an index to the essential message of the play and the cycle as a whole: the relentless pursuit of material gain.

O'Neill revised the play so that the conflict between Sara and Deborah would be more powerful, thus placing the women in the roles of mighty opposites in the drama. Simon's role, although central, becomes more passive, more malleable. The restoration of several speeches in the electric scene in act 4, scene 2, shows how far each woman is willing to go in the battle over Simon. One crucial speech reveals Deborah's extreme "unscrupulousness," her sick mind at work. She tells Sara that Simon has hinted that "I might find some subtle way . . . to poison you!" Then she explodes in a mad frenzy: "I could watch you lashed to death, with the blood running down your gross white back, and never raise a finger to save you!" Without lines such as these both Deborah's viciousness and aspects of O'Neill's "theatricality," however extravagant, are diminished.

In revisions recorded in January 1939, O'Neill contemplated merging acts 1 and 2, but he was by no means certain about such drastic changes. On the first leaf of these revisions O'Neill engaged in the following dialogue with himself: "Combine 4 scenes of present Acts I and II into one act. Time of this Act would be year of present Act II—but would be some months after Harford's death—." Further along in the revision notes he contemplates a different scenario: "Second scene—The Inn—as I–1 now, except Simon's financial & mental condition are those of II–2—his hidden conflict increased by memories dreams give him—. Or at opening condense so Simon and Sara already there, Joel and Abig. home—. Or omit Inn scene entirely—." Since there is strong evidence that O'Neill added to the typescript at least as late as 1942, and that in the passage just quoted he still refers to Deborah as Abigail,[6] it would seem that his indecision ultimately translated into a decision *not* to combine acts 1 and 2.

What remains certain is that O'Neill had no plans to omit the epilogue. The Yale edition ends the play with act 4, scene 2, with Deborah's rejection of Simon and her retreat into the summerhouse. Sara has vowed to divest herself of the Harford Company and all its profits and return to the mothering posture of act 1, scene 1. This ending leaves Sara exclusively in the role of feminine protector and Simon in a state of breakdown, a mental invalid and lost cause. However, O'Neill did not intend his audience to leave the theater with this final impression. He felt the need to add a scene that would take Simon and Sara beyond the limits of their assigned roles at the end of act 4.

The epilogue is carefully designed to recapitulate for the audience the events of the past year. This time Jonathan and Honey, the Harford sons, replace Cregan and Maloy as the harbingers of exposition. Sara, Simon, and their sons have been dispossessed of the previous generation's materialistic trappings and, more important, are ready to begin life anew without the curse of the Harford money. We learn that Simon has been institutionalized for the past year and, now on the road to recovery, is freed from his mother's possessive clutches. These are events that are crucial to our ultimate assessment of the characters.

O'Neill has emphasized the roundness of Sara's character when he depicts her as both nurturer and worker. She typifies the American pioneer woman who—like the protagonist Alexandra in Willa Cather's *Oh Pioneers!*—returns to the land with the strength, initiative, and flexibility commonly ascribed to male American heroes. Simon has recovered, but Sara assures him he "needn't ever lift a hand," and he is free to live in his dreamworld and "write the books you planned here in the old days." This return to the farm allows Sara and Simon to shed the false personae of acts 1 through 4. Sara moves closer to her

---

6. The decision to change Abigail's name to Deborah came late in the creative process—the fall of 1942, when O'Neill was working on *A Touch of the Poet* (hereafter referred to in the notes as *TP*). O'Neill crossed out the name Abigail and wrote the name Deborah on the typescript of *MSM* in several places. The revision notes just quoted and all notes relevant to *MSM* are catalogued under Za O'Neill 108 in the Yale Beinecke Library. These notes and all handwritten material found in this edition were transcribed by me and quoted exactly as O'Neill wrote them.

peasant roots, her true self, and Simon discards the mask of big business and becomes once again a dreamer with "a touch of the poet." Now the tension that informed the aristocracy/peasant opposition is dispelled. Sara, the strong farmer/nurturer, and Simon, the frail gentleman/poet, merge in harmony, not in the home sphere of the Harford mansion but on Sara Melody's farm. Thus O'Neill ends the play with the gender role reversal that informs all of the cycle plays.

In a final scene that foreshadows the pietà in *A Moon for the Misbegotten,* Simon, like Jamie Tyrone, is enticed by Sara to "sleep on my breast." But O'Neill laces her maternal curtain speech with a "brooding" possessiveness. Sara cannot resist indulging in her recurring vision of the American Dream: "Ethan will have a fleet of ships! And Wolfe will have his banks. And Johnny his railroads! And Honey will be in the White House before he stops, maybe. And each of them will have wealth and power and a grand estate—." These are lines that we have heard before in acts 2 and 3, but O'Neill's obsession for refrain and a need to connect subsequent cycle plays with this one cause him to repeat them again. He has Sara say one more time: "Leave it to them to take what they want from life; once they're men!" O'Neill creates an element of unity through the repetition of the familiar "take what you want" motif, a phrase he places strategically throughout the play, one that brings the end of the action back to the beginning. Indeed, notes to succeeding plays confirm that Sara and her sons would have continued their pursuit of money and power, and that each son would, in his own play, assert himself in his chosen field of shipping, banking, politics, or railroads.

O'Neill grounded much of the fictional material in *More Stately Mansions* and the cycle plays in historical fact. Finally titled "A Tale of Possessors Self-Dispossessed," the cycle was to trace the saga of the Harford-Melody family's pursuit of wealth and power from their arrival in the New World in 1755 to the year 1932.[7] O'Neill read widely in American, European, and Irish history before attempting the long

---

7. O'Neill planned to include eleven plays in the cycle. *TP* and *MSM* were the only cycle plays completed by O'Neill. *The Calms of Capricorn* was "developed" by Donald Gallup from O'Neill's 1935 scenario (New Haven, Conn.: Ticknor & Fields, 1982).

cycle, and when designing the sets he made sure they were exact repro-
ductions of their respective periods. There is evidence based on notes
he made before composing early versions of *A Touch of the Poet* and
More Stately Mansions that O'Neill was inspired to create Sara's father,
Con Melody, through his readings in Irish history and his fascination
with the nationalist war heroes of the eighteenth and nineteenth cen-
turies.[8]

Intrigued by Con and his family, O'Neill decided to write a separate
play about them and then merge the Melodys and the Harfords. The
merger of immigrant and patrician—Sara and Simon—in *More Stately
Mansions* allowed O'Neill to return to his own, as well as America's,
beginnings. The strong peasant roots of the Melodys integrated with
the gentility and education of the Harfords reflected similar family
mergers in American history. O'Neill concentrated the action in *More
Stately Mansions* between 1832 and 1842—a period in American history
rarely depicted in drama. According to notes to the play, the Simon
Harfords live in a Massachusetts mill town modeled after Fall River.
Before designing the Harford mansion, situated in a seaport town
similar to Newburyport, Massachusetts, O'Neill researched the architecture and the social and cultural legends of the period. He was well
enough versed in history to have the characters allude to current affairs
of the day: President Andrew Jackson, the banking system, the tariff
laws, and the cotton mill business. O'Neill's interest in the Transcen-
dentalists and the Romantic period is reflected in the many references
in his notes to Emerson, Whitman, and Thoreau. In fact, in notes to
the play entitled "Thoreau in Simon," O'Neill recorded excerpts from
Thoreau's and Emerson's journals. Simon's cabin, described at the beginning of act I, scene 2, is a replica of Thoreau's hut on Walden
Pond.[9]

---

8. These and all notes relevant to *TP* are catalogued under Za O'Neill 111 at the Beinecke
Library.
9. In notes to the early versions of *MSM* and *TP*, O'Neill made several notations on the
Transcendental period and described Thoreau's hut in detail (Za O'Neill 111). See also
Van Wyck Brooks' *The Flowering of New England, 1815–1865* (New York: E. P.
Dutton, 1936), p. 359. O'Neill used this book, among others, as a historical source. See
also Virginia Floyd's *O'Neill: A New Assessment* (New York: Frederick Ungar, 1986)
and Frederick Carpenter's *Eugene O'Neill*, rev. edn. (Boston: Twayne, 1979), p. 139.

In a letter to Leon Mirlos O'Neill expressed his rationale for accumulating so much factual data from each period in American history before composing his cycle plays: "As you can imagine it involves a tremendous amount of reading and note-taking—for even if I find it beside my point to use as much historical fact background, still I wish to live in the time of each play while writing it."[10]

Woven into the historical fabric of *More Stately Mansions* is O'Neill's own experience. Central to the action of the play is the tension between peasant and patrician—the same tension that dogged the O'Neill family in New London, the Tyrones versus the Harkers in *Long Day's Journey,* and the Hogans versus the Harders in *A Moon for the Misbegotten.* In *A Touch of the Poet,* the first play of the cycle to include the Irish Melody family, there are strong resemblances between Con Melody and James O'Neill. The conflicts between Sara and Con are more than reminiscent of the ones O'Neill experienced with his daughter, Oona. *Work Diary* entries recorded at a time when the tension between O'Neill and his daughter was most intense coincide with the dates of revision notes to scenes involving Con and Sara.[11]

But it is in *More Stately Mansions* that connections between the late plays and O'Neill's personal life abound. For instance, Sara Melody bears more than a coincidental likeness to O'Neill's wife, Carlotta. Louis Sheaffer has pointed to the obvious parallels between Sara and Carlotta, noting that both women were what O'Neill described as "a blend of what are commonly called aristocratic and peasant characteristics." According to Sheaffer, Carlotta's father, "the illegitimate son of a Danish nobleman and a servant girl," recollects Con Melody, whose parents were a mix of peasant and aristocrat. And Carlotta, like Sara Melody, "looked patrician from the waist up, but she had strong hands, short sturdy legs, and a peasantlike capacity for hard work."[12] The

---

10. The Mirlos letter is quoted in Virginia Floyd's *Eugene O'Neill at Work* (New York: Frederick Ungar, 1981), p. 217.
11. Eugene O'Neill's *Work Diary* was transcribed and edited by Donald Gallup, prelim. edn. (New Haven: Yale Univ. Library, 1981). It consists of a daily record of composition data and brief entries describing what O'Neill did each day during his productive years. The first volume covers the years 1924–33, while the second spans the years 1934–43 and the 1925 "Scribbling Diary."
12. Louis Sheaffer, *O'Neill: Son and Artist* (Boston: Little, Brown, 1973), p. 482.

marriage between Simon and Sara recalls that of the O'Neills when Sara tells Deborah Harford, in *More Stately Mansions,* that Simon "has nothing left but me and my love. I'm mother, wife, and mistress in one." It is commonly known that O'Neill often said that Carlotta simultaneously fulfilled for him these three roles. Simon possesses the requisites of the poetic, frail O'Neill figure who accepts Sara's mothering. As Carlotta was for O'Neill, Sara is the power behind Simon's ego, taking charge of both domestic and business matters.

Not only do Simon and Sara Harford reflect Eugene and Carlotta O'Neill, but Deborah Harford finds her source in O'Neill's mother. Deborah's description is not far from Mary Tyrone's in *Long Day's Journey.* Although slightly different wording is used in the two descriptions, the women are unequivocal lookalikes: youthful, pretty, white-haired, full-lipped, with high foreheads, deep-set eyes, long fingers, nervous gestures, and so on. The mother/son tensions that pervade *More Stately Mansions* are the very ones that plague the Tyrones, and thus O'Neill himself.[13]

With the composition of this sixth cycle play O'Neill sharpened the contours of the ghosts that haunted his last plays: Deborah Harford, Mary Tyrone's double and shadow of Carlotta; Sara Melody Harford, Carlotta's twin; and Simon Harford, O'Neill himself. All confront one another in the garden—a tainted Eden, a metaphor for the O'Neill family life and the promise of America turned sour. But Deborah's garden differs from O'Neill's other locales of escape and torment: the Hogan farm, Harry Hope's bar, the New London summer cottage where the Tyrone men trim hedges and drink and Mary takes drugs in "the spare room." Deborah's garden is a type of the garden at Tao House, where *More Stately Mansions* and O'Neill's late plays were composed and where, according to her diary, Carlotta taught "Gene to

---

13. Several scholars have drawn comparisons between the Harford women and O'Neill's wife and mother. Travis Bogard, in *Contour in Time* (New York: Oxford Univ. Press, 1972), p. 387, cites several similarities between Deborah Harford and Mary Tyrone. Louis Sheaffer makes detailed comparisons between Sara and Carlotta and Deborah and Mary as they occur in *MSM* and *LDJ* and sees the author's resentment of his mother depicted "more bluntly, more violently" in the former play (pp. 481ff.). Michael Manheim also draws comparisons between Deborah and Mary in *Eugene O'Neill's New Language of Kinship* (Syracuse, N.Y.: Syracuse Univ. Press, 1982).

prune things!" (4-14-39). There is the oriental formality, border hedges, and high wall with gate in both Deborah's and Carlotta's garden. The red-lacquered door that decorates the "Temple of Love" mirrors the Chinese interior doors at Tao House. Like Deborah, who sought to possess Simon's soul and his creative self, Carlotta was able to coax O'Neill away from the sea, to the high hills of Danville, California, behind the locked gate at the foot of the long drive, to ensure that he would not be distracted from writing his last great plays. There she served his genius, as mother, wife, mistress, nurse, and typist. Thus in this play the boundaries that separate mother from wife dissolve. Deborah becomes a projection of both Ella O'Neill and Carlotta Monterey, and Sara resembles Carlotta as well.

The 1939 revision notes to the play, mentioned earlier, demonstrate O'Neill's growing preoccupation with his mother/son demons. *More Stately Mansions,* begun as a simple struggle between spiritualism and materialism, grew to include not only the dimensions of a mother/son/ wife rivalry but also a mother/son fixation. By means of his characters O'Neill psychoanalyzed his own neuroses in revision notes to the play, coming to the conclusion that "the underlying plot of this play is the duel to the death between mother and son."[14] In the two published plays about his family, *Long Day's Journey* and *A Moon for the Misbegotten,* O'Neill subverts this "duel" by assuming a passive role in one and absenting himself altogether in the other. Much of this confessional material is buried in the almost impenetrable writing found in the revisions to *More Stately Mansions.* However, in the typescript of the play O'Neill has camouflaged some of his most bitter resentments and secrets in the characters of Sara, Simon, and Deborah Harford.

This is O'Neill's longest play, one that contains expansive interior monologues, protracted set descriptions, and a myriad of interruptions in the form of stage directions. These elements seem to persuade the reader that he or she is experiencing a new genre—a novel-drama, perhaps. Deborah Harford's long soliloquy in act 1, scene 2, and Sara's soliloquy in act 4, scene 1, seem to enter the realm of Molly Bloom in

---

14. This comment is found in notes to *MSM*. See n. 6.

James Joyce's *Ulysses*. But part of the rationale for the play's overly long speeches, repetitions, and overstatements resides in O'Neill's return to the expressionistic style of his middle years, a compulsion to animate the setting—Simon's office is described as "a painted loud-mouthed bawd"—and to probe relentlessly beneath the surface to expose the multilayered human imagination, a technique that allowed O'Neill to explore his own psyche. However novelistic *More Stately Mansions* may appear in its interior probings and philosophical sermonizing, in the last analysis the play remains a document for the theater, one that can stand alone as an interesting self-sufficient vehicle or as an integral part of a far more complex structure.

I see *More Stately Mansions* not as an "unfinished work"[15] but as a play that O'Neill edited with a sense of artistry and logic. Doubtless O'Neill had more work to do and would have continued to revise the play, as he did all of his works, during its staging and production. But, with the exception of one missing page—absent when Carlotta sent the script to Yale—the play is complete and the action whole. And if it is to be published at all, perhaps O'Neill would rather we read the whole script than a fraction of it.

In this, the O'Neill centennial year and the bicentennial of the ratification of the U.S. Constitution, it seems most appropriate that we rediscover a play that was primarily shaped by events in O'Neill's own life as well as those belonging to history. O'Neill's analysis of the American industrial landscape of the 1830s and its obsessed inhabitants not only serves as a chronicle of that period but also encapsulates the future of America. Although far from being a model of Aristotelian unity, *More Stately Mansions* has passion and perception and contains scenes that excite us to pity and fear. Through O'Neill's tragic vision we are confronted with a very contemporary depiction of women, and of violence in the home as well as in the workplace. It is a vision that bares O'Neill's soul and reveals the truth about ourselves. The revelation is dark, yet it is penetrated by the occasional light of the American pioneer spirit.

---

15. O'Neill had slipped a piece of paper into the typescript that read "Unfinished Work. This script to be destroyed in case of my death!"

SCENES

CHARACTERS

JAMIE CREGAN

MICKEY MALOY

NORA MELODY

SARA [Mrs. Simon Harford], her daughter

SIMON HARFORD, Sara's husband

JOEL HARFORD, his brother

DEBORAH [Mrs. Henry Harford], mother of Simon and Joel

ETHAN

WOLFE

JONATHAN ⎱ children of Simon and Sara Harford

OWEN [Honey]

NICHOLAS GADSBY, an attorney

CATO, the Harford's coachman

Act One, Scene One

———

SCENE *The dining room of Melody's Tavern, an Inn in a Massachu-setts village near a city. The Tavern is over a hundred years old. It had once been a prosperous haven for travellers, a breakfast stop for the stagecoach, but the stage line had been discontinued years ago and the Inn fallen upon lean, unprosperous days.*

The dining room, and what is now the barroom, had once been a single spacious room, low-ceilinged, with heavy oak beams and pan-elled walls. It is now divided into two rooms by a pine partition, the barroom being the section off left. The partition is painted in a poor imitation of the panelled walls, which only makes it stand out more as an eyesore.

The appearance of the dining room gives evidence of a poverty-stricken neglect. Nothing in it has been repaired or freshened in years. The tablecloths are dirty and stained. On the partition at left, front, is a cracked mirror, hanging askew. Farther back, near the door leading to the Bar, a cupboard is fixed to the partition. In the rear wall, center, is the door leading to the street with two windows on either side of it. In the right wall, toward front, is a door to a little hallway off the kitchen, where the stairs to the upper floor are. At extreme front, right, is a high schoolmaster's desk with a stool.

Four tables are placed around the room, one at left, front, one at rear, to the left of the street entrance, one at right in back of the door to the hall, and the fourth at center, front. The two which are at left, front, and at right are square with four chairs. The other two are larger with three chairs to each long side and a chair at each end. It is night of a day in Fall, 1832. The room is lighted by three cheap lamps in brack-ets, one to each wall, and a candle on the table at center, front.

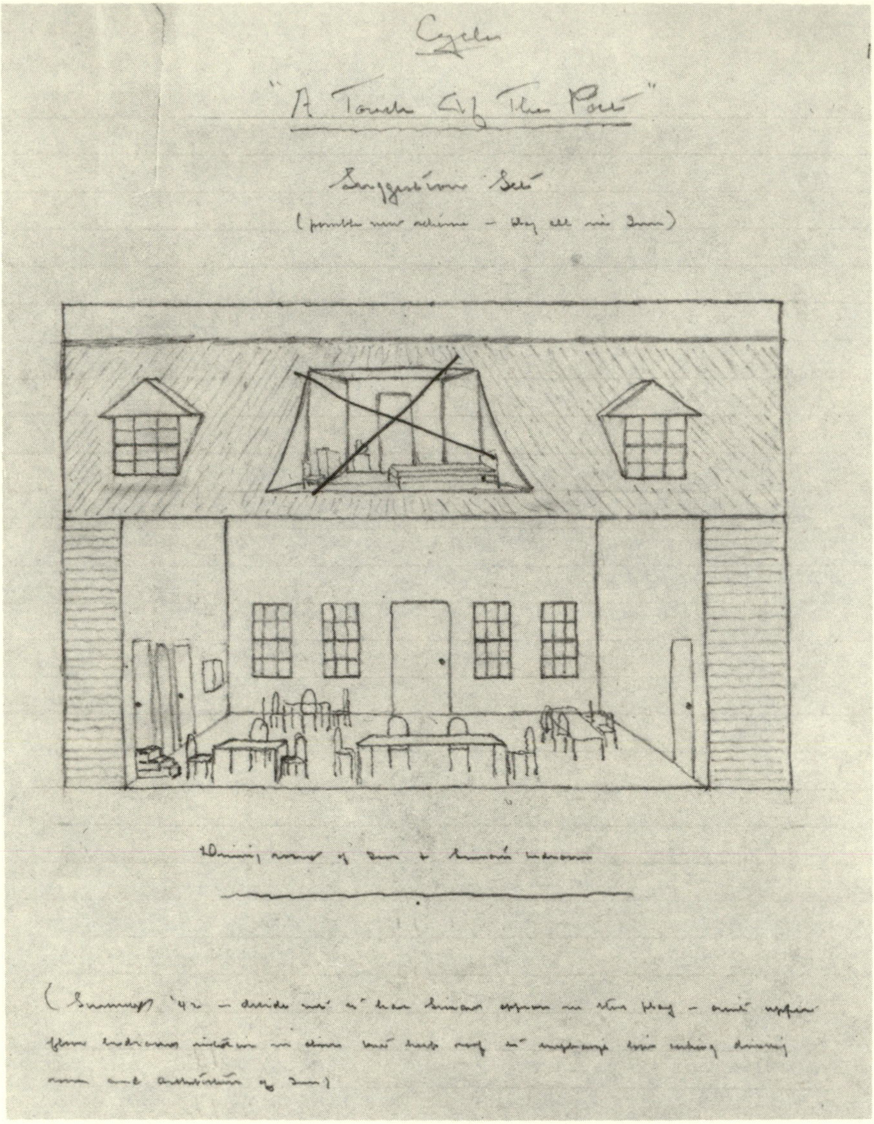

Melody Inn—Act One, Scene One

Yale Collection of American Literature, Beinecke Rare Book and Manuscript Library, Yale University

*Jamie Cregan is discovered sitting in the chair at front of the table at
left front. He is fifty-two but drunkenness has aged him and he looks
in his sixties. An obviously Irish peasant type, he is tall and emaciated.
His face is long, hollow-cheeked and lantern-jawed with small dark
eyes, a wide, loose-lipped mouth, a twisted broken pug nose. There
is the scar of a saber-slash over one cheekbone. His ragged hair is a
dirty white. He is dressed in old black clothes that are worn thread-
bare. A drunkard, there yet remains in him something likable, a
fundamental decency, the dim flicker of an old soldier's courage and
devil-may-care spirit. He sits slumped forward in his chair, sober now,
in a stupor of melancholy, staring before him. A decanter of whiskey,
three-quarters full, and several empty glasses are on the table in front
of him.*

*For a moment after the rise of the curtain, there is silence. Then from
the floor above comes the sound of voices and the rising and falling
wail of an Irish keen for the dead. Cregan stirs and mutters to himself
resentfully.*

CREGAN Ah, keen with your mouths and pretend, but there's divil a
one in the world but miself and Nora cares in their hearts he's gone.
[*He slumps into brooding dejection again. The door from the Bar is
opened and Mickey Maloy, the barkeep, comes in. Mickey is as typically the Irish peasant as Cregan. He is thirty-four with a sturdy
physique beginning to run into fat. He has a healthy, honest, common, fresh-complected face with curly dark hair and small blue eyes,
twinkling with an amiable cunning. His mouth is set in the half-
leering grin of a bartender's would-be, worldly-wise cynicism. He
glances at Cregan with a look of mingled liking and contempt for
his weakness.*]

MALOY [*automatically appraising the decanter—grinning*] Glory be,
it's three-quarters full yet! Are ye sick, Jamie? [*Cregan gives no
sign of having heard the jibe. Mickey sits in the chair opposite it.*]
I've been takin' stock of what liquor's left. There's enough for Nora
to kape on. With me to help her— [*grudgingly*] and you too, if
you'd stay sober—she'll have a livin' from this place. [*He pauses,*

then goes on resentfully.] We'd have no cause to worry for Nora if it wasn't for the debts himself run up in the days he was playin' the grand gentleman.

CREGAN [*starts from his stupor and pounds his fist on the table angrily*] Let you close your big mouth—and him dead upstairs! I'll not hear a word against him!

MALOY [*unimpressed—contemptuously*] To hell wid you. [*Cregan relapses into dejection again. Maloy glances at him with a grudging sympathy.*] But I know how ye feel, Jamie, and I'm glad for him there's one to mourn him widout lyin'! [*From upstairs there comes again the wail of the keen. Maloy glances up.*] Well, it's a beautiful wake Nora's givin' him, anyways, and a grand funeral tomorrow. [*He gives Cregan a nudge.*] Let you rouse yourself, Jamie, and not sit there half dead. Come on, have a taste wid me like Con Melody'd want you to if he was alive here. You know he'd only laugh at you and call you a liar for pretendin' grief at his death.

CREGAN [*with a change of mood—resentfully*] He would, damn him! He couldn't believe there was decency in anyone. [*He pours out a big drink from the decanter which Mickey has shoved toward him.*]

MALOY [*pours a small drink for himself*] Because there was none in him. [*raising his glass*] Here's health. [*They drink.*]

CREGAN [*melancholy again*] Poor auld Con. The dew don't taste the same, an' him not here.

MALOY [*sardonically*] He's needin' a drink bad where he is now.

CREGAN [*with a shudder*] Don't say it.

MALOY [*smacking his lips judiciously*] The dew tastes right to me. It's his private stock and he knew whiskey, if it did kill him.

CREGAN [*somberly*] It wasn't the dhrink killed him.

MALOY [*grins*] You'll be tellin' me next it was something he ate.

CREGAN [*angrily*] Yerrah, don't make fool's jokes an' Con Melody a corpse. It wasn't whiskey killed him, I'm sayin'. He was strong as a bull an' his guts was made of iron. He could have drunk a keg a day an' lived for twenty years yet if the pride and spirit wasn't killed inside him ivir since the night he tried to challenge that Yankee coward, Harford, to a duel, and him and me got bate by the police and arrested. And then his own daughter turnin' traitor and marryin'

Harford's son. That put the final shame on him! He's been a walkin' corpse ivir since, drinkin' to forget an' waitin' for death, while he'd be talkin' in brogue wid all the bog-trotters came in, tellin' stories an' roarin' songs, an' dancin' jigs, pretendin' he had no edication an' was no bhetter 'an they were.

MALOY [*stubbornly*]   He wasn't better. It was in the days before that happened, when he used to lie about bein' a gintelman, an' his father only a Galway shebeen-keeper, that he was pretendin'.

CREGAN [*harshly*]   Arrah, don't talk! Didn't he go to the College in Ireland, and hadn't he his own estate till he ruined himself! Wasn't he as fine an Officer as you'd find in Wellington's Army when he was a Major of Dragoons in Spain and I served under him? To hell wid what his fader was! He raised Con to be a gentleman, and Con Melody was a gentleman! [*He adds, making the sign of the cross.*] May God rest his soul in peace.

MALOY [*crosses himself automatically*]   Amen. I'll say no more. It's bad luck to spake ill of the dead, anyways. [*He pauses.*] Will Sara come for the funeral, d'you think?

CREGAN [*viciously*]   God's curse on her if she don't! Nora wrote her when himself was bad took, and she's had plenty of time.

MALOY   I doubt she'll come. She hated him. You know as well as me there's nivir been a word between them in the four years since she married. And, anyways, she was always stuck up and givin' herself airs. I'll wager by this she's so high and mighty she'd feel shame to visit her poor Irish relations even for her father's funeral.

CREGAN [*fiercely*]   Poor relations, is it? Her own mother! [*The door from the hall at right is opened and Nora Melody appears.*]

MALOY [*warningly*]   Whist!

[*Nora walks slowly toward them. She is forty-five, a typical Irish peasant woman with a shapeless, heavy figure. She must have been extremely pretty as a girl—she still has beautiful eyes—but drudgery has worn her down, constant weariness of body and spirit has made her too tired to care about her appearance, so that, even now dressed in her best black mourning, she appears older and more unattractive than she really is. She has a round head with thinning grey hair, almost white, ar-*

ranged with a half-hearted attempt at neatness. Her face is broad with high cheekbones, the complexion a blotchy pallor. Everything about her body appears swollen—her neck, her nose, her lips, her sagging breasts, her legs, feet, ankles, and wrists, her hands with fingers knotted by rheumatism. Yet despite her appearance, there is a spirit in her that shines through her grief and exhaustion, some will behind the body's wreckage that is not broken, something kindly and gentle and unselfish, an essential humble fineness of character, a charm.]

NORA [*as she comes to them—complaining but without bitterness*] Faix, it's a great help you are, Mickey, sittin' here takin' your ease.

MALOY [*gets to his feet guiltily*] I've been makin' a list av the stock—

NORA [*wearily*] Arrah, who cares now? Go up to the wake, that's a good lad, and see people have what they're wantin', an' lave me a chance to rest. My legs are broken under me. [*She sits down exhaustedly in Mickey's place at the table.*]

MALOY I'll go, surely. But be damned if I'll ask what they're havin'! They'll drink ye out of house an' home wid any encouragement. [*He goes to the door at right and goes out, grumbling to himself. Nora sags in her chair with a weary sigh. Cregan relapses into his mood of depression, staring before him. Nora glances at him.*]

NORA You've nivir been up to the wake at all, Jamie.

CREGAN [*dully*] I don't want to look on him dead. [*with bitterness*] An' I don't want to see the crowd av thim pretendin' sorrow to his corpse, who hated and mocked him livin'.

NORA [*gently reproachful*] You're bitter. [*He doesn't reply. She looks at him with understanding sympathy—gently.*] You're missin' himself, Jamie?

CREGAN I am, Nora.

NORA [*pats his hand consolingly*] He's grateful for your sorrow, I know. You were the one friend he had in the world.

CREGAN [*bitterly*] I'm thinkin' now I was maybe only a drunken sponge who helped him kill himself.

NORA Don't think it. Sure, you know as well as me, it was the broken heart of his pride murthered him, not dhrink. Think only of what good you did him. It was only wid you he'd forgit once in a while and let himself remember what he used to be. An' wid me. [*her voice breaking*] I'm missin' him, too, Jamie. [*She sobs softly.*]

CREGAN [*pats her shoulder gently*] Don't cry. We'd ought to be glad for his sake. He's where he longed to be now in the peace of death. [*changing the subject abruptly to distract her mind*] Sara'd ought to come soon, don't you think?

NORA [*has stopped crying—dully*] Yes—if she'll come.

CREGAN [*without conviction*] Av course she'll come.

NORA I don't know. What do I know of her now? It's four years since I've laid eyes on her. I've only her letters, an' what are letters? It's aisy to remember to write to hide you're forgettin'. An' Sara had great pride in her, her father's own pride, and great ambition to raise herself in the world, and maybe she's grown shamed of me.

CREGAN God curse her, thin!

NORA [*immediately reacting defensively*] Let you not curse my Sara, Jamie Cregan! But it's my fault. I should be shamed to talk wrong of her, an' her so sweet in every letter, beggin' me kindly to visit her, an' her husban', too, God bless him, an' I nivir had the dacency to go, even when her children was born, but always was afeered to lave Con alone. An' she always asked if I needed money.

CREGAN She nivir sent any.

NORA If she didn't, it was because she knew I'd send it right back to her. So don't you be sayin'—

CREGAN [*sullenly*] I'll say divil a word. [*a pause*] What'll you do, Nora, now himself is gone?

NORA [*dully*] Kape on here. What else? It'll pay better now himself is gone. I'll kape on until all his debts is paid. [*She sighs wearily.*] It'll take a long time.

CREGAN Arrah, why don't you let them whistle for their money, like he did. [*admiringly*] It's little Con Melody ivir let debts bother him! [*then with a change of tone*] All the same I know, if he didn't, that the men he owed would have kicked him out in the gutter, if they hadn't liked and trusted you.

NORA [*simply*] I never let Con know that. [*proudly*] True for you. They trusted me. And I'll pay every penny. I've my pride, too.

CREGAN   Ye have. You're a good woman, Nora, an' the rist av us are dirt under your feet.

NORA   [*with a touching, charming, pathetic little smile of pleased co-quetry that lights up her face*]   It's you have the blarneyin' tongue, Jamie.

CREGAN   [*with an answering grin*]   I have not. I'm a great one for telling the truth, ye mean. [*with a change of tone*] Maybe Sara'll pay off his debts for you.

NORA   [*defensively*]   She'll not, then! Do you think I'd ask her?

CREGAN   Why not? She's his daughter. She's a right—

NORA   Well, I've no right. She has her husband an' three young children to think of, an' another comin'. An' if I would take her money, what she's got is her husband's not hers. [*with scornful pride*] Do you think I'd let a Harford pay for Con Melody? Even if I had no pride, I'd be afeered to. Con would rise from his grave to curse me!

CREGAN   [*with grim appreciation*]   Aye, divil a doubt, he would! His rage'd bring him back from the flames of hell! [*then hastily*] I'm jokin'. Don't heed me, Nora. [*Someone tries the handle on the bolted street door at rear. Then there is a knock.*]

NORA   [*wearily*]   Go tell them it's the side door for the wake. [*Cregan goes and unbolts the door—then backs away as Sara with her husband, Simon Harford, behind her, step into the room.*]

Sara is twenty-five, exceedingly pretty in a typically Irish fashion, with a mass of black hair, a fair skin with rosy cheeks, and her mother's beautiful deep-blue eyes. There is a curious blending in her appearance of what are commonly considered to be aristocratic and peasant characteristics. She has a fine thoughtful forehead. Her eyes are not only beautiful but intelligent. Her nose is straight and finely modeled. She has small ears set close to her head, a well-shaped head on a slender neck. Her mouth, on the other hand, has a touch of coarse sensuality about its thick, tight lips, and her jaw is a little too long and heavy for the rest of her face, with a quality about it of masculine obstinacy and determination. Her body is concealed by the loose dress of mourning black she wears but, in spite of it, her pregnancy, now six months along, is apparent. One gets the impression of a strong body, full breasted, full of health and vitality, and retaining its grace despite her condition. Its bad points are thick ankles, large feet, and big hands, broad and strong with thick, stubby fingers. Her voice is low and musical. She has rid her speech of brogue, except in moments of extreme emotion.

Simon Harford is twenty-six but the poise of his bearing makes him appear much more mature. He is tall and loose-jointed with a wiry strength of limb. A long Yankee face, with Indian resemblances, swarthy-complected, with a big straight nose, a wide sensitive mouth, a fine forehead, large ears, thick brown hair, light brown eyes, set wide apart, their expression sharply observant, and shrewd but in their depths ruminating and contemplative. A personality that impresses one incongruously as both practical and impractical. He speaks quietly, in a deep voice with a slight drawl. He is dressed in black. He is carrying in his arms the youngest of his three sons, Jonathan, just a year old.

At first sight of Sara and Simon as they enter the room, the impression one gets of their relationship, [sic] one feels that here is as loving and contented a marriage as one could find.

SARA [*as she enters—to Cregan with genuine warmth*] Jamie! [*She holds out her hand.*]

CREGAN [*takes it coldly, bitter resentment in his voice*] Better late than never.

SARA [*hurt and resentful*] I came as soon as—

NORA [*has jumped to her feet—with a happy cry*] Sara, darlin'—

SARA [*rushing to meet her*] Mother! [*They meet at left rear of the table at front and embrace and kiss. Meanwhile, Simon Harford stands just inside the door, smiling a bit embarrassedly. He turns to Cregan, who is closing the door, meaning to greet him pleasantly, but Cregan avoids his eye and leaves him standing there while he goes and sits sulkily in the chair at front of the table at left, rear.*]

NORA [*weeping with joyous relief*] You've come, God bless you! [*She cries sobbingly but triumphantly over Sara's shoulder.*] Didn't I tell you she'd come, Jamie Cregan!

SARA [*soothingly*]   Of course I've come. There now, Mother dear, don't cry. You're making me cry, too. [*She breaks away from her mother's embrace, smiling and brushing tears from her eyes.*] And here's Simon waiting to greet you, Mother.

SIMON [*comes toward them, smiling at Nora with a genuine affection*] It's good to see you again, Mother.

NORA [*aware of him for the first time is embarrassed and instinctively bobs him an awkward curtsy—respectfully*]   Good evening to you, Sor. [*then a smile of humble gratitude and pleasure as she diffidently takes the free hand he holds out to her*] Mother, did you call me? That is kind of you. [*then forgetting everything as her eyes fall on the baby*] Glory be, you've brought the baby.

SARA   I had to, Mother. The other two are old enough to leave with the servant. But he's too little yet.

NORA [*officiously maternal*]   Arrah, ain't he as welcome as the flowers in May, the darlin'. Here! Give him to me, Sor. [*rebukingly to Sara*] Did you make your poor husband carry him, you lazy girl?

SARA [*laughingly*]   No, Simon just took him outside the door. But he likes to, anyway. [*then solicitously as Nora cuddles the baby in her arms*] Careful, Mother. Don't wake him.

NORA   Teach your grandmother! If I didn't know how to carry babies, where would you be? [*then to Simon, mindful of her duty as hostess*] Take a chair, Sor. Sit down Sara Darlin'. [*She sits at right of the small table at left, front. Sara in the chair at left end of the long table at front, center. Simon in the first chair at the same table to right, rear, of Sara. Nora croons over the baby.*] Wake you, would I, Acushla? It's little she knows. My, haven't you a fine handsome face! You're the image of your grandfather— [*She stops abruptly.*]

SARA [*sharply resentful*]   He's not! There's not the slightest resemblance— [*She stops abruptly, too.*]

NORA [*half to herself, her eyes sad and haunted*]   Never mind, never mind. He's gone now. [*She forces her attention on the baby and talks hurriedly.*] What's your name, Darlin'? Your mother wrote me. Let me see can I remember. The first was Ethan. That's a quare Yankee name you'd not forget. The next was Wolfe Tone. That's

a grand Irish hero's name you can't forget nather.[1] And yours is—
wait now—another Yankee name—ah!—Jonathan, that's it.

SARA [*maternally tender now*]   And the one that's coming, if it's a boy,
we're going to call Owen Roe.[2]

NORA [*solicitously*]   Ah, I was forgettin' you're— How are you feelin',
Darlin'?

SARA [*embarrassed, with a glance at Simon*]   As fine as can be, Mother.
I'm so healthy it never has bothered me at all. [*changing the subject abruptly*] It was Simon's idea, the Irish names. He likes the
sound of them. It's the poet in him. [*Simon starts and gives her a
strange suspicious glance.*] Only he wanted to call them all Irish,
but I wouldn't let him, it wasn't fair. [*She laughs.*] So we agreed
to divide, and I'd choose the American ones, and he could—

CREGAN [*breaks in jeeringly*]   So it was your husband had to shame
you to give Irish names to your children, was it? [*They all start,
having forgotten his presence.*]

SARA [*stung*]   Mother! I'll not stand Jamie insulting—

SIMON [*quietly admonishing*]   Sara. [*She glances at him and bites her
lip.*]

NORA [*angrily*]   Jamie! Hush your blather! [*Cregan subsides sullenly.
She turns to Simon apologetically.*] Don't mind him, Sor. [*From
upstairs, at the wake, comes the sound of a wailing keen of sorrow.
Sara starts and her face hardens. Nora's face grows dully grief-
stricken. She mutters miserably.*] We're all forgettin' him. [*She
looks at Sara appealingly.*] Sara. You'll want to come up and see
him now.

SARA [*stiffening—coldly*]   If you want me to, Mother.

NORA [*sadly reproachful*]   If *I* want?

SIMON [*quietly*]   Of course, Sara wishes to pay her last respects to her
father.

---

1. Theobald Wolfe Tone (1763–98) was one of the leaders of the United Irishmen, a
nationalist organization that sought to make Ireland a republic (modeled after the one in
France) and to sever ties with England. Tone persuaded the French to aid the Irish in
their rebellion against the English and was captured aboard a French warship by the
English at the battle of Bantry Bay in 1796. Tone committed suicide in prison.
2. Owen Roe O'Neill (1590?–1649) was another Irish nationalist hero. He is best known
for his courageous victory over the Scots in 1646 at the battle of Benrub.

SARA [*again glances at him—then quietly*]   Yes, I do, Mother.

NORA [*relieved—quickly, as if afraid Sara may change her mind*]   Then come now. [*She and Sara rise.*] We'll leave the baby in the back room I've fixed for you. He won't hear the noise there to wake him. [*She goes to the door at right. Sara starts to follow, her face set to face an ordeal. As she passes Simon he takes her hand and pats it reassuringly. For a moment she looks down into his eyes. Then her face softens with love and she bends over and kisses him impulsively.*]

NORA   Are you comin', Sara?

SARA [*all hostility gone from her voice*]   Yes, Mother. [*She goes quickly over and follows her mother off, right. A pause. Simon stares before him abstractedly. Cregan, from his chair at left, rear, regards him, frowning. He has been watching everything and is having a struggle with himself. He begins to feel liking and respect for Simon and he bitterly resents feeling this. Finally he gets up and comes to the table at left, front, ignoring Simon, and defiantly pours himself a big drink. Simon gets up and approaches him smilingly with outstretched hand.*]

SIMON   How are you, Mr. Cregan? I guess you've forgotten me. I met you here once with Major Melody.

CREGAN [*placated in spite of himself, takes his hand—a bit stiffly*]   I hadn't forgotten but I was thinkin' maybe you had. [*then punctiliously polite*] Will ye sit down and drink wid me, Mr. Harford?

SIMON   With pleasure, Mr. Cregan. [*They sit down, Cregan at left— Simon at right of table. Simon pours a small drink and raises his glass.*] Your good health, Sir.

CREGAN   Drink hearty. [*Suddenly a fierce look of suspicious distrust comes over his face—harshly*] Wait! I've a better toast for you! To Ireland and the Irish and hell roast the soul of any damned Yank that wud kape thim down!

SIMON [*gravely*]   Amen to that, Mr. Cregan. And may they gain what they have longed for and fought for so long—liberty! [*He touches his glass to Cregan's and drinks. For a moment Cregan stares at him in comical confusion, then he gulps his own drink hastily.*]

CREGAN [*wiping the back of his hand across his mouth—abashed and respectful*]   Thank ye, Sor. [*then in a burst of honest admiration*] You're a man, divil a less, and Sara has a right to be proud she's your wife.

SIMON [*embarrassed in his turn*]   Oh no, it's I who should be proud to be her husband.

CREGAN [*flatly*]   I don't agree with you. [*He hesitates, staring at Simon uncertainly—then impulsively and appealingly, lowering his voice and speaking rapidly*] Listen, Sor. I've somethin' to say to you, before Nora comes. She's a grand woman! [*As Simon is about to assent*] Oh, I know you know that or I'd not be talkin'. An' she's had hell's own life wid Con. Nora deserves peace in the days that's left her, if ivir a woman did. An' now he's gone, she's her chance. But there's his debts. It's her honor to pay them, but it'll take years of more slaving— [*Again there is a wailing keen from the room above and suddenly his expression changes to a guilty self-contempt and he stares at the ceiling with a haunted, frightened look and mutters to himself.*] Did you hear me, Con? It's a black traitor I am to your pride—beggin' from a Harford! [*He turns on Simon fiercely threatening.*] You'll forget what I've said, d'ye hear? I'm dead drunk; It's the whiskey talkin'! [*then as he hears a sound from the hall—imploringly*] Whist! Here's someone. For the love av God, don't let on to Nora I told ye or she'd nivir spake to me again! [*then quickly changing his tone as Sara enters from the hall at right*] It's a pleasure to drink wid ye, Mr. Harford. Will ye have another taste?

SIMON [*playing up to him*]   Not now, thank you, Mr. Cregan. [*Sara comes to them. She is white and shaken, her eyes have a stricken look, and her lips are trembling. Simon rises and puts his arm around her protectingly. She clings to him.*]

SARA [*in a trembling voice*]   You shouldn't have made me go, Simon. I'd forgotten him—almost. Now he's alive again—lying there in his Major's uniform I remember so well, with the old sneer I hated on his lips! [*She shudders. Simon pats her shoulder but can find nothing to say. She goes on.*] I couldn't stay. I can't bear the sight of death. It's the first time I've seen it and I hate it! It's life with you I love. I don't want to think it can ever end. [*She stares before her *strangely.*] He was lying there with the old sneer—like death mocking at life!

SIMON [*soothingly*]   Don't think of it. It's over now.

SARA [*controlling herself*]   Yes, I know, I won't. [*forcing a smile*] You and Jamie seem to have gotten friendly all of a sudden. Don't you think I've got the best husband a woman could have, Jamie?

CREGAN   He's a man—if he is a Harford. [*Sara resents this but sees that Simon is smiling and she smiles too. Cregan goes on hesitantly.*] Askin' your pardon, Sor—but, av ye plaze, all them above at the wake will be gossipin' you're here, an' they'll take it bad if you don't go up—

SARA [*angrily*]   Let them think what they please!

SIMON [*ignoring her—to Cregan*]   I'll go right away. [*He turns.*]

SARA [*clings to his arm*]   No! I don't want death seeing you. We—we're so happy now. It'll bring bad luck.

SIMON [*smiles teasingly and pats her cheek*]   Now, now. Remember what you promised me about your superstitions.

SARA   That I'd forget all but the good luck ones. [*She forces a smile.*] I'll try again, Simon. [*She kisses him.*] Go up then—only don't stay long. [*Simon goes out right. Sara's eyes follow him. Then she sits in the first chair at left rear of the long table at center, her expression again strained and fearful. Cregan pours another drink and downs it, regarding her frowningly. Then he gets up and takes the chair on her right, at the end of the table.*]

CREGAN [*with thinly veiled hostility*]   You've changed, Sara.

SARA [*resenting his tone*]   Have I? [*then resolved not to quarrel, forcing a smile*] Well, I hope it's for the better—for Simon's sake.

CREGAN [*sneeringly*]   You've made yourself a fine, high-toned, Yankee woman, God pity you! It's great shame you must feel to have to come here an' associate wid us poor Irish.

SARA [*stung*]   Jamie! You know that's a lie! You know it was Father I was always ashamed of and he's dead now.

CREGAN [*bitterly*]   Thank God, you're saying.

SARA   You know I was ashamed of him just because he was such a crazy snob himself, with all his lies and pretenses of being a gentleman, and his being ashamed of my poor mother.

CREGAN [*grimly*]   He had none of his auld lies and pretenses wid him the past years since you married an' broke his heart.

SARA   Are you trying to blame me—?

CREGAN   He pretended to be one av us, instead. He never spoke except in a brogue you could cut with a knife, like an ignorant bog-trotter had just landed—except when he was too drunk to watch himself.

SARA [*with a shrinking movement*]   I know. Mother wrote me. [*suddenly deeply moved in spite of herself*] Poor Father! God forgive him. He never knew what he was himself. He never lived in life, but only in a bad dream. [*then with an abrupt change to disdainful scorn*] You don't have to tell me, Jamie. Didn't I see him, before I left, own up life had beaten him and lose the last speck of pride?

CREGAN   An' you scorned him for it, and still do, even while you say it was his lyin' pride shamed you! Faix,[3] you're his daughter still, as you always was! You're like him, inside you, as he was at his worst!

SARA   It's a lie! [*controlling her temper—quietly*] You've been drinking or you wouldn't be so unfair to me. I haven't changed, Jamie, not in the way you suspect.

CREGAN   We'll soon see. Tell me this, are you goin' to help your mother now in her troubles?

SARA   What do you think me? Of course, I'll help her! Don't I love her more than anyone in the world, except Simon and the children!

CREGAN [*eagerly*]   That's the talk! Then you'll give your word to pay off his debts?

SARA [*stiffening*]   His debts?

CREGAN [*misunderstanding*]   Faix, ye didn't think he'd ivir paid them, did ye? He didn't change that much, divil a fear. He owed ivry one in creation—two thousand or more, it must come to. But I know how well your husband's bin doin' in his business. It'd be aisy for you to—

SARA   Would it, indeed! Do you think I'd ever ask Simon to give the money we've slaved to save to pay the debts of his drunken squan-

---

3. This is a variant form of "fegs," an archaic form of "faith" and a distortion of the word "fay."

dering? Two thousand! And just when we're planning to buy out Simon's partner—and us with children to bring up and educate! Do you think I'm a fool?

CREGAN [*his anger rising*]   It's for your mother's sake. They might take the roof from over her head.

SARA   A fine roof! Let them! It'll be a good thing to free her from it. She's been a slave to this drunkard's roost too long. And I'll look after her, never fear, and see she wants for nothing.

CREGAN   Ye think Nora'd take charity from you? It's plain you've forgot the woman your mother is. [*losing his temper*] You've become a Yankee miser wid no honor ye wouldn't sell for gold! [*furiously*] God's curse on your soul, an' your mother's curse—!

SARA [*with a cry of superstitious fear*]   No! Don't! [*then flying into a rage herself and lapsing unconsciously into peasant brogue*] Hold your gab! Is it the likes of a drunken fool like you, who's sponged on my father for whiskey since the time you came to America, just because you're his cousin—is it you has the impudence to be talkin' to me about honor?

CREGAN [*delighted at having broken her control—bitingly*]   Someone has to—seein' you haven't any. [*with a grin of vindictive pleasure*] I'm glad to hear ye talk in your natural brogue an' forget the grand lady. Faix, there may be some red blood in ye yet beneath your airs!

SARA   Shut your mouth or I'll— [*She rises and seems about to strike him. Cregan chuckles. She controls herself—quietly*] I am sorry I lost my temper, Jamie. I ought to know better than to mind you.

CREGAN [*enraged again*]   Arrah, to hell wid your lady's airs! I'd rather have your insults! [*He stops abruptly as Nora appears in the doorway at right—getting to his feet, suddenly*] Here's herself. I'll be goin' up to the wake. [*He passes Nora as she comes in and goes out right. Nora sits wearily in the first chair at rear of the center table, right.*]

NORA [*dully*]   Was Jamie quarreling wid you? Don't heed him.

SARA   I don't, Mother. [*She sits in the chair at her mother's right.*]

NORA [*sadly*]   He's wild wid loneliness, missin' your father. [*A pause. Nora's face lights up.*] Mr. Harford came up to the wake.

SARA [*annoyed*]   Don't say Mr. Harford. You must call him Simon.

NORA [*humbly*] It sounds too familiar, and him such a gentleman.

SARA Nonsense, Mother! I don't like you to play humble with him— as though you were a servant. *He doesn't like it either.*[4]

. . . .

NORA [*resentfully*] Why wouldn't I?

SARA Because it's crazy. To give up life for a living death! I'd rather kill myself!

NORA Don't be sneerin' just because your father, God forgive him, brought you up a haythen. [*stubbornly*] I would do it—and I will!

SARA [*with a mocking smile*] There's no worse thing you could do if you want to make Father turn over in his grave.

NORA [*triumphantly*] He'll not, then! I've been waitin' to tell you. He came back to the Faith before he died.

SARA [*startled*] He never did! I don't believe you!

NORA It's God's truth, Sara! Afther the doctor said he was dyin' I begged him. He wouldn't answer for a long time, until I said, "Con, if you've ivir felt one bit av love for me, you'll do this for me now!" an' I cried my heart out. Then he opened his eyes an' there was a quare smile in them, an' he spoke, forgettin' to put on the brogue. "Yes," he says, "I still owe you that last bit of pride to pay for your love, don't I? An' I'm a gentleman about debts of honor, at least. So call in your priest." An' I did, an' he died with the rites av the Church. So ye needn't talk av his turnin' over in his grave.

SARA [*her face hard—with intense bitterness*] No. I needn't. There's not that much pride left in him now. Even his spirit is dead.

NORA [*resentful and a bit frightened*] Why do you make that bitter talk, God forgive you? Ain't you glad his soul's found peace, at last?

SARA Not the peace of death while he was still alive. Oh, I know he

---

4. Beginning with the end of Sara's speech, "He doesn't like it either," there is a page missing from the typescript (p. 16). It is the page where Nora tells Sara that she is going to enter a convent. The next line ("Why wouldn't I?") is apparently in answer to Sara's negative response to Nora's news.

died long ago—the spirit in him. But maybe I hoped, in spite of hating him, that he'd kept that last pride! Maybe I admired that one thing in him—his defiance of a God he denied but really believed in! [*She gives a bitter little laugh.*] Well, I know now why he died with that sneer on his lips. It was at himself!

NORA [*protesting pitifully*] It's no sneer at all! It's the smile av his soul at peace! [*She breaks down and sobs.*] Don't take that from me, Sara!

SARA [*moved and ashamed—patting her shoulder*] There Mother, don't. I—forgive me— [*changing the subject*] When will you go in the Convent?

NORA [*sadly*] God knows. Tomorrow if I could. But there's a pile av debts to be paid first. I want no dishonor on his name, an' I'd feel it was cheatin' to go in the Convent widout a clear conscience. [*then hastily*] But nivir mind that. You've your own troubles. And it's nothin' at all.

SARA [*hesitates—then blurts out*] I can ask Simon—

NORA [*stiffening—proudly*] You'll not! You'll be kind enough to mind your own business av you plaze!

SARA [*relieved and hating herself for being relieved*] But we'd be only too happy—

NORA [*gently*] I know, Darlin'—an' God bless you. But I'd nivir be able to look myself in the face if I held you back when you're just startin' in life.

SARA But we could afford—

NORA [*roughly*] No, I'm sayin'! To the divil wid me! My life is done. All I ask for myself is a bit av peace before the end. But I'm askin' more for you! I want you to rise in the world, an' own the things your father once owned an' you was born to—wealth an' a grand estate an' you ridin' in your carriage like a Duchess wid coachman an' footman, an' a raft av servants bowin' an' scrapin'.

SARA [*her face lighting up—with a determined confidence*] I'll have all of that, Mother, I take my oath to you.

NORA [*enthusiastically*] So ye will, Darlin'! I know it! An' won't I be proud, watchin' you rise, an' boastin' to the world! Even in the Convent, I'll be prayin' the Blessed Virgin to help you! [*guiltily*]

God forgive me, maybe I shouldn't say that. [*reassuring herself*] Ah, I know Almighty God will find it enough if I give up all worldly thoughts for myself an' He'll forgive my pride in you! [*dismissing this eagerly*] Tell me now—how is the business doin'? You haven't written in a long while.

SARA [*eagerly—unconsciously lapsing a little into brogue*] It's doing fine, Mother. We've just finished building an addition to the mill and the cottons we're weaving are as good or better than any foreign ones. By we I mean Matthew, too, but it'll soon be only us, because Simon is buying him out.

NORA [*proudly*] So he's buyin' out his partner, is he? The last you wrote, you didn't know if you could persuade him.

SARA [*with a smile*] I had a hard time, he's that stubborn. I had to plead with him it was for my sake and the children's. He's so afraid of getting in too deep. And it's so silly because after I get his mind made up, there's no stopping him. [*with a proud toss of her head*] And don't think it's just a wife, blind with love, boastin'. It's common talk of our town he's the ablest young merchant in the trade and has a great future before him.

NORA [*admiringly*] Ah, ain't that grand, now! You'd nivir think it to meet him—I mean, he's so quiet and gentle.

SARA [*with a laugh*] Let you be a man meetin' him in business, and tryin' to get the best of him, you'd find him different. [*practically*] Of course, it doesn't do to boast yet. We're only on the first step. It's only a small mill that you wouldn't notice at all compared to the big ones. But business is leapin' up and once we have Matthew out of it—he wants to travel in Europe and he's only too anxious to sell at a bargain—we'll have all the profits for ourselves.

NORA [*teasing admiringly*] Musha, you have grand business talk! To hear you, you'd think it was you was his partner, no less!

SARA So I am! I'm no fool, Mother. I've got brains for more than just sleepin' with the man I love an' havin' his children an' keepin' his house. Ask Simon. He talks over everything with me. I've made him. At first, he was all for never sayin' a word about business at home, and treatin' me like a stuffed bird in a glass case he had to protect from the world, but I soon got him over that. Now he depends on me, an' I'll say for myself I've never advised him wrong. [*She smiles.*] The only foolish thing he ever did he did without askin' me. He had someone buy the old farm here for him where he used to live in the cabin by the lake.

NORA   Did he, now? I heard tell it was sold. Ivery one was wonderin' who was the fool— [*hastily*] I mane, they say divil a one has ivir made it pay.

SARA [*frowning*]   I know. It was foolish. But he was that shamed when I found out—like a little boy caught stealing jam—that I couldn't scold. And he had all kinds of excuses that it was a wise notion because, if the worst happened, it'd be easy to fix up the old farm-house on it, and you could at least raise a living from it, and we'd always have it to fall back on. Then when I laughed at him and said that was no fear it'd ever come to that, he owned up he'd really bought it for sentiment because it was there we first loved each other.

NORA [*guiltily embarrassed*]   Arrah, don't think av that now. Wasn't you married right after? God forgave you the sin.

SARA [*proudly defensive*]   I've never asked His forgiveness. I'm proud of it. [*changing the subject abruptly*] So, of course, when he told me that, I forgave him. And maybe it'll come in useful in the end. There's over two hundred acres, and he bought it for a song, and the little lake on it is beautiful, and there's grand woods that would make a fine park. With a mansion built on the hill by the lake, where his old cabin was, you couldn't find a better gentleman's estate.

NORA [*with admiring teasing*]   Glory be, but you're sure av havin' your way!

SARA [*determinedly*]   I am, Mother, for this is America not poverty-stricken Ireland where you're a slave! Here you're free to take what you want, if you've the power in yourself.[5] [*a pause—her expression*

---

5. This is the first of several instances where the phrase "take what you want" occurs. It is an index to the theme of greed in the play and the cycle. Sara's words to Nora here echo her speech to Nora in *TP*. In act 1 she explains to Nora that "this is a country where you can rise as high as you like, and no one but the fools who envy you care for what you rose from, once you've the money, and the power goes with it." *The Later Plays of Eugene O'Neill*, ed. Travis Bogard (New York: Random House, 1967), p. 150.

suddenly becomes uneasily thoughtful] I think Simon had other reasons for buying the farm he didn't tell me—maybe that he didn't tell even himself. He has queer lonely spells at times when I feel he's in a dream world far away from me.

NORA   Yes, he's a touch av the poet, God pity him—like your father. [*A wailing keen comes from the floor above. Nora's face becomes sorrow-ridden. She shivers, and makes the sign of the cross.*]

SARA   [*her thoughts made more uneasy by this disturbance—irritably*] Why do you let them keen, Mother? It's old ignorant superstition. It belongs back in Ireland, not here! [*Then, as her mother doesn't hear her, she goes on uneasily.*] Sometimes I feel he's thinking that if it wasn't for me and the children he'd be living alone back in his cabin by the lake writing poetry like he used to, or else writing the book he was planning, to show people how to change the Government and all the laws so there'd be no more poor people, nor anyone getting the best of the next one, and there'd be no rich but everyone would have enough. [*She finishes scornfully.*] He doesn't talk about that anymore, thank God! I've laughed it out of him! I've told him you can make new laws but you can't make new men and women to fit them, so what's the use of dreaming? I've said, even if he could make it come true, it would be a coward's heaven he'd have, for where is the glory of life if it's not a battle where you prove your strength to rise to the top and let nothing stop you! [*She says this last with exultance. Then she smiles fondly.*] But I'm a fool to take his dreams seriously. Sure, when he's himself, there's no one takes more joy in getting ahead. If you'd see his pride sometimes when he comes home to tell me of some scheme he's accomplished. [*She laughs.*] Oh, he's a queer mixture. [*then intensely*] And I love him, every bit of him! I love him more than ever any woman loved a man, I think. I'd give my last drop of blood to make him happy! And he is happy! [*Again there is the wailing keen from the wake above. Nora gets to her feet, wearily.*]

NORA   [*dully*] I'd better go up to the wake. They'll think it wrong I'm staying away from him so long. [*She hesitates—feeling she must make some comment on what Sara has said, which she has only half heard.*] I wouldn't worry over Simon bein' happy. Sure, you've only to see the love in his face when he looks at you. [*then inconsequently*] Does he ever hear from his people?

SARA [*resentfully*]   From his father? No fear. He won't ever let Simon's name be spoken in their home. But Simon's mother writes him letters. Not often, though. I'll say this for her, she's never tried to interfere. [*then cynically*] Maybe it's because Simon's father never gives her the chance. [*then honestly*] No, that's not fair. I ought to feel grateful to her. It was the two thousand dollars she sent Simon after we were married gave us our start. [*resentfully*] Not but what we didn't pay her back every penny as soon as we'd saved it. I made Simon do that, for all his saying she wanted it to be a gift and we'd hurt her feelings. [*with a toss of her head*] I have my feelings, too. I'm accepting no gifts from her.

NORA [*has not been listening to this at all—dully*] I'll go up to him now. [*She starts for the door at right as Simon enters it. He smiles at her and she forces a smile in return and goes out. He comes over and sits beside Sara, giving her a pat on the cheek as she smiles up at him.*]

SARA   How's the baby?

SIMON   Sound asleep. [*he hesitates—then making up his mind—uncomfortably*] Listen, Sara. There's one thing we ought to talk over and decide right away—for your mother's sake.

SARA [*stiffens, glancing at him suspiciously*]   What's that?

SIMON [*quietly*]   About your father's debts.

SARA [*angrily*]   How do you know? Was Jimmie Cregan begging to you?

SIMON [*placatingly*]   Now don't blame him.

SARA [*angrily*]   Ah, if that drunken fool would only mind his own business!

SIMON [*quietly*]   It's your business, isn't it? And we're partners, aren't we? So it's my business, too. Please don't feel bitter toward Cregan. He may have his faults. Who hasn't? [*smiling*] Perhaps even you and I have some. [*She glances at him with quick guilty suspicion.*] But he is a good friend to your mother.

SARA [*sneeringly*]   As long as she has free whiskey for him to sponge!

SIMON [*frowns—a bit sharply*]   Sara! That's not— [*He controls him-*

self and pats her hand—gently] I hate to hear you sneering and full of bitterness. That isn't you, you know.

SARA [*clasps his hand—humbly*]   No. It isn't the me who loves you. I know that, Simon. [*resentfully*] It's coming here does it to me. It brings back the past. It makes Father live again. Ah, why can't he be dead, and not have his ghost walk in my heart with the sneer on his lips!

SIMON [*repelled*]   Sara! [*then more gently—slowly*] One must forgive the dead, for their sakes, but even more for our own.

SARA [*squeezing his hand*]   Oh, I know!

SIMON [*persuasively*]   Try and forget him. It's of your mother we must think now. She has had a hard life. How hard you know better than anyone.

SARA [*sadly*]   I do. Poor Mother! Not an hour of joy or peace did he give her since the day she married him, but only slavery. [*then hurriedly—and guiltily*] But the debts come to two thousand dollars. That's a pile of money, Simon. No matter how much we wanted to, we couldn't afford right now—

SIMON [*easily*]   Oh, I think we can. You're forgetting what we've put aside to buy out Matthew. We can use part of that.

SARA [*tensely*]   And not buy him out, after all our plans? [*angrily*] No! I won't have it!

SIMON [*sharply*]   Sara!

SARA [*hastily*]   I mean it means so much to your future that you'd never forgive yourself!

SIMON [*quietly*]   What about your mother's future? Could we forgive ourselves if we deliberately ignored that?

SARA [*hurriedly*]   And anyway, it's no use talking, because I've already talked to her. I said I'd ask you to pay his debts for her.

SIMON [*his face lighting up*]   Ah, I knew you—

SARA [*an undercurrent of triumph in her voice*]   And she told me to mind my business for my pains! She was mad and insulted. So you might as well put it from your mind. [*with incongruous pride*] My mother may be an ignorant, simple woman but she's a proud woman, too. If you think she'd ever let a Harford pay Father's debts, you're badly mistaken.

SIMON [*quietly*] I know your mother's pride and I admire her for it. [*then with a smile—calculating*] But I think we can get around her, if we go about it shrewdly. In the first place, before we let her know, I'll look up all the creditors and pay them. Then we'll face her with an accomplished fact. She will resent it, of course, but I've been figuring out a way to put it to her so that she'll be reconciled—that it's a sin for her to put her duty to God off just because of pride and that if she waited she might not live to enter a Convent. I can even see the Priest and persuade him to talk to her. I'll ask her, too, if it's fair of her to keep on the feud with my father against me, and if it isn't time, now your father's dead, to forgive and forget, for her grandchildren's sake, who have both Melody and Harford blood in them. I'll—

SARA [*with a helpless sigh—exasperatedly*] Arrah, you needn't go on! [*her manner changing—with a trembling tender smile*] Don't I know better than any, without your boasting, that you're a sly one to look into a woman's heart and see her weakness and get your own way. [*proudly*] And don't I love you for it, and for being kind and sweet and good, and putting shame on me for a greedy selfish pig. [*She raises his hand impulsively and kisses it.*]

SIMON [*tenderly*] Don't say that! You're the dearest, most precious— [He hugs her to him.]

SARA [*stubbornly*] I'm not! I'm a fool always dreaming of wealth and power and pride, even while I know in my heart that doesn't matter at all, that your love is my only wealth—to have you and the children. [*pitifully*] But I can't help dreaming, Darling. I've known what you haven't—poverty—and the lies and dirt and hurt of it that spits on your pride while you try to sneer and hold your head high!

SIMON [*soothingly*] I know, Dear.

SARA You don't. You couldn't. [*pleadingly*] But please know, Simon Darling, that for all the greed in me, I was only fooling myself. My conscience—and my honor, for I have honor, too—would never have rested easy until we paid the debts for Mother. [*She laughs.*] So thank you kindly, Sir, for beating me and saving me having to beat myself. [*She kisses him.*]

SIMON [*teasing tenderly*]   Maybe I guessed that. [*He laughs.*] You can't fool me.

SARA [*teasing, with a note of taunting coming in*]   No. And you can't fool me. Don't I guess that, besides all your goodness of heart, you're glad of the excuse not to buy out your partner, because you're afraid of the whole weight of the business on your shoulders.

SIMON [*starts—sharply*]   What makes you say that! It's not true. I should think I'd already given you ample proof. If I'm afraid it's not for that reason, as you well know. [*bitterly*] But, do you know, I wonder? Will you ever understand—?

SARA [*alarmed now*]   Darling, I was only teasing. [*pulling him to her—with rough possessive tenderness*] Come here to me. Don't push away, now! Don't you know I wouldn't hurt you for the world?

SIMON [*giving in—but stiffly*]   I don't like that kind of teasing. [*She kisses him. He relaxes against her body. His face softens. Finally he forces a laugh.*] Forgive me, I'm a fool. [*then almost boastfully*] To show you how wrong you are, I've already figured out how we can pay your father's creditors, and still buy out Matthew's interest.

SARA [*eagerly*]   Ah, don't I always tell you you've the brains to beat the world!

SIMON   I'll simply get him to take my note for the difference.

SARA [*uncertainly*]   I don't like notes. My father always—

SIMON [*tauntingly*]   Who is being afraid, now? [*then eagerly*] But you needn't be. With the profits from the business, as I intend to reorganize it, I can pay him in no time, and then—

SARA [*gloatingly*]   Oh, then I know you'll make the money come flying in! [*She suddenly looks guilty and forces a laugh.*] There I go with my greedy dreaming again. But it's because when we were married it was such a hurt to my pride that I knew your family and their friends thought you'd lowered yourself through me. I swore then I'd help you rise till you were bigger than your father or any of them.

SIMON [*his face hardening*]   It would be a satisfaction to me, too, to prove to Father, in the only terms he can understand—

SARA [*aggressively*]   And to your mother.

SIMON [*his expression changing—in a tone that is tinged with self-contempt*]   Mother? I hardly think my achievement on that plane could impress her greatly.

SARA   Why not, I'd like to know?

SIMON [*frowns and shrugs his shoulders*]   Well, her point of view is a bit different from yours—ours, I should say.— [*He is interrupted by a knock on the door at rear.*]

SARA [*irritably*]   Someone for the wake, I suppose. I'll go. [*She goes and unbolts the door—then starts back with a surprised gasp as she sees a tall, black, powerfully-built negro in a coachman's uniform standing before the door.*] What do you want?

CATO [*removes his hat—with polite dignity*]   Mister Simon Harford, Ma'am. Is he heah?

SIMON [*astonished*]   Why hello, Cato. [*He goes back to meet him.*] It's all right, Sara. Let him come in. [*She steps aside and Cato enters. He is about fifty-five with whitening, crinkly hair. Simon, smiling with genuine pleasure, holds out his hand. Cato takes it embarrassedly.*] It's good to see you again, Cato.

CATO [*grinning*]   Thank you, Mister Simon. I'm happy to see you. [*They come forward. Sara follows them, her expression uneasy and suspicious.*]

SIMON   This is my wife, Cato. She's often heard me speak of you. [*Cato bows respectfully. Sara forces a smile.*]

SARA   Yes, indeed, Cato. He's never forgotten how good you were to him when he was a boy.

SIMON   Oh, Cato and I are old friends, aren't we, Cato?

CATO [*grins embarrassedly*]   Thank you, Suh. Thank you, Ma'am. Your mother sent me, Suh. I'se got a letter she tol' me give in your hands and only your hands. [*Sara stiffens resentfully. Cato takes a letter from his inside pocket and hands it to Simon.*] She say wait til you read it and you tell me de answer and I tell her.

SIMON [*opens the letter. It is only a few lines. As he reads his face lights up.*]   Tell her my answer is, of course I'll meet her there.

CATO   Yes, Suh. I'll tell her. Now I better git back quick. She tell me sneak out and sneak in so nobody see and tell yo father. [*He bows *to Sara.*] Good night, Ma'am. Good night, Suh. [*He hesitates—then blurts out*] Effin you don't mind, I'se wishin' you happiness!

SIMON Thank you, Cato. Good night.

SARA [*touched, her face softening*] Thank you, Cato. Good night. [*Cato makes a hurried sidling-backwards exit through the door at rear, closing it behind him. Sara sits in the chair at right end of the table at center, front, her face again stiff and resentful. Simon stands with the letter in his hands, sunk in a smiling reverie. Then his eyes fall on Sara and he starts as if awakening.*]

SIMON Here's Mother's letter, if you'd care to read it.

SARA [*stiffly*] No. It was meant for you alone.

SIMON Nonsense. I'll read it to you. It's only a note. [*He reads.*] "I have your letter telling me you are coming up for your father-in-law's funeral and it occurs to me that we might take this opportunity to see each other again, if only for a moment. If you agree, and if Sara will consent to a brief leave-of-absence for you—"

SARA Why shouldn't I consent? Does she think I'm afraid?

SIMON [*resentful in his turn*] Don't be silly. She's only joking. [*He goes on reading.*] "—let us meet at your old cabin tomorrow afternoon at three o'clock. I hope you can come. I am most curious to see how much you've changed, and I promise you will discover me to have changed, too, though not by evidence of the ravages of time on my poor face, I trust." [*Then he laughs.*] Hello. Here's a joke on her. I didn't notice before, but she's signed it "Deborah." She must have been in such a hurry—

SARA It seems a strange letter to me.

SIMON [*impatiently*] I've always told you you can't judge anything she does by ordinary standards. [*He smiles.*] She takes a childish pride in being fancifully willful and eccentric. You surely saw that, the one time you met her, even though you only talked with her a moment.

SARA I saw it, yes. And I guessed beneath it she was a woman with a will of iron to get her own way.

SIMON [*laughs*] Iron and Mother! That's funny, Sara. Quicksilver would describe her better.

SARA Maybe. But she promises you she's changed.

SIMON [*smiling*] She couldn't change if she tried. From her letters of the past year or so, I'd say she had simply become more herself, if that were possible.

SARA   Maybe. [*She hesitates—then slowly*] I wish you wouldn't go, Simon.

SIMON [*astonished*] Not go? When she asks me to? When we haven't seen each other in four years? Surely you wouldn't want me to hurt her like that? [*then shortly*] Anyway, I've already said I would go.

SARA   You could send a note by Jamie. You could lie and make an excuse.

SIMON [*sharply*] Sara! [*He stares at her frowningly.*] I can't understand— [*His face softens and he puts his arm around her.*] Here, here. This won't do. What has come over you?

SARA [*doggedly*] Why does she want you to meet her at your old cabin?

SIMON [*cajolingly*] Because it's out of the way and she won't be seen going there. She can't take any chance that Father might find out, you know. And I suppose it naturally suggested itself. I wrote her I had bought the property, so she knows she won't be trespassing.

SARA [*resentfully*] It's mine. You put it in my name. I hope you told her that. [*with sudden agitation*] Oh, I know I'm stupid, Simon, but I can't help suspecting she hates me in her heart and would like nothing better than a chance to come between us.

SIMON [*stares at her—then laughs teasingly but with a note of taunting*] Ah, who's the one who is afraid now? [*then with increasing sharpness*] You have absolutely no justification for talking of Mother like that. It's not only absurd, it's ungrateful. She favored our marriage. It was her money that helped us. And now you want me to lie out of seeing her! I don't know what to think of you, Sara, when you act like this!

SARA [*frightened*] Please don't think badly, Simon. I know it's crazy. Maybe it's being pregnant makes me nervous and afraid of everything.

SIMON [*immediately shamefaced*] I, —I'm sorry, Dear. [*He kisses her with awkward tenderness.*]

SARA   It's because I love you so much, and I never can believe my good luck in having you. I'm always afraid of something happening.

SIMON [*hushing her—tenderly*] Foolish One! As if anything could— [*He kisses her.*]

SARA [*Presses him to her with a fierce possessiveness and kisses him. Then she pushes him back and jumps to her feet with a happy laugh.*] There! The craziness is all gone. Of course, you must see your mother. She's been good to us, and I'll never stop being gratefull, and you're to give her my best respect and love. [*then bullying him lovingly*] And now, quick with you, and go to bed. I want you to have a good rest so you'll look healthy and handsome and she'll see how well I take care of you. [*She pulls his arm and he gets to his feet smilingly.*] Go on. Get along with you. [*She urges him toward the door at right.*] I'll be in as soon as I've had another word with Mother. But mind you're fast asleep by then!

SIMON [*laughingly*] Oh, I'll mind. Don't I always obey like a devoted slave? [*He goes out.*]

SARA [*looks after him, smiling fondly, then sits down, sighing. She stares before her, deep in thought. Her expression suddenly becomes uneasy, suspicious, and calculating*] She's still got her hold on him. She's up to some trick. [*with smouldering anger*] Well, I'll fool her! I'll go there and hide. I can easy get the key from his pocket— [*then guiltily*] What would he think of me? But he won't ever know. [*scornfully*] Ah, the divil take honor! It's something men made up for themselves! As if she'd ever let honor stand in her way!

* * * CURTAIN * * *

Tao House
April 12, 1938
May 11th[6]

6. Carlotta typed in dates at the end of some of the scenes, indicating when she completed typing the scene. I have included these dates when they occur. However, O'Neill inserted revisions into many of the scenes after they were dated by Carlotta.

Cabin—Act One, Scene Two

*Yale Collection of American Literature, Beinecke Rare Book
and Manuscript Library, Yale University*

Act One, Scene Two

—

SCENE *A log cabin by a lake in the woods about two miles from the village. It is just before three in the afternoon of the following day.*

The cabin is ten feet by fifteen, made of logs with a roof of warped, hand-hewn shingles. It is placed in a small clearing, overgrown with rank, matted grass. The front of the cabin, with a door at center, and a small window at left of door, faces front, overlooking the lake.[1] Another window is in the wall facing right. At the left side is a stone chimney. Close by the left and rear of the cabin is the wood—oak, pine, birch, and maple trees. The foliage is at the full of brilliant Autumn color, purple and red and gold mingled with the deep green of the conifers.

The cabin gives evidence of having been abandoned for years. The mortar between the stones of the chimney has crumbled and fallen out in spots. The moss stuffing between the logs hangs here and there in straggly strips. The windows have boards nailed across them. A weather-beaten bench stands against the wall at left of the door. It is home-made, heavily constructed, and is still sturdy.

The clearing is partly in sunlight, partly shadowed by the woods.

As the curtain rises Sara appears by the corner of the cabin, right, having come by a short-cut trail from off rear, right, along the shore of the lake. She has evidently hurried for she is breathless and panting. She looks around the clearing furtively. Her expression is a mixture

---

1. This description of the cabin coincides with the one found in Brooks' *The Flowering of New England*. See n. 9 of Introduction.

of defiant resentment and guilt. She wears the same mourning of Scene One. She hastily unlocks the door and changes the key to the inside. Leaving the door ajar, she comes stealthily to the edge of the woods at left, front, and peers up a path which leads from the clearing into the woods. She starts and darts back to the door, enters the cabin and closes the door noiselessly behind her and locks herself in. For a moment there is silence. Then Simon's mother, Deborah Harford, steps into the clearing from the path, at left, front.

Deborah is forty-five but looks much younger. She is small, not over five feet tall, with the slender, immature figure of a young girl. One cannot believe, looking at her, that she has ever borne children. There is something about her perversely virginal. Her face is small, heart-shaped, olive-complected, astonishingly youthful, with only the first tracing of wrinkles about the eyes and mouth, a foreshadowing of sagging flesh under the chin, and of scrawniness in the neck. It is framed by a mass of wavy white hair, which by contrast with the youthfulness of her face, gives her the appearance of a girl wearing a becoming wig at a costume ball. Her nose is dainty and delicate above a full-lipped mouth, too large and strong for her face, showing big, even white teeth when she smiles. Her forehead is high and a trifle bulging, with sunken temples. Her eyes are so large they look enormous in her small face. Beautiful eyes, black, deep-set, beneath pronounced brows that meet above her nose. Her hands are small with thin, strong, tapering fingers, and she has tiny feet. She is dressed daintily and expensively, with extreme care and good taste, entirely in white. Her habitual well-bred manner is one of mercurial whimsicality—a provocative unconventional frankness of speech. But one senses that underlying this now is a nervous tension and restlessness, an insecurity, a brooding discontent and disdain.

DEBORAH [*looks around the clearing—bitterly*] And I hoped he would be here, eagerly awaiting me! [*She forces a self-mocking smile.*] What can you expect, Deborah? At your age, a woman must become resigned to wait upon every man's pleasure, even her son's.

[*She picks her way daintily through the long grass toward the bench, answering herself resentfully.*] Age? I am only forty-five. I am still beautiful. You harp on age as though I were a withered old hag! [*mocking again*] Oh, not yet, Deborah! But now that the great change is upon you, it would be wise, I think, to discipline your mind to accept this fate of inevitable decay with equanimity. [*She gives a little shiver of repulsion—determinedly*] No! I will not think of it! I still have years before me. [*She breaks a leaf off the branch fastidiously and sits down—sneeringly*] And what will you do with these years, Deborah? Dream them away as you have all the other years since Simon deserted you? Live in the false life of books, in histories of the past? Continue your present silly obsession with scandalous French Eighteenth Century memoirs?[2] Dream yourself back until you live in them an imaginative life more real than reality, until you become not the respectable, if a trifle mad, wife of the well known merchant, but a noble adventuress of Louis's Court, and your little walled garden, the garden of Versailles, your pathetic summerhouse a Temple of Love the King has built as an assignation place where he keeps passionate tryst with you, his mistress, the unscrupulous courtesan, forsooth, greedy for lust and power! [*She laughs softly with sneering self-mockery—tauntingly*] Really, Deborah, this latest day dream is the most absurd of all the many ridiculous fantasies in which you have hidden from yourself! I begin to believe that truly you must be more than a little mad! You had better take care! One day you may lose yourself so deeply in that romantic evil, you will not find your way back. [*answering herself with defiant bravado*] Well, let that happen! I would welcome losing myself! [*abruptly—angry*] But you distort and exaggerate, as you always do! You know I do not take it seriously. I am lonely and bored! I am disgusted with watching my revolting body decay. Anything to forget myself. Besides, there is a perfectly rational explanation. I have seriously taken up the study of Eighteenth Century France to occupy my mind. I have always admired

---

2. Perhaps Deborah is referring to one of several memoirs, such as those of Duchess Gontaut, mistress to Louis XIV. See *Memoirs of the Duchesse Gontaut, 1773–1836* (New York: Dodd, Mead, 1894).

the Bourbons—perhaps because Father's stupid adoration of Napoleon prejudiced me against Napoleon, I suppose, and made me want to love his enemies. [*impatiently*] No, no, don't be absurd! That has nothing to do with it. I admire the manners and customs of that period, that is all. I would like to have lived then when life was free and charming and fastidious, not vulgar and ignoble and greedy as it is in this country today. [*She stops abruptly— exasperatedly*] But how stupid! These insane interminable dialogues with self! [*with a sudden tense desperation*] I must find someone outside myself in whom I can confide, and so escape myself. If I only had a close woman friend,[3] someone strong and healthy and sane, who dares to love and live life greedily instead of reading and dreaming about it! What a mistake it was to warn off friendship from my life like a prying trespasser! [*answering herself mockingly*] Quite true, Deborah, but don't tell me you hope to make Simon into such a friend—a man and your son. [*argumentatively*] Well, that is not so absurd as it appears. He always had a sensitive, feminine streak in him. He used to sense so much intuitively, to understand without my putting into words, and I hope he still— [*then derisively*] You forget he has changed, as you know from his letters. You are thinking of the Simon that was, your Simon, not the contented husband of that vulgar Irish biddy, who evidently has found such a comfortable haven in her arms! [*with bitter sadness*] Yes, it is hopeless. What am I doing here? Why did I come? And he keeps me waiting. Perhaps he is not coming. Perhaps she would not permit him— [*in a burst of anger*] Am I to sit all afternoon and wait upon his pleasure? [*springing to her feet*] No! I will go! [*controlling herself—in a forced reasonable tone*] Nonsense, he told Cato to tell me he would come. He would never break his word to me, not even for her. I know, from his letters, he still loves me. [*She sits down again.*] I must stop my ridiculous, suspicious worrying. He is not late. It is I who am early. I have only to be patient—keep my mind off bitter thoughts—stop

---

3. This line is, of course, an echo of the line Mary Tyrone speaks in *LDJ*. See n. 5 of Introduction.

thinking—wile away the time—with any dream, no matter how absurd, if it serves the purpose of comforting me until he comes— shut my eyes and forget—not open them until he comes— [*She relaxes, her head back, her eyes shut. A pause. Then she dreams aloud to herself.*] The Palace at Versailles—I wear a gown of crimson satin and gold, embroidered in pearls—Louis gives me his arm, while all the Court watches enviously—the men, old loves that my ambition has used and discarded, or others who desire to be my lovers but dare not hope—the women who hate me for my wit and beauty, who envy me my greater knowledge of love and of men's hearts—my superior talents for unscrupulous intrigue in the struggle for power and possession—I walk with the King in the gardens—the moonlight sobbing in the fountains—he whispers tenderly: "My Throne it is your heart, Beloved, and my fair kingdom your beauty, and so of all Sovereigns of the earth I am most blessed"—he kisses me on the lips—as I lead him into the little Temple of Love he built for me— [*There is a sound from up the path at left, through the woods, front. She starts quickly and opens her eyes as Simon comes into the clearing.*]

SIMON [*his face lighting up*] Mother! [*He strides toward her.*]

DEBORAH [*rising—still half in her dream—in a tone of arrogant displeasure*] You have been pleased to keep me waiting, Monsieur.

SIMON [*disconcerted—then decides she is joking and laughs*] Not I, Madame! I'm on the dot. It's you who are early. [*He kisses her.*] Mother, it's so good to—

DEBORAH [*her arrogance gone—clinging to him, almost hysterically*] Oh, yes! Yes! Dear Simon! [*She begins to sob.*]

SIMON [*moved*] Don't! [*tenderly chiding*] Here, here! You crying! I can't believe it. I don't remember ever seeing you cry.

DEBORAH [*stops as suddenly as she had begun—pulling away from him*] No. And it is a poor time to begin. Tears may become a woman while she's young. When she grows old they are merely disgusting. [*She dabs her eyes with her handkerchief.*]

SIMON [*gives her another puzzled look*] Oh, come now. [*smiling*] You're only fishing for compliments, Mother. You're as young and pretty as ever.

DEBORAH [*pleased—coquettishly*] You are gallant, Sir. My mirror tells me a crueler story. Do you mean to say you don't see all the wrinkles? Be truthful, now.

SIMON   I can see a few, just beginning. But for your age it is amazing—

DEBORAH [*flashes him a resentful glance*] It is true, I am well preserved. [*abruptly*] But how foolish of us to waste precious moments discussing an old woman's vanity. [*She puts her hands on his shoulders.*] Here. Turn about is fair play. Let me examine you. [*She stares into his face critically.*] Yes. You have changed. And quite as I had expected. You are getting your father's successful merchant look.

SIMON [*frowns and turns away from her*] I hope not! [*changing the subject*] Sit down, Mother. [*She does so. He stands examining the cabin.*] I shall have to send someone out here to repair things. I wish I could do it myself. [*He passes his hands over the logs lovingly.*] What labor it cost me to build this without help. Yet I was never happier. [*He tries the door—searches his pocket*] Funny, I could have sworn I had the key. But perhaps it is better. It would only make me melancholy.

DEBORAH [*cases a sharp appraising glance at his face*] Yes, it is always sad to contemplate the corpse of a dream.

SIMON [*answers before he thinks*] Yes. [*then defensively*] Unless you have found a finer dream.

DEBORAH   Oh, I know. Love is worth any sacrifice. I told you that, if you will remember. How is Sara?

SIMON   Well—and happy.

DEBORAH   You are as much in love?

SIMON   More. I cannot imagine a marriage happier than ours.

DEBORAH   I am glad. But, of course, I knew. You have protested in every letter how happy you were. [*He flashes a suspicious look at her. She goes on casually.*] And the children? Sara expects another before long, I believe you wrote.

SIMON   Yes.

DEBORAH   All this child-bearing. It must be a strain. Is she pretty still?

SIMON   More beautiful than ever.

DEBORAH   There speaks the devoted husband! I was wondering if you would bring her with you today.

SIMON [*surprised*] You said nothing in your note about bringing her. I thought you wanted to see me alone.

DEBORAH I did. But perhaps I see now it might have been as well— [*quickly*] I had begun to think perhaps Sara might not permit you to come—

SIMON [*frowning*] Permit me? You talk as though I were a slave.

DEBORAH Well, one is, isn't one, when one is in love? Or so I have read in the poets.

SIMON [*smiling*] Oh, to love I am a willing slave. But what made you think Sara—?

DEBORAH Well, a woman's love is jealously possessive—or so I have read—and she knows how close you and I used to be in the old happy days. You were happy in those days with me, weren't you, before you graduated from Harvard and had to leave me and find your own life in the world?

SIMON [*moved*] Of course I was, Mother—never more happy.

DEBORAH [*tenderly*] I am glad you still remember, Dear. [*She pats his hand.*]

SIMON And I am grateful for all you did afterwards—your approval of our marriage, your generosity in helping us financially to make a start.

DEBORAH It was Sara, wasn't it, who insisted on your paying back as a loan what I had meant as a gift?

SIMON [*uncomfortably*] Yes, she didn't understand— She is very sensitive and proud— [*hurriedly*] But she is as grateful to you as I am. She will never forget your kindness.

DEBORAH [*with a trace of disdain*] I am grateful for her appreciation. [*changing the subject abruptly*] Tell me, do you ever think now of the book you were so eager to write when you resigned in disgust from your father's business and came out here to live alone—the one inspired by the social philosophy of Jean Jacques Rousseau—your Utopian plan for a new society where there would be no rich nor poor, where all would be content with enough and live in perfect amity without envy or greed. You never mentioned it in your letters. Have you abandoned the idea entirely?

SIMON [*reluctantly*] For the present. I have so little time now. [*defensively*] Oh, I think of it often and some day I'll write it.

DEBORAH I see.

SIMON [*suspiciously*] What made you ask about that now, Mother?

DEBORAH [*carelessly*] Nothing. This place reminded me, I suppose. And you really should write it. The times are ripe for such a book, in these days when our republic is sinking into a corrupt decline. With four years more of Mr. Jackson in power—and even your father admits he is sure of re-election—the precedent will be irrevocably set. We shall be governed by the ignorant greedy mob for all future time. [*She laughs with malicious amusement.*] Your poor father! He wishes Massachusetts would secede from the Union. One has but to mention the name of Jackson to give him violent dyspepsia.

SIMON [*grinning*] I can imagine. [*then scornfully*] It's ridiculous snobbery for him to sneer at the common people. He should remember his grandfather was only a Welsh immigrant farmer. Not that I hold any brief for Andrew Jackson. His spoils system is a disgrace to the spirit of true Democracy. [*He shrugs his shoulders.*] But it is also an inevitable development of our system of government. That system was wrong from the beginning. It confused freedom with separation from England, and then mistook the right to vote for Liberty. To be truly free, we must start all over again. In a free society there must be no private property to tempt men's greed into enslaving one another. We must protect man from his stupid possessive instincts until he can be educated to outgrow them spiritually. But at the same time, we must never forget that the least government, the best government. We must renounce the idea of great centralized governments, and divide society into small, self-governing communities where all property is owned in common for the common good. In my book I will prove this can easily be done if only men—

DEBORAH [*cynically*] Ah, yes, if only men—and women—were not men and women!

SIMON [*frowns, then smiles*] Now you're as cynical as Sara. [*She stiffens.*] That is her objection, too. [*then with embarrassment*] But I'm afraid I'm boring you with my perfect society.

DEBORAH   No. I'm only too happy to discover the old idealistic dreamer still exists in you.

SIMON [*self-consciously*] I haven't spoken of such matters in so long— [*He forces a laugh.*] Your influence, Mother! You were always such a sympathetic audience.

DEBORAH [*quietly*] I still am. But are you, I wonder?

SIMON [*preoccupied, ignores her question, and goes on doggedly as if he had to finish expressing his ideas*] I still believe with Rousseau, as firmly as ever, that at bottom human nature is good and unselfish. It is what we are pleased to call civilization that has corrupted it. We must return to Nature and simplicity and then we'll find that the People—those whom Father sneers at as the greedy Mob—are as genuinely noble and honorable as the false aristocracy of our present society pretends to be!

DEBORAH [*bitingly*] No doubt. However, I would still be nauseated by their thick ankles, and ugly hands and dirty finger nails, were they ever so noble-hearted! [*She suddenly cries with a desperate exasperation.*] Good Heavens, did I come here to discuss politics, and the natural rights of man—I, who pray the Second Flood may come and rid the world of this stupid race of men and wash the earth clean! [*She gets to her feet—with curt arrogance*] It is getting late, I must go.

SIMON   Go? You've just come! [*pleadingly*] Mother! Please! Forgive me if I've bored you. But it was you who brought it up. [*coaxingly*] Come. Sit down, Mother. [*She sits down again.*] You haven't told me a word about yourself yet.

DEBORAH [*bitterly*] I am afraid, though you might listen kindly, you could not hear me, Simon.

SIMON [*gently reproachful*] I used to hear, didn't I?

DEBORAH [*bitterly*] Once long ago. In another life. Before we had both changed.

SIMON   I haven't changed—not in my love for you. [*sadly*] It hurts that you can believe that of me, Mother.

DEBORAH [*bitterly*] Oh, I no longer know what to believe about anything or anyone!

SIMON   Not even about me?

DEBORAH   Not even about myself.

SIMON   [*regards her worriedly—gently*]   What has happened, Mother?
[*frowning*] Is it anything Father has done?

DEBORAH   [*astonished*]   Good Heavens, no!   [*She bursts into genuinely
amused laughter.*] My dear boy, what an absurd idea! It is easy to
see you have forgotten your old home. Your father is much too
worried about what President Jackson will do or say next, and what
effect it will have on imports and exports, to bother with me, even
if I would permit him to.

SIMON   Is it anything Joel—?

DEBORAH   Worse and worse! If you could see your brother now! He
is head of the bookkeeping department, which is about as high as
his ability can ever take him, to your father's disgust.

SIMON   [*with satisfaction*]   I knew Joel had no ability. Father must be
disappointed.

DEBORAH   Joel has become a confirmed ledger-worm. I think he tried
once to find me listed on the profit side of the ledger. Not finding
me there, he concluded he must merely be imagining that I existed.
[*Simon laughs.*] I invited him to visit me in my garden not long
ago—

SIMON   [*with a boyish scowl—jealously*]   Why? What could you want
with him?

DEBORAH   [*with a sharp interested look at him*]   Anyone for company!
You don't know how lonely I have grown since you— Poor Joel!
He looked as astounded as if a nun had asked him to her bedroom.
And when he came—with the air, I might say, of a correct gentleman who pays a duty call on a woman of whom he disapproves—
he determinedly recited impeccable platitudes and stared the flowers
out of countenance for half an hour, and then fled! You would have
laughed to see him.

SIMON   [*resentfully*]   Yes, he must have been out of place.

DEBORAH   [*smiles with satisfaction at his tone*]   He was indeed. So you
need not be jealous, Dear. I remembered you and all our old happy
days there. [*She pauses—then slowly*] No, I have not changed because of anything Joel— Hardly!

SIMON   [*gently*]   Then what is it, Mother?

DEBORAH   Why, nothing has happened, Dear, except time and change.

SIMON   You seem so lonely.

DEBORAH   [*patting his hand*]   I am glad you know that. Now I feel less lonely.

SIMON   It's hard to believe that about you. You were always so independent of others, so free and self-sufficient. All you ever needed was the solitude of your garden, or your room—your books and your dreams.

DEBORAH   [*bitterly*]   Yes, that was my arrogant mistake, presuming myself superior to life. But a time comes when, suddenly, all that security in solitude appears as weakness and cowardice, a craven running away, and hiding from life. You become restless, and discontent gnaws at your heart while you cast longing eyes beyond the garden wall at life which passes by so horribly unaware that you are still alive!

SIMON   How can you say Life has passed you by, Mother? That's foolish. You—

DEBORAH   [*unheeding*]   While you are still beautiful and life still woos you, it is such a fine gesture of disdainful pride, so satisfying to one's arrogance, to jilt it. But when the change comes and the tables are turned and an indifferent life jilts you—it is a repulsive humiliation to feel yourself a condemned slave to revengeful Time, to cringe while he lashes your face with wrinkles, or stamps your body into shapelessness, or smears it with tallow-fat with his malicious fingers! [*anticipating his protest*] Oh, I realize I am hardly as bad as that yet. But I will be, for I constantly sense in the seconds and minutes and hours flowing through me, the malignant hatred of life against those who have disdained it! But the body is least important. It is the soul, staring into the mirror of itself, knowing it is too late, that it is rejected and forever alone—seeing the skull of Death leer over its shoulder in the glass like a roué in a brothel ogling some life-sick old trull!

SIMON   [*shrinking with repulsion*]   Mother! That's—that's too morbid!

DEBORAH   [*seeing his shocked face, gives a little mocking laugh*]   Poor Simon, I warned you I had changed. Have I shocked you dreadfully? Mothers should never have such thoughts, should they? Not even while dreaming to themselves? [*She laughs again.*] Forgive me. I am afraid my mind has been corrupted by reading so many French Eighteenth Century memoirs of late. I believe I wrote you that I had started studying history. But perhaps you did not take it seriously. I was always studying something, wasn't I? The time I wasted hiding in my mind!

SIMON [*rebukingly*] Don't tell me you regret— [*abruptly*] You didn't write me it was that kind of history.

DEBORAH [*smiles at him teasingly*] No doubt I was ashamed to confess. But I find the French Eighteenth Century the most instructive and congenial period in modern history for me.

SIMON [*abruptly changing the subject*] What of your old passion for Hindu Philosophy? Don't tell me you have given that up!

DEBORAH Yes. Long ago. Or, to be exact, a year ago. This past year of change has seemed so long! It happened I awoke one day from my dream of self-renunciation, and indifference to the opposites, to find Life sneaking out my door renouncing me, taking the indifferent opposites along with him. From that moment the Sacred Books became for me merely a rubbish of lifeless words. And Brahma nothing at all but a foreign name for Death. [*She smiles bitterly—self-mocking*] As I have said, it is pleasant to your superior disdain to renounce life, but an intolerable insult when life renounces you. As for my excursions into Oriental wisdom, I see it now as the flight of one who, bored at home, blames the surroundings, and sails for far lands, only to find a welcoming figure waiting there to greet one—oneself! [*She smiles bitterly.*] And straightaway the exotic palms turn into old familiar elms or maples, the houses are the same old houses, the gardens the same gardens, and the natives only one's old neighbors with fewer clothes and a darker sunburn— [*Simon chuckles amusedly.*] —and one is as bewilderedly at home and not at home as ever! [*She pauses—then shrugging her shoulders*] I should have known I could have no enduring faith in any other-life religion. Being a Minister's daughter killed that in me. My father's life and his beyond-life expectations were too absurdly incongruous. [*She smiles mischievously.*] Poor man, how dreadfully embarrassed he would have been if Christ had ever called

even that I had started studying~~,history~~. But perhaps you did not
take it seriously. I was always studying something, wasn't I? The
time I have wasted ~~instructing~~ my mind!

Simon: (rebukingly) ~~Mother! That! too bitter.~~
Don't tell me you regret -- (abruptly) You didn't write to me that
kind of history.

Abigail: (Smiles at him teasingly) No doubt I was
ashamed to confess. ~~Oh,I have been studying Roman history ,too,
especially the lives of the Roman Empresses.~~ But I find the French
Eighteenth Century the most instructive and congenial. ~~It is still so
near - at least,to me.~~ I can conjure it back to life at home in it.

Simon: (Abruptly changing the subject) ~~But~~ What of
your old passion for Hindoo Philosophy? Don't tell me you have given
that up!

Abigail: ~~(with defensive curtness)~~ Yes. Long ago.
Or,to be exact, a year ago.

Simon: (looking at her - puzzledly) Why? You seemed
to believe in the doctrine of Brahma so enthusiastically. The Sacred
Books of India were like a Bible to you.

Abigail: (with a bitter smile) ~~I have always has an
infinite capacity for deluding myself -- until Life rudely awakens me.
Then I awoke one day to see Life sneaking out my door resisting me,
and the Sacred Books became merely a rubbish of holy words. Just anoth
er hiding place,in which I had implacably discovered myself. Brahma
had failed me. Or I had failed Brahma. There was no faith left in my
soul,but only the ghost of an intellectual conception in my brain of the
vague All which is the Nothing-At-All. I could not loose myself in
Brahma. Brahma was lost in me. In the end there was only I as an absurd celebrant offering the sacrifice of self in worship before the al-
tar of myself. (She laughs wryly) A sufficiently ridiculous tableau,
if you like - and not without humor,if one can have the hardihood to
laugh. And there was an end to Brahma,and the cowardly swindle of self
renunciation.~~

Simon: (worried and puzzled - matter of factly) ~~Yes.
I don't think Eastern philosophy is suited to our Western souls. We
are too young,too in love with the world of appearances and possessions.~~
(He adds slowly) Too wise,perhaps.

Abigail: (impatiently) East,West. I see no differ-
ence,except a superficial one. Hindu or Yankee,there is in the end only
oneself,a man or woman,a lonely animal ~~who dreams~~. As for my excursion
into Oriental ~~thought, it was like~~ the flight of one who,bored at home,
blames the surroundings,and sails for ~~the~~ farthest lands,only to find
a welcoming figure waiting there to greet one - ~~and the figure is~~ oneself! (She smiles bitterly) And straightaway the exotic palm ~~trees~~

Page 42 from typescript—Act One, Scene Two
*Yale Collection of American Literature, Beinecke Rare Book
and Manuscript Library, Yale University*

on him, especially if he came to the front door, with all the neighbors peering spitefully from behind curtains; hoping this Jacobin tramp would turn out to be a poor relation whose existence Father had concealed from them.

SIMON [*laughs*] Poor Grandfather! You're always so hard on him.

DEBORAH [*with gloating malice*] He was so proud of having sprung from an aristocratic old family. And yet he did try so hard to identify himself with Christ. But there was no point of resemblance except his poverty, and he was ashamed of that. And he couldn't help bearing God a grudge because He never kept His promise and let the meek devour the earth. Father's real idol was Napoleon. *He* didn't wait on promises, *he* wasn't meek, *he* took the earth! Father worshipped him. He used even to have the newspaper *Moniteur* sent him from France—his one extravagance—and gloat over each new victory. [*She sneers spitefully.*] Poor man! If you could imagine anyone less like Napoleon! Except in bodily stature. Poor Father was plump and insignificant.

SIMON I wish I remembered him. He must have been a strange character.

DEBORAH Extremely commonplace, you mean. Don't you recognize the symptoms? He was one of the great mob of greedy meek. He was Everyman. [*then with a sudden exasperation*] Great Heavens, why do I recall him? And what a stupid conversation! Politics, first and now, religion and family gossip about the dead! It was silly of me to come! [*She makes a move to rise but Simon catches her arm.*]

SIMON [*soothingly*] Now, Mother! It isn't stupid to me. If you knew how delighted I am to sit and hear you talk again. It's like old times! It brings back all the happiness of the past—the hours together in your garden, as far back as I can remember.

DEBORAH [*moved—pats his hand*] I am happy you have not forgotten, Dear.

SIMON [*smiling musingly*] Are you still as incorrigible a dreamer as ever, Mother? [*She stiffens and gives him a suspicious, defensive look.*] I can remember times—I must have been very little, then— when you would sink into a dream, your eyes open but no longer seeing me. I would speak to you but you wouldn't hear me. You were off somewhere. Then I'd be frightened—

DEBORAH [*relieved, smiling tenderly*]   That was silly, Dear. I was probably dreaming about you, of how, when you grew up, you and I—

SIMON [*again with a musing smile*]   Are you still as accomplished an actress as you used to be?

DEBORAH [*starts—forcing a laugh*]   Why, what a thing to say, Simon!

SIMON   Oh, I meant it admiringly, Mother. I was remembering—I must have been very little then, too—how you used to act out each part when you'd read me fairy stories. One moment you'd be the good fairy, or the good queen, or the poor abused little Princess— That was wonderful. But the next moment you'd be the evil Queen, or the bad fairy, or the wicked witch, and I'd be all gooseflesh with terror! [*He chuckles.*]

DEBORAH [*gives him a strange glance—almost tauntingly*]   You were extremely sensitive and imaginative—as a child.

SIMON [*frowning*]   The trouble was, your acting confused my mind about you. Sometimes I got bewildered trying to keep you distinct and separate from the part you played.

DEBORAH [*strangely*]   Yes, I have experienced that bewilderment, too— when trying to reconcile my opposites.

SIMON [*suddenly looks at her—smilingly*]   What role do you play nowadays, Mother?

DEBORAH [*stiffens, avoiding his eyes and forcing a laugh*]   I? What nonsense, Dear. You forget I have no audience now.

SIMON [*teasingly*]   Oh, you were always your own audience, too. I felt that. So tell me—

DEBORAH   No, I assure you I've foresworn dream dramas. I'm too painfully conscious of reality these days, and its banality is too grotesquely in contrast—

SIMON   Now, don't tell me you've given up imagination and resigned yourself to the dull humdrum of being merely Mrs. Harford. I won't believe it. You couldn't if you tried. I'm sure you still fly from that deadly boredom into a secret life of your own—or at least, into the life in books—

DEBORAH [*gives him a quick searching glance—with feigned carelessness*]   Oh, if that's what you mean, yes. I'll confess there are times now when I become so bored with myself that I do try to escape into Eighteenth Century France. Life was so much more romantic and exciting for a woman then, don't you think? As the Memoirs depict it, anyway, and as I recreate it from them in my imagination. [*more decidedly*] Yes, if I had had the choice, I would have chosen to live then. In fact, there are moments when I become so absorbed in the life of that period that I lose all sense of the present and feel that I did live then, that I am living there again. [*forcing a careless smile*] Perhaps my study of Eastern wisdom left me with a desire to believe in reincarnation. Sometimes I feel— [*forcing a careless laugh*] But that is very silly, of course.

SIMON   Why is it silly? Who knows? Anyway, about the life in books, I know I have often felt it more real to me than reality. [*He adds with an undercurrent of resentment.*] Or I used to in the old days when I had time for books. Especially the poetry you would read aloud to me. [*He smiles musingly.*] Remember Byron, Mother, and your favorite Childe Harold stanza? [*He recites.*]

> I have not loved the World, nor the World me;
> I have not flattered its rank breath, nor bowed
> To its idolatries a patient knee
> Nor coined my cheek to smiles,—nor cried aloud
> In worship of an echo: in the crowd
> They could not deem me one of such—I stood
> Among them, but not of them—

[*He breaks off—tenderly*] Do you remember, Mother?

DEBORAH   I do now. I forgot Byron after you had gone. I remember now, too, the stanza that begins: "But quiet to quick bosoms is a hell." And then, in the following one: "—all unquiet things which stir too strongly the soul's secret springs." [*She forces a smile.*] I fear loneliness is making me into a most unquiet thing. [*then with a laugh*] Your memories of the past encourage me to carry confession further and admit I do still have the childish habit of daydreaming and acting romantic roles in my mind to wile away the time.

SIMON [*grows teasing*]   I knew it. I know you.

DEBORAH [*lightly*]   You did, but do you? You forget time has changed me. [*still lightly, but with an undercurrent of taunting*] And you. You are a contented husband and father now, a successful merchant, so like your father! [*Simon frowns with annoyance.*] I greatly fear you would be horribly shocked if I should tell you the nature of the part I play in my Eighteenth Century past!

SIMON [*grins*]   I'll chance it, Mother. Remember your old wicked witches led me always to be prepared for the worst!

DEBORAH [*playfully but a growing undercurrent of compulsive, deadly seriousness as she goes on*]   Oh, I warn you this is more wicked than any witch. She was a creature of pure fantasy, a fairy tale. But this is real life, even though it be past—and perhaps Time is but another of our illusions, and what was is forever identical with what is, beneath the deceiving, changing masks we wear.

SIMON [*a bit impatiently*]   Well, out with the terrible secret, Mother. I promise not to be too horrified. Are you an evil Queen of France who never was?

DEBORAH [*suddenly seems to lose herself—arrogantly*]   No. I could be if it were my whim, but I prefer to be the secret power behind the Throne—a greedy adventuress who has risen from the gutter to nobility by her wit and charm, by the sale of her beauty, by her talent for marvelous intrigue—who uses love but loves only herself, who is entirely ruthless and lets nothing stand in the way of the final goal of power she has set for herself, to become the favorite of the King and make him, through his passion for her, her slave! [*She ends up on a note of strange, passionate exultance.*]

SIMON [*startled and repelled—sharply rebuking*]   Mother! [*She starts dazedly. He goes on quickly with a curt resentful contempt.*] No, I am not shocked. It is too damned idiotic! [*She gives a shrinking, cowering movement as though he had struck her in the face. Suddenly the absurdity strikes his sense of humor and he grins.*] No, that's a lie. You really did shock me for a second, Mother. Stunned me, even! [*He chuckles.*] But now I have a picture in my mind of you sitting in your walled-in garden, dressed all in white, so sedulously protected and aloof from all life's sordidness, so delicate and fastidious and spiritually remote—and yet in your dreams playing make-believe with romantic iniquity out of scandalous French memoirs! [*He laughs almost derisively.*]

DEBORAH [*stung to fury, a flash of bitter hatred in her eyes, drawing herself up with fierce, threatening arrogance*] You dare to laugh at me, Monsieur! Take care—! [*Then as he stares at her in petrified amazement, she controls herself and forces an hysterical laugh.*] There! You see! I can still be a convincing actress if I wish! Poor Simon, if you could see your horrified face! Don't you see this is all a joke, that I made up that nonsense on the spur of the moment just to tease you?

SIMON [*relieved, grins sheepishly*] You did fool me. For a moment I thought you were serious—

DEBORAH Serious! My dear boy, I hope you don't think your poor mother has gone quite insane! [*abruptly*] But let's forget my stupid joke and return to common sense in the little time left us. I must go. Tell me, how is your business progressing these days? Judging from your letters, you must be making a great success of it.

SIMON [*reluctantly*] Oh, only in a very modest way as yet, Mother.

DEBORAH You hope to do even better? I am sure you will—with Sara to inspire you.

SIMON Yes, it is all for her. Everything I have is in her name.

DEBORAH [*gives him a searching look—smiling curiously*] I see.

SIMON See what? I owe it to her—

DEBORAH Of course you do. [*She smiles.*] But I didn't mean that. My thought was fanciful—that perhaps thus you contrived to hide from yourself.

SIMON [*resentfully*] You are right to call that fanciful.

DEBORAH [*teasingly*] And I think you're playing modest with me about your success. Why, in one of your letters, you boasted that the town considered you the most talented of its young merchants.

SIMON I wasn't boasting, Mother. Good Heavens, what is there to boast about? It requires no high order of talent to be a successful tradesman—merely a cunning acquisitiveness. I meant my boasting humorously. I thought it would make you laugh.

DEBORAH Oh, I did laugh then. Now I see there is nothing incongruous about it. After all, you are your father's son. It is natural you should have inherited his ability. You are so like him now, in many ways, it's astonishing.

SIMON [*irritated*]   Oh, nonsense, Mother.

DEBORAH   It's true. It struck me the minute I saw you. And do you know, although he never permits himself to speak of you, I am sure he keeps informed of all you do, and is quite proud of you.

SIMON [*coldly*]   I can dispense with his approval.

DEBORAH   What a strange boy you are! One would think you were ashamed of your success.

SIMON   Why should I be ashamed?

DEBORAH   Why, indeed? Unless you regret your lost poet's dream of a perfect society.

SIMON   I haven't lost it! And it isn't just a dream. I can prove—

DEBORAH [*carelessly*]   Oh, I know. Your book. But you said you had given that up.

SIMON   I said I had had no time lately—

DEBORAH   Four years is a long "lately." But why should you be ashamed of that? You must learn to laugh at your dreams if you hope ever to be happy.

SIMON [*defensively*]   I am happy now!

DEBORAH   We all pass through a callow period when our vanity prompts us to believe we may become poets or philosophers or saviours of mankind—when we dream of spiritual beauty and a greedless world. But we soon discover the world we must live in is greedily practical and could bitterly resent being saved from its gross appetite, that we must eat or be eaten, and an ounce of flesh is worth a ton of spirit.

SIMON [*repelled*]   I never thought I'd ever hear you—

DEBORAH   I am trying to drive the nonsense from your head, for your own peace of mind, and Sara's. You must forget what you once wanted to be and face yourself as you are, and not be ashamed.

SIMON   I am not ashamed! Why do you keep insisting?— [*then suddenly giving in—moodily*] Well perhaps, now and then, I do feel a little guilty.

DEBORAH   Ah!

SIMON   But I remind myself that what I am doing is merely a means. The end is Sara's happiness. And that justifies any means!

DEBORAH   I've found the means always becomes the end—and the end is always oneself.

SIMON   I propose to retire as soon as we have enough. I'll write my book then.

DEBORAH   You have agreed with Sara how much is enough?

SIMON   [*hesitates—then lies*]   Yes, of course. [*A pause. He frowns and goes on moodily.*] I'll admit I do get deathly sick of the daily grind of the counting house—the interminable haggling and figuring and calculation of profits, the scheming to outwit the other man, the fear that he may outwit you—a life where Mammon is God, and money the sole measure of worth! It is not the career I would have chosen. I would have lived here in freedom with nature, and earned just enough to support myself, and kept my dreams, and written my book. [*somberly*] Yes, sometimes I feel spiritually degraded, and a traitor to myself. I would confess that only to you, Mother.

DEBORAH   Ah.

SIMON   [*hastily*]   But when I come home and see Sara's happiness and hold her in my arms, then my discontent seems mean and selfish and a petty vanity.

DEBORAH   [*fights back an expression of repulsion*]   Yes. Of course. [*then calculatingly*] The danger is that your discontent will grow and grow with your success until— But, good heavens, I sound like Cassandra! Forgive me! And now I really must go, Simon. [*She gets up and they come to the path front at left. Suddenly she says, strangely.*] No, you go first.

SIMON   But why don't we walk together as far as the road?

DEBORAH   [*with strange arrogant petulance*]   No! That would be meaningless. Please obey me. It is my whim to send you away. [*then forcing a joking tone*] Goodness, how alarmed you look! You have forgotten me, I think. Can't I be whimsical, as of old, if it please me?

SIMON   [*puzzled but smiling*]   Of course you can.

DEBORAH   [*kissing him*]   Goodbye, Dear. Write me frankly of your discontents. There should be no secrets between us. I shall be, as

ever, your Mother Confessor. [*Then she gives him a little push.*]
Now go!

SIMON [*hesitates—moved*] I— Goodbye, Mother. [*He turns reluctantly.*]

DEBORAH [*suddenly overcome by contrition and a tender love*] Wait!
[*She embraces him again.*] My dear son! Forgive me for trying to
poison your happiness. Forget all I have said! Have no regrets!
Love is worth everything! Be happy! [*She kisses him—then pushes
him away down the path—sharply commanding*] No! Don't speak!
Go! [*She turns away. Simon stares at her for a moment, deeply
moved—then turns and disappears down the path. Deborah turns
back to look after him—with a wry smile*] I honestly meant to take
back the poison—but I fear it served only to inject it more surely
into his soul. [*then self-mockingly*] Bosh, Deborah! You over-
estimate your powers for intrigue! You confuse life with stupid
dreams. He will forget in her arms. [*her face hardening*] Besides,
it is ended. I have dismissed that Irish biddy's husband from my
life forever. I shall never see him again. [*Then she smiles to herself
with a perverse pride.*] At least I have proven to my own satisfaction, how easy it would be to steal happiness from her, if it were
my whim, and I were given the opportunity.

[*As she says this last the cabin door is silently unlocked and opened
and Sara comes out. She stands outside the door for a moment hesitantly. Then, her face set and determined, she advances noiselessly until
she stands a few paces from the oblivious Deborah. She takes her in
from head to foot with a searching glance, her eyes narrowing. But
there is no hatred or anger visible in her expression. If she feels any,
she has forced it back beneath the surface, and there is a certain calm
dignity and strength of character in her face and whole attitude. Whatever the battle with her passions has been, she has fought it out inside
the cabin.*]

SARA [*speaks quietly in a polite, carefully considered and articulated
English*] I beg your pardon, Mrs. Harford. [*Deborah gives a
frightened gasp, whirling to face her. For a moment the two stare*

at each other, Sara steady and calm, Deborah recovering from her surprise, her face hardening into a haughtily-questioning mask. Sara makes her a little bow. A hint of a mocking smile on her lips.] I am happy to meet you again and to know you at last, Mrs. Harford. I feel I do know you now, you see, because I was in the cabin all the while since you came.

DEBORAH [*with a flash of arrogant fury*]   You dared to listen!

SARA [*quietly*]   I did. I came on purpose to listen. I suspected you were up to some trick. I wanted to know what it was so I could guard against it. [*a trace of contempt creeping into her voice*] Though after all I've heard, I know now I was a fool to be afraid of you.

DEBORAH [*stammers guiltily*]   So you heard— [*then with biting contempt*] You have the effrontery to boast of it! You have so little shame! You are so ignorant of all honor!

SARA [*her face beginning to flush—but still quietly*]   I am, yes.

DEBORAH   Well, I expected you to be low and unscrupulous, considering your origin, but I never thought you'd boast of it!

SARA [*stung—her inward anger beginning to show, and with it her brogue, but still keeping her voice quiet*]   I have my honor and it's a true woman's honor that you don't know but you'd give your soul to know! To have love and hold it against the world, no matter how! That's my honor! [*gradually losing her control and lapsing more and more into brogue*] As for what you're after saying about my origin—don't put on your fine lady's airs and graces with me! Do you think you'll fool me after what I've heard? [*with a savage, jeering scorn, advancing a threatening step*] God pity you for a fool, then! [*Deborah in spite of herself, shrinks back. Sara gloats triumphantly.*] Ah, you shrink away, don't you? You're afraid! I'm too strong for you! Life is too strong for you! But it's not too strong for me! I'll take what I want from it and make it mine! [*mockingly*] And aren't you envyin' me that strength now in your heart, for all your pretendin'? Aren't you thinkin' that if you could have my strength to love life, and your brains for schemin' and dreamin' of power, you'd make yourself Queen of the world! Oh, I know you now! I know you well! You to put on the airs of a Duchess wid me! You to talk of honor when in your dream what are you but a greedy, contrivin' whore! [*Deborah shrinks back cowering still farther. Sara goes on more quietly but with a derisive taunting.*] But it's only in a dream! You've the wish for life but you haven't the strength except to run and hide in fear of it, sittin' lonely in your garden, hearin' age creep up on you, and beyond the wall the steps of Life growin' fainter down the street, like the beat of your heart, as he strolls away forgettin' you, whistlin' a love tune to himself, dreaming of another woman!

DEBORAH [*stammers*]   That's a lie! [*She sways weakly as though she were about to faint—exhaustedly*] I—I feel a little faint—I— [*She starts weakly for the bench.*]

SARA [*with an abrupt change to her quiet polite manner, takes her arm*] Let me help you, Mrs. Harford. [*She leads Deborah to the bench.*] You must rest a while. It's a long walk back to the road.

DEBORAH [*sinks down on it—quietly*]   Thank you.

SARA [*stands looking down at her*]   I ask your pardon for losing my temper, Mrs. Harford. I'd promised myself I would not. But the things you said—

DEBORAH [*quietly*]   I know. Please forgive me.

SARA   I came out of the cabin because there's a lot of things I want to say to you. [*defiantly*] And I'm going to say them. [*She pauses but Deborah remains silent. She stares at her and suddenly a look of pity comes over her face. She speaks gently.*] But before that I want to tell you how sorry I was when Simon laughed. [*Deborah gives a little shrinking shudder.*] I was listening. I could feel it coming. I waited, praying he wouldn't. When he did, it was like a knife in me, too. [*Deborah raises her eyes for a second to stare at her with an instinctive grateful wonder. Sara goes on.*] I want to apologize for him. He didn't know. How can a man know about the truth of the lies in a woman's dreams?

DEBORAH [*lifts her eyes to stare at her wonderingly again—with a faint smile*]   I thought you were a fool. I am afraid I am beginning to like you, Sara.

SARA [*embarrassedly—forcing a joking tone*]   Oh, don't try to fool me with blarney. You hate me worse than poison, that's the truth. And I hate you. [*then with resentment and now and then a trace of brogue but quietly*] I want to say I'm glad I listened. I've told you I was afraid you were up to some trick. And you were. Oh, I saw through your reminding him about that crazy book of his, although I didn't blame you for trying to get back at him after he'd laughed. You wanted to put doubt and disgust for himself in his mind, and make him blame me for a greedy fool who'd made him a slave and killed his fine poet's dream. [*She laughs scornfully.*] It's you who are the fool. It's little you know Simon, if you are his mother. Sure, what man doesn't complain of his work, and pretend he's a slave, but if you ever saw him when he comes home to me, so proud and happy because he's beat someone on a sale, laughing and boasting to me, you wouldn't hope you could use his old dream of a book that'll change the world to dissatisfy him. I know what he really likes—the world as it is—and I'm not worried by what he thinks he ought to like. [*She pauses. Deborah sits in silence, her eyes on the ground, as though she didn't hear or was completely indifferent. Sara goes on more resentfully.*] But what I wanted to say is, you don't know me. I may have a greed in me. I've had good reason to have. There's nothing like hunger to make you greedy. But the thing you don't know is that there's great love in me too, great enough to destroy all the greed in the world. If I thought it meant his happiness, I'd live here in this hut, or in a ditch with him, and steal praties[4] from the farmers to feed him, and beg pennies with my children, on the road, to buy pen and ink and paper for his book, and still I'd laugh with the joy of love! [*She pauses again. Deborah remains silent. She goes on.*] I heard you, when he said he'd retire to write his book when we had enough, sneer to him that I'd never have enough. It's little you know me, if you think I want him all his life to dirty his hands with trade, when all I'm dreaming of is to make him retire, a landed gentleman the minute we've enough, and to bring my children up as gentlemen. You sneered at my origin. You think in your Yankee pride and ignorance, because my father ruined himself with drink and gambling in Ireland, that the dirty Inn he came down to own here, is

---

4. Irish word for potatoes.

all I've known. But I was born on a great estate that was my father's, in a grand mansion like a Castle, with sloos [*sic*] of servants, and stables, and beautiful hunters. My father was a gentleman, and an officer, who served with honor in Spain under the great Duke of Wellington. [*abruptly with exasperated self-scorn*] Arrah, what am I sayin'? Am I boastin' of him? [*with a sudden return to her quiet correct manner*] I beg your pardon, Mrs. Harford, for boring you with talk of my father. The truth is, I am not proud I am his daughter. He was a drunken fool, full of lying pretensions— [*hastily, with stubborn defiance*] But what I've said is true all the same!

DEBORAH [*without raising her eyes—smiling strangely*] Did I think you were strong and unscrupulous? But you are also very weak and honorable, I'm afraid. [*She laughs softly.*]

SARA [*stares at her uneasily—then defiantly*] You'd better not think I'm weak, or have any honor but one. I'll tell you something to prove it. You'll remember the night your husband sent his lawyer to buy off my father from any claims I had on Simon, and my father got mad with rage at the insult and went to challenge him to a duel. I was afraid there'd be a row you'd use as an excuse to keep Simon from marrying me, but I knew Simon would feel bound to me in honor if— So I came out here in the night to make him take me. [*She smiles tenderly.*] I found I didn't need to. He loved me so much, nothing could take him from me. And then I felt guilty and confessed how bad I'd been. And then we— But it was for love only. [*abruptly defiant again*] But I would have done it for the other reason if I'd had to!

DEBORAH [*raises her eyes to stare at her with hate—scornfully*] You need not convince me you are capable of any vileness to get what you want. [*Then she drops her eyes—with a strange little mocking laugh*] You are boasting, Sara. Oh, I don't doubt you would have. That's your strength. But afterwards your weak honor would have made you confess to him—perhaps even tell him he need not marry you, anyway.

SARA [*taken aback—blurts out*] Yes, I told him that before—

DEBORAH [*laughs*] I am beginning to know you, Sara.

SARA [*again stares at her uneasily—resentfully threatening*] I don't care what you know. I've only this left to say to you. Stay in your dreams and leave me and mine alone. Simon is mine now. [*then politely*] I must go. Simon will be wondering where I have gone. I promise you I won't confess that. I'll bid you goodbye now, Mrs. Harford.

DEBORAH [*looks up—coldly*] Goodbye. I promise you, in turn, I never intend to see your husband again, or even write to him. [*with arrogant disdain*] Do you presume to think I would touch anything of yours?

SARA [*contemptuously*] No. You know I wouldn't let you. [*She smiles mockingly and goes off right, rear, to the short cut along the lake.*]

DEBORAH [*her face full of bitter hatred*] Vulgar, common slut! Boastful fool! If I wished—if I had the opportunity— [*sneeringly*] And now her honor will make her remind him constantly of his book, when he wants to forget— [*She laughs spitefully.*] I could not have contrived it better! [*abruptly*] No. It is ended. Forgotten. Dead. It is cheap and mean and sordid. Like life. I will not let it touch me. [*She frowns as if desperately concentrating her mind. Gradually her tension relaxes and her eyes become dreamy and she stares before her unseeingly. Finally she murmurs happily to herself.*] The Palace at Versailles—the King and I walk in the moonlit gardens— "My Throne it is your heart, Beloved, and my fair Kingdom your beauty"— [*A faint smile of arrogant satisfaction forms on her lips. Then abruptly she starts awake and springs to her feet, furious at herself.*] No! I have done with that insane romantic vaporing! I will never dream again! Never! Not if I have to pluck my idiot brain from my skull! I will face change and loneliness, and Time and Death and make myself resigned! [*A bitter ironical smile comes to her lips.*] After all, what else can you do now, Deborah? You would always hear his laughter.

* * * CURTAIN * * *

Tao House
May 10th '38

Act Two, Scene One

SCENE   *A corner of the garden of Deborah Harford's home in the city on a warm moonlight night in June, 1836.*

The corner is formed by a brick enclosing wall, eight feet high, at rear and right. This wall borders a neighboring property at rear, a quiet street lined with elms at right. At center is an octagonal summerhouse, its walls and pointed roof entirely covered by ivy. At left and right of the summerhouse are shrubs with a line of Italian cypresses behind them along the wall. The shrubs, of various sizes, are all clipped into geometrical shapes, cones, cubes, cylinders, spheres, pyramids, etc. They give the place a curious artificial atmosphere. It is like a fantastic toy garden magnified, in which nature is arrogantly restricted and arbitrarily distorted to form an appropriate setting for a perversely whimsical personality.

In the side of the summerhouse facing front is a narrow arched door, painted a Chinese lacquer red.[1] The floor is raised from the ground and three steps lead up to the door. In front of these steps is lawn, with two small stone benches, facing right-front, and left-front, on the edge of a narrow brick-paved walk which surrounds a little oval pool. From this pool two paths lead directly right and left, the left one passing behind a spherical shrub at left-front to the house. The right one leads to an arched door, painted green, in the wall at right, opening on the street. There is a wrought iron lantern hanging from a bracket in the wall above the door, in which a little lamp burns brightly. There is a sound of men's voices from down the path off left, and a moment later

---

1. In *The Flowering of New England* Van Wyck Brooks describes "summer-houses in the Chinese style" (p. 21). This is most likely O'Neill's inspiration for Deborah's summerhouse.

Garden with summerhouse—Act Two, Scene One
*Yale Collection of American Literature, Beinecke Rare Book
and Manuscript Library, Yale University*

*Nicholas Gadsby, the Harford lawyer, appears accompanied by Deb-
orah's younger son, Joel. Gadsby is a short, tubby man of fifty-six,
with a head almost completely bald, a round red face, and shrewd little
grey eyes. Every inch the type of conservative, best-family legal advisor,
he is gravely self-important and pretentious in manner and speech,
extremely conscious of the respect due his professional dignity. He is
dressed with a fastidious propriety in mourning black.*

*Joel Harford is twenty-nine, tall and thin, with a slight stoop in his
carriage. His face is pale and handsome. Judged by its separate features,
each of which has an aristocratic distinction, it should possess distinction. But it remains the face of a methodical mediocrity, who within*

*his narrow limits is not without determination, and a rigid integrity,
but lacks all self-confidence or ambition beyond these limits. His whole
character has something aridly prim and puritanical about it. He has
brown hair, cold light blue eyes, a pointed chin, an obstinate mouth.
His voice is dry. A voice prematurely old. His mourning suit is well
tailored. They stop as they come to the pool. Gadsby stares around
him, looking for someone. His manner is shocked and indignant, and
at the same time pathetically confused, as though he'd just been confronted by a fact which he knows to be true but which is so outrageous
he cannot bring himself to accept it.*

GADSBY [*trying to conceal his shattered poise behind a fussy, impatient
air*] Well? She isn't here. I didn't think she would be. Under the
circumstances. At this time of night. But you insisted—

JOEL [*dryly, indicating the summerhouse*] You will find her hiding
in there, I think.

GADSBY [*stares at the summerhouse—with a sort of bewildered offended
dismay*] In there? God bless me. I cannot believe—? I know how
eccentric your mother— But at such a time, one would think—

JOEL [*dryly*] You have not seen her for some time. She has grown
increasingly eccentric. And since the night Father died she has appeared— Well, to be frank, deliberately deranged is the only way
I could truthfully describe—

GADSBY [*appalled*] Deranged? [*rebukingly*] Come, come, Joel. Naturally, the shock—her grief.

JOEL [*coldly*] No. Whatever the cause be, it is not grief.

GADSBY [*shocked*] Come, come. A shocking statement for you to
make. I refuse to— [*then bewilderedly*] You said "deliberately."

JOEL I have felt it was deliberate. You may judge for yourself.

GADSBY [*with defensive asperity*] Ridiculous. I have known your
mother since before you were born. Eccentric, yes. Deliberately and
provokingly unconventional. Childishly self-willed. Irresponsibly
whimsical and fanciful. But always a well-bred, distinguished gentlewoman, a charming hostess, witty and gay—and beautiful.

JOEL [*stiffens resentfully*] I have never considered her beautiful. And

I think even you will not think her beautiful now. [*with thinly concealed relish*] She looks her full age now, and more. [*then guiltily, with abrupt cold reproof*] But you are forgetting the business which brings us here.

GADSBY [*guiltily*] Yes, of course. We must see your mother at once. [*then explosively*] By heaven, I wish I could forget. Joel! I still cannot believe that your father could—

JOEL [*interrupts sharply*] It would be better if you were the one to call her out. I have never been welcome here.

GADSBY [*turns to the summerhouse and calls*] Deborah! [*There is no answer. He goes to the foot of the steps—fussily impatient, more sharply*] Deborah! This is Nicholas! I must see you at once. A matter of the gravest importance has come up. [*He pauses, then turns to Joel uneasily.*] God bless me, Joel, you don't think anything can have happened to her?

[*But even as he is speaking the door is slowly opened outwards and Deborah appears. Her back is to the door as though she had groped backwards in the darkness, her hand behind her feeling for the knob, keeping her face turned toward something from which she retreats. As the door opens her body, pressed against it, turns as it turns until it faces toward left, front, as the door is two-thirds open. But she keeps her head turned so that she is still looking back over her shoulder into the dark interior. Gadsby takes a step back, regarding her bewilderedly. Joes stares at her with a cold emotionlessness. Suddenly a little shudder runs over her; she gives a smothered gasp and wrenches her eyes from the darkness inside and pushes the door back against the house, wide open, and faces front. As he sees her face, Gadsby cannot restrain a startled exclamation of shocked alarm and even backs frightenedly away from her a step or two. For there is a shocking transformation in her appearance. Where she had always before looked astonishingly youthful for her age, she now seems much older than her forty-nine years. Her olive complexion has turned a displeasing swarthy. The dry skin is stretched tightly over the bones and has the lifeless sheen of a shed snakeskin. Her black eyes are sunk in deep hollows beneath their heavy brows and have an unhealthy feverish glitter. They appear more*] *enormous than ever in her small oval face. There are deep lines from her nose and the corners of her mouth, between her eyes and across her forehead. Her lips appear contracted and shrunken over her still perfect set of big, even teeth. There are hollows under her cheekbones and in her slender neck. The skin sags under her chin. There is the quality of a death's head about her face, of a skull beginning to emerge from its mask of flesh. Wherever her figure had been slender it is now thin, but it is still graceful in all its movements, and by contrast with her face, youthful. She is dressed all in white.*

DEBORAH [*staring at Gadsby but with eyes that are still fixed inward, frightenedly and fascinatedly, something in her own mind—in a low voice that has lost its old musical quality and become flat and brittle*] I am glad you came, Nicholas, I must never go in there again! [*She gives a little shudder.*]

GADSBY [*trying to recover from his shocked surprise at the change in her*] There is something in there that frightens you, Deborah?

DEBORAH [*strangely, as if talking to herself*] Something? Outside me? No, nothing is there but I. My mind. The past, Dreams. My life, I suppose you might call it, since I have never lived except in mind. A very frightening prison it becomes at last, full of ghosts and corpses. Yes, in the end, and I have reached the end, the longing for a moment's unthinking peace, a second's unquestioning acceptance of oneself, become so terrible that I would do anything, give anything, to escape! [*Her voice had become lower and tenser.*] That is what frightened me. After you called. Oh, not before. Before, I was so longingly fascinated, I had forgotten fear. The temptation to escape. Open the door. Step boldly across the threshold. [*bitterly*] And, after all, good God, why should I be frightened? What have I to lose except myself as I am here.

GADSBY God bless me, Deborah, you cannot mean—

DEBORAH Death? Oh, no. There is a better way—a way by which we still may live. As one has always wished to live. As the woman one has always desired to be. One has only to concentrate one's mind enough, and one's pride to choose of one's own free will, and one can cheat life, and death, of oneself. It would be so easy for me!

Like pushing open a door in the mind and then passing through with the freedom of one's lifelong desire! [*tensely her eyes glowing*] I tell you, before you called, I saw that door, as real as the door I have just opened, and I was reaching out my hand to— [*then with a frightened shudder*] No, I am glad you called. Because I am not sure that one completely forgets then. If I were, I would have gone. [*abruptly shaking off this thought—trying to force a natural tone but still strangely*] No, do [not] fear, Nicholas, that I will outrage your sense of propriety by suicide. I assure you Henry's dying completely disillusioned me with death.

GADSBY [*partly regaining his fussy self-importance—rebukingly*] That is hardly a befitting attitude— [*then solicitously*] It is very bad for you to come out here to brood over Henry's death.

DEBORAH [*strangely*] Brood? No. But I have tried to make it real to myself—to examine it as a fact. I have said to myself: "Why can't you face the new fact, Deborah? Your husband is dead. He was buried this morning. These are facts." "Oh, I know. But I can't comprehend them as facts yet." "Why not, Deborah. You surely should be experienced in facing facts by this time." "Yes, God knows I should. I have lived with reality many years now. That afternoon at the cabin with Simon seems a lifetime ago, and he is more dead to me than Henry. I have kept the oath I made to myself then. Have not allowed myself to dream. Have not hidden from my life. Have made myself accept it as it is. Made myself a decently resigned old woman, saying to myself: 'So is so, and you must not hope it could be more.' Made myself each morning and night confront myself in the mirror and bow a well-mannered bow to age and ugliness. Greet them as my life-end guests. As elderly suitors for my body, roués in their bored withered hearts, their smiles insinuating the desire of Death. Not charming company, but a hostess must honor even unwelcome guests." So all day for years I have lived with them. And every night they have lain abed with me. [*smiling strangely with a bitter satisfaction*] Oh, yes, indeed! I have disciplined my will to be possessed by facts—like a whore in a brothel!

GADSBY [*shocked*] Deborah!

DEBORAH [*goes on as if she hadn't heard*]   I have deliberately gone out
of my way to solicit even the meanest, most sordid facts, to prove
how thoroughly I was resigned to reality. Joel will remember one
night at supper when I actually asked my husband: "How is trade
these days? Tell me. I feel a deep interest. Has President Jackson's
feud with the Bank of the United States had an adverse effect on
your exports and imports?"[2] A silence that shrank back, stamping
on its own toes. In his eyes and Joel's a wondering alarm. Has this
alien woman gone completely insane? No, she is merely being
fantastical again. Deborah has always been fantastical. [*She gives a
little mocking laugh.*]

JOEL [*coldly hostile*]   That is what you are being now, Mother. And
we have no time to listen—

GADSBY [*who has been staring at Deborah fascinatedly, bewilderedly
uncomprehending but disturbed because he senses her despair, now
attempts to regain a brisk, professional air, clearing his throat im-
portantly*]   Humph. Yes, Deborah. We must—

DEBORAH [*ignoring this—with the same strange inward stare, and the
air of talking aloud to herself*]   And now Henry is dead. Gone
from life forever. I am free. Can't you understand that? [*She shakes
her head slowly.*] No. His death will not live in me. It is meaningless. Perhaps I am too dead myself— And yet I witnessed his dying.
The dutiful wife sat by his bedside. He seemed not to suffer but to
be impatient and exasperated. As though he had an important appointment with God to discuss terms for the export of his soul,
and Life was needlessly delaying him. And then came nothing. An
expiring into nothing. And that was death. Is that why it cannot
live for me? Did I think death would be something in itself—a beginning, not just the end of life? What did I expect? What was
I hoping? For Death to open the door and enter the room, visible
to me, the good King of Life come at last to escort one into his

---

2. Andrew Jackson, as President of the United States (1829–37), warred against the Bank
of the United States, a national bank that favored the rich and powerful, and one that
held eight million dollars of the government's money. Jackson vetoed a bill sponsored by
Henry Clay that would have renewed the bank's charter. Clay misread the will of the
American electorate when he lost to Jackson by a landslide vote in 1832.

palace of peace, a lover keeping a life-long promised tryst? [*She smiles with a taunting self-mockery.*] I regret to see living as a mistress of facts has not entirely killed your fanciful imagination, Deborah! You and your lover-Kings! Had you, perchance, personified your own death in your whimsical imagination, and fallen in love with it?[3] Then Henry's extinction should richly disillusion you! Oh, it has. There was nothing at all but a meaningless ceasing to breathe, and I suppose that is only logical and reasonable. If Life had meaning then we might properly expect its end to have as much significance as—as the period at the close of a simple sentence, say. But it has no meaning and the sentence, worn out by futile groping within its own stupid obscurities, stammers haltingly to an unintelligible end—and that is all. Like an aimless improvisation on a far-off, out-of-tune piano that tinkles into silence. And death is no more than a muddy well into which I and [a] dead cat are cast aside indifferently! [*Suddenly she presses both hands to her temples with an agonized, distracted gesture—tensely*] Ah, good God, can I never stop this everlasting thinking and questioning, this sneering and jeering and spitting at my own heart—a helpless slave to a mind that runs on and on like a mad perpetual motion machine I cannot stop? [*wildly*] Ah, and you wonder I was tempted to open that door and escape! I tell you I am still tempted—that I will not endure being the tortured captive of my mind much longer—whatever the cost of release—

GADSBY [*alarmed and bewildered*] Deborah. I beg of you, compose yourself. This—this is most unsuitable conduct—even when I consider the natural shock of grief. I cannot condone—such—such lack of decent control—

DEBORAH [*stares at him—a sudden transformation comes over her as she forces her obsession back and becomes her usual self again. She smiles at him—an amused, derisive smile*] Your rebuke is well taken, Nicholas. I fear I was boring you as surely as I was myself.

---

3. Deborah's allusion to death is very much like Edmund's in *LDJ*. Edmund says in act 4, "As it is, I will always be a stranger who never feels at home, who does not really want and is not really wanted, who can never belong, who must always be a little in love with death!" (Yale edn., p. 154).

[*dryly*] May I ask to what I owe the honor of your visit, Gentlemen? It is a rare pleasure indeed to see you in my garden, Joel.

JOEL [*stiffly*] I assure you, Mother, I would never intrude unless circumstances—

GADSBY [*interrupts worriedly, his mind now occupied with the matter at hand*] The circumstances are these, Deborah: In going over Henry's private papers, we made the astounding discovery— [*He interrupts himself—indignantly*] Upon my soul, I could not credit the evidence of my own eyes! I knew Henry since we were boys together. I would have sworn he would be the last man on earth to indulge in such outrageous folly!

DEBORAH [*astonished and interested*] Outrageous folly? No, that does not sound like Henry, Nicholas. [*coolly*] I think we could discuss this mystery more calmly if we sat down. [*She sits on the step of the summerhouse. Gadsby and Joal on the stone benches by the pool, at left-front and right-front of her, respectively. She notices the look of disapproval Joel gives her white dress.*] I see you disapprove of my changing back to my accustomed white, Joel. Please remember, although I detest mourning and think it ridiculous, I did wear it at the funeral before the world. That is all your father would consider my duty. Never that I should play the hypocrite to myself.

GADSBY [*frowns rebukingly*] Now, now. It is no time— [*overcome with indignation again*] I tell you, Deborah, this is incredible!

DEBORAH What is "this"?

JOEL [*coldly*] We found two letters in Father's strong-box, one addressed to Mr. Gadsby, the other to me. They were written some weeks ago. He had a premonition he might die suddenly. The letters are practically identical. They—

GADSBY [*feels it incumbent on him to take over now—in his best family-lawyer manner*] I must warn you, Deborah, to be prepared for a dreadful surprise. [*He pauses. She stares at him calmly. He is thrown off stride by her lack of reaction and becomes even more portentous*] These letters are confessions that Henry had been secretly gambling in Western lands.

DEBORAH [*incredulously*] Gambling? Henry?

GADSBY [*nods solemnly*] Yes, Deborah. Unbelievable!

JOEL [*coldly*]   As a result, Mother, the Company stands on the brink of bankruptcy.

GADSBY   It appears he had overreached his resources during the past few years. Sunk too much capital in new ships. Borrowed too freely, and then yielded to the temptation to regain a sound position by making a quick profit in Western lands. He lost, of course. What could an honorable, conservative merchant like Henry know of such wild speculation? [*giving way more and more to indignation and rabid political partisanship*] And what a time he chose to expand the activities of his Company. With his reputation for shrewdness and caution! When the country is in turmoil, with uncertainty the only certainty, thanks to that idol of the scum, that criminal lunatic in the White House! And, even with Jackson's passing, there will be no relief from this damnable demagoguery! It seems tragically probable his jackal, Van Buren, will succeed him!

DEBORAH [*cuttingly but with an amused twinkle in her eye*]   An excellent Whig electioneering speech, Nicholas. But wasted on a poor widow who has no vote.[4] And hardly in the spirit so soon after a funeral, do you think, although I know Henry would agree with every word.

GADSBY [*crushed*]   I—forgive me. I—er—I am greatly upset—and I blame conditions for Henry's folly.

DEBORAH [*staring before her strangely*]   It would appear I have spent my life with a stranger. If I had guessed he had folly hidden in his heart and a gambler's daring— Who knows? [*She shrugs her shoulders with a bitter little smile.*] Too late, Deborah.

JOEL [*stares at her with chilly disapproval*]   I said, Mother, that the Company is faced with ruin. That is what we came to discuss with you.

DEBORAH [*looks at him with distaste*]   Discuss with me? You know I haven't the slightest knowledge of trade.

JOEL   I know you have never taken the slightest interest. But now you must.

---

4. Women were given the right to vote in 1919, when Congress passed the Nineteenth Amendment. Tennessee became the thirty-sixth state to ratify the amendment, in 1920, so that women were able to vote in the presidential election that year. Van Buren won the 1836 election Deborah refers to in this scene.

DEBORAH [*arrogantly*]   Must?

GADSBY [*interposing*]   What Joel means, Deborah, is that in his letters Henry suggests certain steps should be taken which, if they can be successfully negotiated, may save the firm.

DEBORAH [*indifferently*]   Then you have only to take the steps, Nicholas.

GADSBY   They can be taken only with your consent, since Henry's will bequeaths the Company jointly to you and Joel. I may add that Joel has given his consent.

JOEL [*stiffly*]   I consider it my duty to Father's memory. What he proposes is the one possible way to preserve the honor of his name. For that I am willing to make any sacrifice of my personal feelings.

DEBORAH [*stares at him exasperatedly*]   If you only knew, Joel, how many times I wish to pinch you to discover if you're stuffed!

JOEL   I have long realized I bore you, Mother. You will doubtless find Simon more congenial.

DEBORAH [*stiffens startledly—in a flash her face becomes as hard and cold as Joel's*]   Pray, what has your brother to do with this?

GADSBY   If you will permit me to explain, Deborah. Simon has everything to do with it.

DEBORAH [*tensely*]   He shall have nothing to do with anything that concerns me. You know his father's attitude regarding him. It was in obedience to what I knew would be my husband's wish that I did not inform Simon of his death, nor invite him to the funeral. I forbid you to bring his name into this discussion. I have forgotten him. [*Joel regards her with a cold surprise. Gadsby is astonished and taken aback.*]

GADSBY   I did not realize you felt so bitterly toward Simon.

DEBORAH   I do not feel bitter. I feel nothing.

GADSBY   I had thought, and Henry must have thought, or he would never—

DEBORAH   I never let Henry know my thoughts. Simon is dead to me. And I will not have him resurrected. That is final.

GADSBY [*with a trace of asperity*]   It cannot be final, Deborah. If you will pardon my saying so, it is no time for personal feelings. It is a time to consider what you owe, in honor, to your husband's good name.

DEBORAH   I cannot believe Henry would ever—

GADSBY [*with dignity*]   I trust you are not doubting my word, Deborah. If you will only let me explain—

DEBORAH   Very well. I will listen. But I warn you—

GADSBY   No, I cannot accept that. You must keep an open mind for the sake of the Company, and—

DEBORAH   I care nothing for the Company!

JOEL [*coldly resentful*]   You forget what you owe it, then—your home, the comforts you have enjoyed, the privacy you cherish, the aloofness from life you pride yourself upon! I think you have not yet faced what has happened as it will affect your own future, Mother. You will have to sell this home. You will have nothing. What will you do? Go and beg Simon and his wife to let you live on charity with them?

DEBORAH [*passionately*]   I would rather beg in the gutter!

JOEL   Of course, you may always have a home with me. But on a bookkeeper's wage—

DEBORAH [*scornfully*]   Can you possibly imagine—?

JOEL [*coldly*]   No. So I advise you to listen to Mr. Gadsby, as he requests, with an open mind.

GADSBY   Joel is right, Deborah. Your position is—er—precarious, unless— [*plunging into his subject*] What Henry suggests is this: [*He hesitates a bit—uncomfortably*] He realized that Joel has not had the requisite executive experience to take control under such difficult circumstances.

JOEL [*emotionlessly*]   I am not grateful to you for sparing my feelings, Mr. Gadsby. It is my practice to face the truth about myself. Father knew I have not the ability to be head of the Company under any circumstances. In my narrow sphere, no man could serve the Company more faithfully. But, beyond that, I am worthless to it.

DEBORAH [*stares at him wonderingly—slowly*]   There are times when I almost respect you, Joel. [*He gives no sign of having heard her.*]

GADSBY [*clears his throat embarrassedly*]   Humm. [*then briskly*] Henry appears to have had complete confidence in Simon's ability, in spite of his disapproval of his personal conduct. He seems to have carefully followed Simon's career.

JOEL He did. He obtained constant, confidential reports on the condition of my brother's business. I know that because the reports were made through me. Father did not wish to appear in the matter.

DEBORAH [*with a sincerely pitying glance*] Poor Joel, your father never had time to spare others' feelings.

JOEL [*seems to become more frozen—icily*] I dislike pity, Mother.

GADSBY [*embarrassedly again*] Henry's suggestion is that you and Joel approach Simon—

DEBORAH [*flaring up again*] I? Go begging to Simon? Never, I tell you! I did that once— [*abruptly stops, as Joel fixes a cold inquisitive stare on her*]

GADSBY [*testily*] If you will let me continue, you will see Henry did not suggest you ask Simon for favors. What he recommended is a straight business deal which involves no personal obligations whatever, which will be equally to Simon's advantage and yours. He knew that Simon's business is still a small local affair. Nothing to compare to the Harford Company, which is known and respected wherever our trade is carried. To be its head is to be a leading figure in commerce—as Simon, who once worked under his father and knows the business, will be the first to appreciate.

DEBORAH [*tensely*] So I am to ask Simon to accept the leadership of the Company, is that it?

GADSBY Yes. A controlling interest. That is only just if he saves it from ruin. And Henry believed he has the means to save it. According to him, the condition of Simon's business is astonishingly sound from a cash standpoint. He has been shrewd enough to anticipate conditions, and foresee the ruin which is gathering around us. He has been putting all his profit into specie. Of course, from such a small business, it is no tremendous sum, but—

JOEL It is enough. Specie has become rare and highly prized.[5] A payment in specie here and there will restore confidence.

GADSBY Henry appreciated, too, that many people here in the city have

---

5. Deborah's reference to the popularity of specie relates to President Jackson's 1836 Specie Circular, which forbade the Treasury to accept anything but gold and silver (specie), or bank notes based thereon, in payment for public lands. This Specie Circular was the straw that broke the back of the speculators' market.

kept an eye on Simon's success. Because he was Henry Harford's son. The announcement that Simon will assume control will have a very salutary effect. There will be no inclination to grow uneasy and take to prying into conditions—which would be fatal just now. It will be taken for granted the Company is as sound as ever. Henry had learned, too, that Simon had been made a very favorable offer to sell his mill. So there should be no difficulty on that score. [*He hesitates—then uncomfortably*] Humm— Of course, Henry foresaw that there might be difficult personal aspects. He knew that Simon still feels a resentment—

DEBORAH   If we are facing facts, let us face them. Simon hated him.

GADSBY   But Henry evidently believed that you and Simon still felt a mutual affection, and that you could persuade—

JOEL [*coldly*]   Simon will not wish you to be ruined, Mother.

DEBORAH [*tensely*]   So I am cast in the role of chief beggar! [*controlling herself—dryly*] Henry must have lost his shrewdness in more ways than one. He fails to consider the one person who can laugh at his calculations, and who will take great pleasure in doing so—Simon's wife! It is she who controls his affairs. He does nothing without consulting her, and if you think she will ever consent— Oh no, you will find she has never forgiven Henry for humiliating her pride, and this will be a glorious opportunity to revenge herself! And you will discover everything Simon possesses is in her name.

GADSBY   Henry knew that. He—er—evidently relied on your tact and diplomacy, Deborah, to convince her how advantageous for her own future it would be—

DEBORAH   I? She hates me like poison!

GADSBY   I am sure, if you wished, you could easily win her confidence. A woman of her type would be no match for you, with your intelligence and charm.

DEBORAH [*suddenly struck by a thought—with a strange, almost eager, little laugh*]   My talent for intrigue? Yes, this could be the opportunity— [*then with a start—violently*] No! That has no meaning now! It is dead and forgotten!

GADSBY [*stares at her puzzledly—then in his lawyer's tone*]   One further thing Henry suggested, to make his proposal as equitable as

possible for Simon and his—er—family. He thought, as they would
have to sell their present home and come to the city, and as this
home, which he bequeaths to you Deborah, is much too large for
you and Joel, that—

DEBORAH [*tensely*]   That I should invite that vulgar Irish biddy and her
brats to live with me! [*again suddenly struck by her thought, with
almost a gloating smile*] Yes, that would be a greater opportunity
than I had ever hoped— [*then resisting more violently than before—
furiously*] No! How dare you insult me like this! How dare you
make such a shameless proposal!

JOEL [*with cold bitterness*]   It is Father who proposes it, Mother. You
owe it to him to do all in your power—

DEBORAH [*stares at him—bitterly*]   And I hoped I had at last escaped
the dunning of wifely duty! [*with a strange desperate anguish*] For
the love of God, hasn't his death even that meaning?

JOEL [*coldly relentless*]   We are waiting for your consent, Mother.

DEBORAH [*bitterly hostile*]   What an implacable bill-collector you would
make, Joel! [*violently*] No, I will not have it! What have I to do
with the Company? Let it be ruined! Do you think I fear poverty?
What have I ever cared for things outside me? And I have experienced poverty before and did not let it touch me—the most degrading form, that of a minister's household, where one must pretend
one welcomes it as a mark of kinship with God! [*desperately*] No!
He is dead! All my debt to him is paid! I refuse—!

GADSBY [*embarrassed—clears his throat*]   Humm! As your attorney,
Deborah, I strongly advise you to consent.

DEBORAH [*violently, rising to her feet*]   No! I tell you I swore to myself
years ago I would never involve myself in such a low intrigue! And
I still desired life then. Do you think you can tempt me now when I
am an ugly resigned old woman whose life is only in the mind?
You are wasting your time, Gentlemen. [*She makes a gesture of
arrogant dismissal.*] You will kindly leave me in peace.

JOEL [*with cold condemnation*]   How long are you going to keep us
waiting here on your perverse whims? I have always disliked this
garden. [*He stares around him with dislike.*] Nothing is natural,
not even Nature.

GADSBY [*staring around him in turn—as if fighting against an influence*] Yes, Deborah. The atmosphere is hardly conducive to—common sense, shall I say. [*then strangely and haltingly as if the influence took hold on him, staring at her*] My dear Deborah. Why should you talk of being old? Ridiculous! You, ugly? You are beautiful! [*Instinctively her face lights up with an eager grateful smile.*] Why, you could be the most wooed widow in the city! I myself would jump at the chance— [*Deborah gives a soft, gratified little laugh. He goes on hastily.*] Not that there ever was a chance. I know that. Besides, this is hardly the time to speak of— You will forgive me, Joel. Your father always permitted me a little harmless gallantry. He knew your mother could never take a short, fat man seriously. Nor could any other woman. Of course, there was Napoleon. But I admit I am no Napoleon, although at times I have dreamed— [*abruptly wrenching his eyes from her—grumbles irritably to himself*] Humph! What rubbishy thoughts for a man of my years and profession. Her eyes always did make a fool of me. [*reacts to an extreme professional portentousness*] I must protest against your acting so childishly, Deborah. You know there is one honorable course to take. As a woman of breeding and honor, you have no possible choice.

DEBORAH [*staring before her—with an undercurrent of tense eagerness*] Yes, I suppose it is my duty to see it only in that light. And then there is no choice, is there? It is fate! [*with a strange urgency*] But you must bear witness, Nicholas, that I fought against this opportunity, that I did not desire it and did all in my power to reject it— that it is destiny—my duty as an honorable woman—and there is no way I could possibly avoid—

JOEL [*coldly impatient*] You consent?

DEBORAH [*slowly—as if forcing the words out in spite of herself*] Yes. I consent. [*She suddenly gives a little shiver of dread—strangely*] Ah! I feel tempted to live in life again—and I am afraid!

JOEL [*coldly matter-of-fact now*] It's settled, then. We will go and see Simon tomorrow. I shall arrange for places in the stage the first thing in the morning. [*He bows with cold courtesy to his mother.*] Good night, Mother. I am going in the house. There is much to do. [*to Gadsby*] Are you coming, Sir?

GADSBY   Yes, Joel. [*He starts to go with Joel—then stops, after a glance at Deborah*] Go on. I'll follow in a moment. [*Joel goes. Deborah is staring before her, oblivious. Gadsby looks at her with a pitying, if uncomprehending, sympathy. He coughs embarrassedly—attempting a joking tone*] Upon my soul, Deborah, I—er—I cannot see what there is to be apprehensive about in your consenting to the one sensible course.

DEBORAH   [*strangely*]   I am afraid of myself, Nicholas.

GADSBY   [*puts on a kindly bullying tone*]   Stuff and nonsense! You have done too much brooding alone. It has made you morbid. You should welcome this opportunity to escape—

DEBORAH   I am afraid I do, Nicholas.

GADSBY   It will distract your mind and give you a new, healthy interest in life.

DEBORAH   [*with a bitter intense yearning*]   Ah, if it only could be a new interest, Nicholas, and not an old one risen from my dead. With that joy I would welcome it, then! With what humble gratitude would I give thankfulness to God for the undreamed of miracle! [*passionately*] Oh, if you knew how I have prayed for resurrection from the death in myself!

GADSBY   [*worriedly uncertain and pitying*]   I—I do not understand you.

DEBORAH   [*forcing a smile—contemptuous and at the same time affectionate*]   No, that is why I can safely tell you all my secrets, Nicholas.

GADSBY   [*offended but determined to finish speaking his mind*]   I *do* understand this, Deborah. It is not good to detach onself as completely from the common life as you have done. But now you have a chance to start anew. It depends entirely on your own attitude whether this shall mean the opportunity for a new life of human warmth and companionship and family affection. I remember how devoted you once were to Simon.

DEBORAH   [*stiffening*]   I am afraid I could only pretend ever to forgive Simon.

GADSBY   [*ignoring this—hurrying on*]   You may even find you can like his wife, when you know her. Forgetting prejudice, you must admit she has been an estimable wife and mother. She must have her good points, if you will see them. She is evidently no fool, and it is not fair to blame her for her origin. [*hastily, with an uneasy glance at her*] Oh, I expect you to storm at me for pleading her case, but we must try to be just.

DEBORAH [*to his amazement—calmly*] I will not storm. I could find it much easier to forgive her. I understand her feeling toward me. In her place, I would feel the same. [*She smiles wryly.*] There. You see how just I am.

GADSBY [*astonished—eagerly*] I do, indeed! Why then, there is no obstacle. But I was thinking most of your grandchildren—the opportunity they present to you. You can have no feeling against them, nor blame them in any way for the past. Your blood is in them. They are yours in part. Children in this garden would clear the stifling atmosphere. A little childish laughter and simple joy in being alive. After all, you have given it the aspect of a child's toy garden, made life-size. They would feel at home here. But I am thinking of it from the standpoint of your future happiness, Deborah. Do you see—?

DEBORAH [*slowly with a simple sincerity*] Yes. I do see, Nicholas, like an amazing revelation—a miraculous hope that would never have occurred to me if you hadn't— It could be the chance for a new life—escape from the death within myself, from my mind's torturing treadmill of futility. Resign myself to be a grandmother! That could be a resignation in which I might find a purpose in living and a meaning outside myself. [*She stares at Gadsby wonderingly— mockingly but with affection*] You astonish me, Nicholas. I have heard of wisdom from babes, but who could dream of it from a bachelor! [*teasingly*] I really believe you are trying to make a good woman of me, Nicholas! [*then quickly, seeing he is hurt*] No. Forgive my teasing. I am truly grateful. [*intensely*] If you could know how grateful! And I swear to you I will try. It will not be easy. You do not know how bitterly Sara suspects me. Or how well she understands—what I was. It will be difficult to convince her of my good motives and persuade her to trust me with her children. I shall have to show her I no longer want Simon. [*her face hardening*] But that should be easy because I do not. He ceased to be my son four years

Abigail: (~~they only a moment~~ ~~Those footsteps~~) ~~When~~ footsteps beyond the wall. They ~~have~~ stopped. ∨ I think he remembers he had forgotten me and he is turning back! (She laughs)

Gadsby: (relieved - his dignity ruffled) God bless me! I thought you heard a burglar! What fanciful rubbish, Abigail!

CURTAIN

[The following is a handwritten revision of the scene:]

Abigail (with an abrupt change to a strange bitter air of ~~~~ bravado) And to prove my escape - ~~~~ - as a symbol - Watch and bear witness, Nicholas! - I will ~~~~ cast out my devil, the old Abigail - drag her from her sneering place in my mind and heart - (She makes a movement with her arms and hands of pulling something out or her head and heart and pushing it from her) and push her back where she belongs - in there - in perpetual darkness - (She advances up the steps - with a fixed pride) "~~~~ Depart from me, ye cursed!" (She grasps the doorknob, slamming the door) And ~~~~ shut the door! ~~~~ Lock it! (She does so) ~~~~ There! (Suddenly in a burst of triumphant, vindictive hatred) Now ~~~~, and sneer and laugh at your ~~~~ dreams, and sleep with ~~~~, and deny yourself, ~~~~ I know you feel no love with madness, and for ~~~~ to poison you, and remain in silence, and beat on the walls until you die of starvation. There ~~~~ live long, now you no longer have me to devour, Cannibal!

Gadsby (~~~~) Come, come, Abigail. This is most unseemly!

Abigail (~~~~ ~~~~ ~~~~) ~~~~ it is done! See it done to me. (The door first lighting up - sternly) Hush! Do you hear, Nicholas?

Gadsby (wicked and bewildered) Hear what?

Abigail: The footsteps beyond the wall. They have stopped receding. I think he remembers he had forgotten me and is turning back. (Suddenly she is conscious of the expression on Gadsby's face and she bursts into natural cheering laughter) Heavens, Nicholas! What an alarmed face! Did you think it was a burglar I heard?

Gadsby (relieved - ~~~~, his dignity ruffled) God bless me! Who could know what is struck ~~~~? Silly, indeed! What fanciful rubbish, Abigail!

Curtain

Page 72 from typescript—Act Two, Scene One
*Yale Collection of American Literature, Beinecke Rare Book
and Manuscript Library, Yale University*

ago. She is welcome to her husband. [*with more and more of vitality in her tone*] In a way it will be a great challenge to my talent for successful intrigue. I shall have to be very cunning. Her weakness is she is sentimentally honorable and proud and full of pity. I must be very meek and humble. [*suddenly, angry at herself*] No! I talk as if I were planning to pretend and play a part! But I *am* meek now! I *am* humble! I am willing to beg her on my knees to give me this chance to be reborn! I can love her for it if she does! Because if she can trust me, I can learn to trust myself again! I can make her love me and her children love me! I can find love again! [*She smiles exultantly.*] Oh, I may surprise myself, I think, with my undreamed-of talents as a good woman! Already at the mere prospect of escape, I feel a rebirth stirring in me! I feel free! [*She laughs with a strange self-conscious embarrassment and shyness.*]

GADSBY [*with an approving, benevolent smile*]   Good! Excellent! I am delighted you—

DEBORAH [*with an abrupt change to a strange hectic air of bravado*] And to prove my escape—as a symbol— Watch and bear witness, Nicholas!—I will cast out my devil, the old Deborah—drag her from her sneering place in my mind and heart— [*She makes a movement with her arms and hands of pulling something out of her head and heart and pushing it from her.*] and push her back where she belongs—in there—in perpetual darkness— [*She advances up the steps —with a final push*] "Depart from me, ye cursed!" [*She grabs the doorknob, shutting the door.*] And shut the door! Lock it! [*She does so.*] There! [*suddenly in a burst of triumphant, vindictive hatred*] Now question, and sneer and laugh at your dreams, and sleep with ugliness, and deny yourself, until at last you fall in love with madness, and you implore it to possess you, and scream in silence, and beat on the walls until you die of starvation. That won't take long, now you no longer have me to devour, Cannibal!

GADSBY [*uneasy*]   Come, come, Deborah. This is all most unseemly!

DEBORAH [*turns to him—with the same strange air, but quietly now*]   It is done. She is dead to me. [*then her face lighting up—tensely*] Shhhh! Do you hear, Nicholas?

GADSBY [*startled and bewildered*]   Hear what?

DEBORAH   The footsteps beyond the wall. They have stopped receding. I think Life remembers he had forgotten me and is turning back. [*Suddenly she is conscious of the expression on Gadsby's face and she bursts into natural teasing laughter.*] Heavens, Nicholas! What an alarmed face! Did you think it was a burglar I heard?

GADSBY   [*relieved—huffily, his dignity ruffled*]   God bless me! Who could know what to think? Life, indeed! What fantastic rubbish, Deborah!

* * * CURTAIN * * *

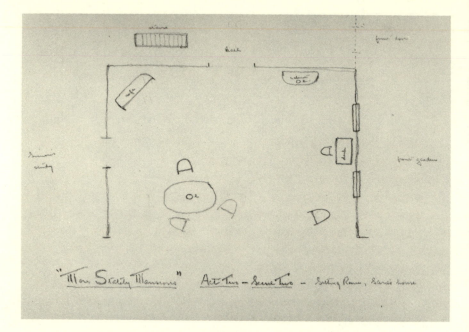

Sitting room, Sara Harford's home—Act Two, Scene Two
*Yale Collection of American Literature, Beinecke Rare Book
and Manuscript Library, Yale University*

Act Two, Scene Two

———

SCENE *Sitting-room of Sara Harford's home in a textile mill town about forty miles from the city. The following night. The room is small, a typical room of the period, furnished without noticeable good or bad taste. The atmosphere is one of comfort and a moderate prosperity.*

At front, to the left of center, is a table with a lamp and three chairs grouped around it. In the middle of the left wall is a closed door leading into Simon's study. In the left corner, rear, is a sofa, facing right-front. The doorway to the entrance hall, and the stairs to the second floor, is in the middle of the rear wall. At right of this doorway is a cabinet with a lamp. There are two windows in the right wall, looking out on the front garden and the street. Between the windows is a desk with a chair. At right-front is a big armchair. A rug covers most of the floor.

As the curtain rises, from the hall at rear the sound of small boys' arguing voices is heard coming down the stair well from the floor above. Then Sara's voice trying to quiet them and, for the moment, succeeding. In this pause, the door from the study at left is opened and Simon enters. Physically, he appears to have changed no more than one would normally expect. His spare frame has put on ten pounds or so but it still has the same general effect of loose-jointed, big-boned leanness. His large-featured Yankee face looks his thirty-one years. But there is a noticeable change in the impression his personality projects—a quality of nervous tension, the mental strain of a man who has been working too hard and put unrelieved pressure on himself. As he comes into the room, he is frowning, his eyes preoccupied. He comes to the table and stands staring down at it preoccupiedly. He is startled from his thoughts by a hubbub from the floor above, a chorus of boys' excited voices, the sound of scuffling coming through the ceiling, followed by a resounding thump and a chorus of laughter. Simon's expression changes. His face lights up. He smiles and chuckles to himself. Then Sara's voice is heard in a commanding tone, and the uproar subsides obediently. Simon sits in the chair at left front of table. He picks up two folded newspapers from the table, puts one paper aside, starts to open the other, hesitates, then determinedly opens it. His eyes fix on one story. As he reads it, his face becomes hard and bitter. He hears Sara coming down the stairs in the hall and at once represses his thoughts and looks back toward the doorway at rear smilingly.

Sara enters at rear. She is flushed, her hair disarranged on one side, her eyes laughing and fondly maternal. She exudes an atmosphere of self-confident loving happiness and contentment. She is much better looking than she had been in her pregnancy. Her figure is buxom, but beautifully proportioned with full breasts, still firm and solid in spite of having nursed four children, and a slender waist.

SIMON   Well! What's been going on up there? I thought the ceiling was coming down.

SARA [*comes forward laughingly*] We had a pillow fight. They were so full of high spirits I thought I'd better let them take it out or they'd never settle down to sleep. If you'd seen Honey! He stood on his bed and aimed a great blow at Ethan and missed and came tumbling off to the floor. I was frightened he'd hurt himself, but not a bit. He sat there laughing to kill himself, and we all had to laugh, too. [*She laughs—then suddenly shamefaced*] But what a way for me—and you in your study trying to write. Simon, I'm sorry, Darling. [*She kisses him impulsively.*]

SIMON [*gives her a little hug*] Nothing to be sorry about. I couldn't get interested in it tonight, anyway. [*He looks away from her. She sits in the chair at right, front, giving him a quick questioning look, trying to read his thoughts.*]

SARA [*notices the paper in his hand for the first time—too casually*] What paper is it you've been reading?

SIMON   Garrison's *Liberator*.[1] [*teasingly but with a resentment under-neath*] I know you don't approve.

SARA [*protestingly*] No, now. I never said that, Simon. I want the poor black niggers set free just as much as you—if they can find a way to do it that won't ruin the country. [*as she sees his smile*] Oh, I know. You think I'm thinking only of us. Well, maybe I am. If you don't look after yourself no one else will. And you are a cotton mill owner who depends on the Southern planters. There's many here envy your success and would play you a mean trick if they could, like telling the planters you were Abolition so they'd black-list you or—

SIMON [*frowning*] I'm not in the habit of advertising my opinions, am I? They're nobody's business but my own.

SARA [*with satisfaction*] I know, and that's all I ask you to remember. [*She looks at him quizzically and smiles with fond amusement.*] It's lucky you don't make speeches about your opinions or you'd have the whole world bewildered. As far as I can make out you're a Massachusetts Whig and a South Carolina Democrat, too. You're for Webster and high tariff—

SIMON [*cynically*] To protect our cotton goods. You approve of that, surely.

SARA   At the same time you were for Calhoun, who hates high tariff, when he wanted Nullification of the Union. I don't approve of that, Simon. I'm all with President Jackson there, that Union must be preserved at any price.

SIMON [*sharply*] I see State rights as a symbol of the individual's right to freedom. [*then quickly*] But why talk of that now. The issue has been settled by a compromise, for the time being.

SARA   I know it's settled. [*then teasingly*] And you're Abolition, too, and that's not Whig nor Democrat. [*She laughs.*] You're a queer man when it comes to politics. You'd better leave them to me. I'm for the party that protects our interests—as long as it protects them and not one minute longer. That's simple enough, isn't it? [*She laughs.*]

---

1. An Abolitionist newspaper called *The Liberator* was published by William Lloyd Garrison in Boston. The first edition appeared January 1, 1831.

SIMON   I'm quite willing to leave them to you. You know very well I am not really interested, that my one true belief is that the whole system is fundamentally rotten, lock, stock and barrel, and— [*He stops abruptly and self-consciously—curtly*] But this argument is ridiculous. I was only teasing you about the *Liberator*. I was reading the newspaper.

SARA [*uneasily*]   Oh, I meant to hide it. I didn't want you to see—

SIMON [*his face hardening*]   Why? I knew Father had died. The report of his funeral means nothing. It seems to have been an eminent occasion. Daniel Webster and every Whig notable in the city were there. That would have pleased Father.

SARA [*resentfully*]   I can't understand your mother not inviting you to the funeral. [*bitterly*] Unless she thought I wouldn't let you go without me, and she didn't want her poor Irish relations shaming her before the notables!

SIMON [*mollifyingly*]   Now, now. Don't let your mind return to that old bitterness. I think it was simply that she knew Father wouldn't have wished me to come and pretend grief for public opinion's sake. He had his virtues and the foremost was his hatred of hypocrisy in any form. [*then with growing bitterness*] As for her having Joel write me he was dead instead of writing me herself, you know I've never had a letter from her since I saw her that time at my cabin, although I kept writing her until it was all too plain she had no further interest— [*He hesitates—then slowly*] I've never told this— it seemed too ridiculous—but I'm afraid I must have done something to offend her, which she's never forgiven, although I can't imagine what. Except one thing, which is too childish— But then, she is childish. She was telling me of some silly flight of her imagination and my sense of humor got the better of my tact, and I couldn't help laughing—

SARA   I know. You shouldn't have laughed, Simon.

SIMON [*staring at her*]   You know?

SARA [*quickly*]   I know you shouldn't have laughed, whatever it was. There's a time when women have to admit to themselves that age and death are real, and they get touchy about their dreams. [*abruptly*] But I think the reason she hasn't written you is because

she's a wise woman and knows it'd do no good for her to interfere—

SIMON I'd hardly call the letters she once wrote me interfering.

SARA She was always reminding you about your book.

SIMON [*stares at her—smilingly*] You objected to that? But for the
last couple of years, who has been encouraging me to write it?

SARA I have. But that's different. That was so you'd have anything
you wish from life to keep you content. And, anyway, I have a
right— [*She grasps his hand and presses it—tenderly possessive*]
Because I love you, and you're mine, and your happiness is my
happiness.

SIMON [*moved*] I know, Dear. And my one happiness is to give you
happiness. [*A pause. He goes on jokingly but with a resentment
underneath.*] Why, often I had forgotten all about the darned thing,
or I'd want to forget, but you would remind me and send me into
my study to work on it like a regular slave-driver!

SARA [*laughingly*] Oh, I'm not as bad as that, Darling. I'd only speak
of it when I'd see you had one of your black lonely fits on, and
I'd be afraid you were regretting—

SIMON [*frowning*] Regretting what? That's silly, Sara. That's all in
your mind. If you'd seen what was really in mine, you'd have discovered it was something to do with the mill that made me preoccupied. [*then jokingly as before*] But I've had a dark suspicion
for some time about the secret motive behind your persistence in
encouraging me to write the book. I think you calculated very cunningly the best way to convince me it was nonsense was to make
me attempt it and then prove to myself—

SARA [*guiltily*] No.

SIMON You were sure the absurdity of it was bound to strike me
finally. There I was at night in my study trying to convince myself
of the possibility of a greedless Utopia, while all day in my office
I was really getting the greatest satisfaction and sense of self-fulfillment and pride out of beating my competitors in the race for power
and wealth and possessions! [*He laughs, bitterly amused.*] It was
too absurd. I couldn't go on forever cheating myself like that, re-
fusing to face myself as I really am. So I made a final decision to-

night to forget the book. [*sharply*] Final, do you hear, Sara? Remember that and don't ever mention the damned thing again.

SARA [*unable to keep a certain triumph from her voice*] You're giving it up forever?

SIMON Yes, to prove that, and wipe the slate clean, I threw all I've done in the fireplace and burned it. Not that there was much beyond notes. I've destroyed so many beginnings at different times. And I can confess to you now that many nights when you thought I was writing, I was simply sitting there with my mind a blank, bored— [*He hesitates—then blurts out*] Yes, why not admit it frankly— bored to death with the idea of it! [*He suddenly casts a quick glance at her face, as if regretting this admission—in a forced joking tone*] You don't have to look so triumphant, Sara.

SARA [*guiltily*] I'm not. I— [*then bluntly*] No, I won't lie. I am glad you have found it out for yourself. You know I've never believed your dream would work, with men and women what they are.

SIMON [*smiling a bit bitterly*] With us as we are, for example? [*quickly*] But you're quite right. My old romantic obsession with Rousseau's fake conception of the inner nature of man was a stupid mistake. Rousseau, as I see him now, was a weak, moral, sentimentalist—a coward who had neither the courage nor ability to live in a world of facts and accept the obvious truth about man—which is that man is compounded of one-tenth spirit to nine-tenths hog— [*quickly*] No. Rousseau was simply hiding from himself in a superior, idealistic dream. [*sneeringly*] As Mother has always done, in a different way. You were right to blame her, Sara. She did have a weakening influence on me when I was young, encouraging me to live in dreams and take a superior scornful attitude about the world of fact and life as it is. It was really her influence that made me first conceive the idea of my book. I can see that now—her haughty disdain for Father because he was naturally absorbed in his business. [*He laughs scornfully.*] And yet all the time she owed everything to his business—the comfort she loved, the protected privacy, her fanciful walled-in garden, the material security which gave her the chance to remain aloof and scornful! It's too idiotic and stupid when you consider it! [*then frowning*] But why think of that now? Except I thank God I freed myself in time, and then met and loved you, who are so simply and courageously and passionately conscious of life as it is, and love it and are healthily eager and happy to be alive and get all you can from it, and don't have to hide from yourself in dreams of what might be in impossible other worlds! [*abruptly*] But I don't know why I'm doing all this talking. All I wanted to tell you was my final decision about the book.

SARA   I'll remember, Darling, and I'll never mention it again. I'm only too happy—

SIMON [*ignoring this—preoccupiedly*]   No, all you have to do to see how sentimentally naive Rousseau's conception was, is to study history—or merely read your daily newspaper and see what man is doing with himself. After all, his deeds constitute the true revelation of his nature. What he desires is what he is. [*with a bitter enthusiasm*] There's the book that ought to be written—a frank study of the true nature of man as he really is and not as he pretends to himself to be—a courageous facing of the truth about him—and in the end, a daring assertion that what he is, no matter how it shocks our sentimental moral and religious delusions about him, is good because it is true, and should, in a world of facts, become the foundation of a new morality which would destroy all our present hypocritical pretences and virtuous lies about ourselves. [*He laughs.*] By God, it's a fascinating idea. I've half a mind to try it!

SARA [*who has been listening uneasily—protesting resentfully*]   Ah now, don't start thinking of another book and getting one of your lonely fits of discontent! What have you to complain of in life? Haven't you love and me and the children? Isn't that enough?

SIMON [*protests guiltily*]   Of course it's enough! I would be an ungrateful fool if— And I'm not discontented or complaining. Don't you see that this new book would show that it was nonsense to complain about oneself or be ashamed of oneself? [*quickly—forcing a laugh*] But you're taking me too seriously, Sara. I was merely amusing myself playing with the idea. I have no intention whatever—

SARA [*relieved, smiling now, maternally amused*]   If it isn't just like

you to start dreaming a new dream the moment after you've woke
up from the old! It's the touch of the poet in you!

SIMON [*resentfully*] Nonsense! Don't be sentimental, Sara. There
never was any poet in me. And I'm through with all idiotic ideas
of becoming an author. I couldn't spare the time, for one thing,
even if I wanted. [*with more and more of a business-like air*] It's
a difficult period for trade this country is in now. I've got to concentrate all my brains and energy on our business affairs. [*frowning*] Conditions are becoming worse every day. [*with a flash of
vindictive anger*] That mad fool, Jackson! What does he know of
business—an ignorant, mob-rousing, slave-dealing plantation owner!
The cowardly tariff compromise[2] he accepted coupled with his insane banking policy are ruining the country!

SARA   Well, he can't ruin us. We've got fifty thousand dollars, the most
of it in gold English guineas. The hard times won't touch that.

SIMON [*with satisfaction*] No. They will make it more valuable.

SARA [*proudly*] And didn't you have the brains to see the hard times
coming before anyone, and guard us against them. I'm so proud of
you, Darling!

SIMON [*pleased*] Well, yes, I did, if I do say it myself. Though I de-
serve no credit except for ordinary horse sense. Any fool should have
seen the crash was bound to come. But they didn't. My competitors
kept on expanding while I was cutting operations down. And now
it's too late. They're caught, poor devils. [*He smiles with satisfaction.*] Yes, we'll weather the storm, Sara. And when the time comes
we will be in a position to take advantage of others' lack of fore-
sight. There will be splendid bargains in bankrupt mill property
to be picked up right here in town. That will be our opportunity
to expand and profit by the inevitable upturn which must follow
the period of stagnation. [*enthusiastically*] And you can bet we will
not be blind to our opportunity, will we?

---

2. In order to pacify the South, represented by John Calhoun and Henry Clay, who were
angered over the tariff law that levied taxes on goods imported from abroad, Jackson
signed a compromise tariff bill in 1833 that reduced the tariff rates over a period of nine
years until they reached the level of the 1816 law. Because Northerners, like Simon in
the play, manufactured their own goods and did little importing, they were in favor of
the protectionist measure.

SARA [*proudly*] *You* won't, I know. It's all your brains.

SIMON [*lovingly, patting her hand*] No, no. There is no you, nor I. There is only we. [*then enthusiastically*] Yes, there are great opportunities ahead of us. It won't take long for us to get the hundred thousand we have set as our goal. Or more.

SARA No. That's enough. We promised ourselves—

SIMON [*smiling*] But wouldn't two hundred thousand, say, be better than one?

SARA [*smiling*] Maybe, but—

SIMON It would give you a fine country estate and greater security for the future.

SARA Give us, you mean. It's for you. I don't want you slaving in trade all your life. I want you to retire a landed gentleman and live at your ease. [*then calculatingly*] Of course, the more you've got to retire on, the safer you'd feel. But I don't want you to take risks and get in too deep.

SIMON You used to laugh at me for saying that. [*He smiles teasingly— with a note of taunting*] Who is being afraid now? [*then earnestly*] You don't realize what extraordinary opportunities there will be, Sara. In shipping, for example, there are many firms, from the rumors I hear, on the verge of bankruptcy already. Later on I know we could buy up one for comparatively nothing.

SARA [*uneasily*] No, stick to your own trade, Simon, whatever you do.

SIMON But it is one of my trades. Don't forget I had my first business training with my father's Company.

SARA [*with a trace of vindictive hope*] You don't think maybe his Company is in trouble?

SIMON [*frowning*] No, of course not. Father was much too cautious and shrewd. He took no chances even in the best times. And I'm sure he had everything arranged for the future, so that in case of his death, all Joel would have to do would be to carry on a traditional ritual of conservative policy—small risks and moderate profits—and be a Harford figurehead, while the real work is done by the competent subordinates Father has trained. [*He sneers.*] That is about all Joel is good for, as Father knew. [*then impatiently*] But all that is nothing to me. What I was going to say is that we can't dismiss the shipping trade as something that doesn't concern us. Properly considered, it is a part of our business—or it ought to be. Our cotton is brought to us on ships, isn't it? If we owned our own shipping company, managed as economically and efficiently as I know I could manage it, it would be of tremendous advantage to our mills—

SARA [*uneasily*] Oh, I see, Darling. It's only that I have a feeling that railroads are bad luck. [*bitterly scornful, lapsing into brogue*] My father, God pity him, was always prating about the great future for the country there was in them, and how he considered them the proper investment for a patriotic gentleman—and him without a dollar to his name! I can hear him now telling my mother— [*Her face suddenly grows sad—scornfully*] Poor Mother! She didn't live long in her Convent to enjoy the rest she'd prayed for. She'd no more than got her wish when she had to die. [*She sighs.*] Ah well, she died at peace, anyway! [*with scorn*] Though it's not the peace of giving up life for a living death I'd ever want for myself. [*then conscience-strickenly to Simon*] But what am I doing, reminding you of death now. Forgive me, Darling.

SIMON [*intent on his own calculating thought, has not been listening— vaguely*] Forgive what? [*then excitedly*] I tell you, Sara, the more I think of it, the more opportunities I foresee. Take banking. Banks are beginning to fail right and left already, and before long I prophesy that some of the strongest and most desirable ones will be so weakened that you could buy control—

SARA [*laughingly*] Stop! You have my head spinning! If you keep on, you'll be dreaming yourself the King of America before you know it!

SIMON [*starts and grins sheepishly*] I was getting a bit beyond myself, wasn't I? [*then with a strange self-compulsive insistence*] Still, if we had that two hundred thousand in specie now, no dream would be too impossible.

SARA [*scolding him as though he were a small boy*] Now, now, you're too greedy. And you mustn't do so much planning and scheming, when it's getting near bed time, or you'll never settle down to sleep. You haven't been sleeping well lately, and I won't have you getting excited and making yourself so tired and nervous.

SIMON [*leans back in his chair, suddenly conscious of weariness*] Yes, I am tired. But I'll sleep soundly again now I've put that damned book out of my mind. [*He closes his eyes. Sara looks at him with tender maternal worry. He opens his eyes to stare before him.*] What a damned fool a man can make of himself by clinging to the irresponsible, sentimental dreams of his youth long after he has outgrown them and experience has proven how stupidly impractical they are! Keep on deliberately denying what he knows himself to be in fact, and encourage a continual conflict in his mind, so that he lives split into opposites and divided against himself! All in the name of Freedom! As if Freedom could ever exist in Reality! As if at the end of every dream of liberty one did not find the slave, oneself, to whom oneself, the Master, is enslaved! [*He chuckles bitterly.*]

SARA [*uneasily*] Ah now, Darling, don't start that black loneliness—

SIMON [*throws off his mood—with a relieved laugh*] Oh, I'm not. That's finished and done with. I promise not to bewilder you with opposites ever again. [*jokingly*] I'll be all high tariff and Whig and Daniel Webster and pro-Union from now on. [*tenderly*] Above all, pro our union, forever one and indivisible, Sara!

SARA [*moved—pats his hand*] Darling! That's my only politics in life, too!

[*They are interrupted by the sound of the knocker on the front door, coming from the hall at rear. They look surprised. Sara starts to get up but Simon is before her.*] I'll go. Now who the devil— [*He goes out, rear, frowning irritably. Sara sits listening. From the hall Simon's voice is heard exclaiming with startled astonishment—"Mother!" and Deborah's voice "Simon." Sara springs to her feet and stands tensely defensive her expression frightened for a second, then hardening into hostility. Deborah's voice again. Then Simon's and Joel's in cold formal greeting to each other. A moment later Deborah and Simon appear in the doorway at rear with Joel behind them. Deborah wears deep mourning. It becomes her, giving her a quality of delicate, fragile sorrow. Outwardly she is all disciplined composure, the gracious well-bred gentlewoman, with just the correct touch of quiet resignation in her bearing which goes with her widow's black. But one senses an inner tense ex-*

citement. At sight of her, Sara instantly puts on her most ladylike manner, as if responding in kind to a challenge.]

DEBORAH [*comes forward with a gracious smile, holding out her hand—simply*] I am glad to see you again, Sara. I hope you remember me from our one meeting just before you and Simon were married.

SARA [*takes her hand, smiling in return—a bit stiltedly*] I do. It is a great pleasure, Mrs. Harford.

SIMON [*indicating Joel—coldly*] This is my brother, Joel, Sara. [*Joel makes her a formal bow, his face cold and expressionless, but remains silent. Sara, following his lead, acknowledges the introduction in silence, then turns to Deborah.*]

SARA Won't you sit down? [*She indicates the chair in which she had been sitting. Deborah takes it.*] You sit there by your mother, Simon. [*She goes to the armchair at right, front. Simon sits in his old place at left, front, of table. Joel takes the chair at rear of table.*]

SIMON [*confused by this unexpected visit—forcing a smile, his tone almost resentful*] When—? This *is* a surprise, Mother.

DEBORAH We arrived on the stage about an hour ago and went to the hotel to make ourselves presentable.

SIMON The hotel? You must stay with us. We have a room for you, if not for Joel—

JOEL [*coldly*] I should stay at the hotel in any case.

DEBORAH No, no. I would not dream of imposing on Sara's hospitality.

SARA [*smiles cordially*] I insist with Simon, Mrs. Harford. [*She goes on in a tone that becomes, in spite of herself, defiantly bragging.*] We've a fine room always ready. We've had Southern planters as our guests, and they seemed well pleased, although they're gentlemen who are used to great mansions on their estates— [*abruptly she is ashamed of her bragging and adds lamely*] We should feel very offended if you refused us, Mrs. Harford.

DEBORAH Why then, since you are kind enough to put it that way, Sara, I accept your hospitality with pleasure. It is the more grateful because it will give me an opportunity of knowing your children. I know when I see them I shall be not only resigned but happy to be an old grandmother. [*For a moment she looks into Sara's eyes with a strange, almost pleading earnestness.*]

SARA [*stares back suspicious and puzzled for a moment—then she soft-ens*] I'm sure you'll like them. No one could help— [*She smiles.*] But, of course, they're mine and I'd be bound to think that.

JOEL [*in his cold emotionless voice*] If you will pardon me, Mother, I think the sooner we make clear the business that brought us here, the better. We must obtain Simon's decision tonight so I can return on the first stage tomorrow.

DEBORAH [*quickly*] And Sara's decision. I suggest Simon take you to his study. You can explain your mission there, and leave me to tell Sara—why I am here. I want her to know that while our reasons for being here have an obvious connection, they are really not the same reasons at all. [*She stares at Sara again with the same earnest, almost pleading, look. Sara reacts as before, at first suspiciously, then puzzledly relenting.*]

SIMON [*frowns—resentfully*] You always take a childish delight in playing the mysterious, Mother. [*turning to his brother—curtly*] My decision on what?

DEBORAH Certain last wishes of your father's, and a bargain he pro-poses. [*She smiles.*] I need not warn you to scrutinize it closely or you may get the worst of it.

JOEL [*coldly rebuking*] Mother!

SIMON [*stares at her and then smiles—dryly*] I naturally would, Mother. But thank you for the warning.

DEBORAH It was your father's wish that you decide this matter solely on its merits as a business opportunity—as though the party of the other part were a stranger. That is my wish, too. I want that clearly understood because Joel is a sentimentalist and will doubtless urge all sorts of fanciful family obligations. You will kindly disregard any nonsense of that kind.

JOEL [*with cold anger*] Mother! I protest!

SIMON [*his face hardening*] I flatter myself I do not need to be re-minded by Joel or anyone of my just obligation.

JOEL [*coldly*] I shall urge no such obligations on Simon, Mother. I am too well aware he is indifferent to them. Besides, there is no ques-tion of obligations. [*He turns to Simon.*] Father's proposal is im-mensely to your advantage.

SIMON [*dryly—getting to his feet*] In your opinion. Perhaps not in mine. We shall see. [*He starts for the study door at the left, Joel following.*]

SARA [*uneasy—warningly*] Simon, remember—

SIMON [*turns back reassuringly*] Don't worry. You know I will make no decision without your consent. [*He turns and opens the study door and bows curtly to Joel to precede him. They go inside and shut the door. There is a pause of silence in which Deborah and Sara stare at each other. Deborah again with the strange earnest, almost pleading, look. Sara suspicious, puzzled, yet impressed by the change she senses in Deborah in spite of herself.*]

DEBORAH [*simply*] It is a long time since our meeting at the cabin. I am sure you notice how greatly I have changed since then.

SARA [*uneasily*] I do. On the outside, I mean. In your looks. [*then with a cruel revengeful satisfaction*] You look an old woman now. [*tauntingly*] But I suppose you still dream you're the King of France's sweetheart, God pity you!

DEBORAH [*winces in spite of herself—then with a quiet smile*] You wish to test me? I cannot blame you for being suspicious. Yes, I look an old woman now, Sara. Well, why not? I am an old woman inside me. And I have not dreamed that dream since that day. Can you believe that, Sara?

SARA [*stares at her—then nods slowly*] I believe you. You couldn't, remembering how he'd laughed. [*then impatiently*] But it's no business of mine. And it isn't telling me why you're here or what you want of me.

DEBORAH [*hesitates—then quietly with a deep pleading sincerity*] I came to beg charity from you, Sara.

SARA [*stares at her, not able to believe her ears*] You! To beg charity from me! [*then with harsh suspicion*] Ah, what trick are you up to now?

DEBORAH No. Can't you feel how I have changed, Sara? Please do! That old Deborah you knew and justly suspected is dead. There is no trick now, Sara. It is the truth that I have come to beg—

SARA [*staring at her believes—then cannot restrain a burst of gloating triumph lapsing into broad brogue*] You, the great lady Harford! Glory be to God, if my father could have lived to see this day.

DEBORAH [*ignores this—with the same pleading sincerity*] I came to beg you for the chance to live in life again, to begin a new second life in which I will welcome reality and not fly from it, in which I will forget as one long dead the old vain selfish greedy fool and coward you knew who hid from herself in ridiculous romantic dreams. Forget, too, the self who succeeded her, whom you have not known, who resigned herself to death-in-life and fell in love with Death, and even with insanity. [*She shudders—then pleadingly again*] There is only one possible chance for me to live again, Sara, and only you can give it to me.

SARA [*moved*] Ah, you poor woman! [*then hastily wary*] No. I'll see. I'd have to know more. I'm buying no pig in a poke, thank you! [*then jeering, not unkindly*] Are you sure you could live if you had the chance? You're a timid dreamy creature and you're not strong like me. [*boastfully*] I'll love life with my last dying groan!

DEBORAH With your help, I would not be afraid. [*pleadingly again*] I want the chance to be unselfish, to live in others' lives for their sake and not my sake. I want to make myself an unselfish mother and grandmother, to learn how to live for others' happiness, to earn their love by giving and not taking! [*She smiles at Sara—a trembling smile pleading for belief.*] I want even to become a loving mother-in-law who can rejoice in your happiness as my son's wife and his happiness as your husband.

SARA [*moved—impulsively with a strange, almost servile, humble gratitude*] Ah, that's good and kind of you, Madam. [*then abruptly hostile—contemptuously*] If you're not lying to play me some trick!

DEBORAH [*ignoring this—pleadingly*] I feel now what I felt that day at the cabin, even when I hated you, that you and I are not natural enemies in our hearts—that in a way we complement each other and each has something the other lacks and needs—

SARA [*resentfully*] If you imagine I have any need for your great lady's airs and graces, you're badly mistaken, Mrs. Harford!

DEBORAH [*continuing as if she hadn't heard*] I feel now what I felt then, that if we gave each other the chance, we could be close friends and allies and even grow to love each other.

SARA [*moved*] Are you begging me for—? [*then with a strange deri-*

sive satisfaction] Indeed and you've changed entirely, when you can lower yourself from the high pride of yourself in your dreams to— [*She stops abruptly and stares at her warily—grudgingly*] Maybe I could like you. I know I don't hate you anymore. I'm too sure of Simon now. I know nothing you could do— And if I could trust you—

DEBORAH [*earnestly*] You can, I swear to you! Don't you feel you can trust me now?

SARA [*moved but warily*] I do—now. But you'd have to prove—

DEBORAH All I ask is a chance to prove it, Sara. [*persuasively*] After all, you won't be risking anything. You would know if I tried to deceive you, and you could always make Simon get rid of me again.

SARA [*grimly*] I could. I'm glad you know that. And I would. I hope you know that, too!

DEBORAH I do know it, and I would be the last to blame you. [*pleadingly*] What I'm begging for above all, Sara, is the chance to find a new life—and unselfish love—through the lives of my grandchildren. I want to become a good, loving grandmother. If you knew how horribly alone I have been for so long, Sara, sitting in my garden with an empty dreamless mind, with only the hope of death for company—a garden where Spring is but the beginning of Winter. It and I need to be reminded that Life is not the long dying of death but the happy greedy laughter of children! [*She pauses—then adds quietly*] Will you give me that chance, Sara?

SARA [*moved*] It's true you have nothing in life, poor woman, and how could I be so cruel and hard hearted as to turn you away, when I'm so rich and you so poverty-stricken.

DEBORAH Then you will! Oh, thank you, Sara. I am more grateful than you can know! It means the difference between life and death to me!

SARA [*uneasy, as if already regretting her consent*] I'm only doing it because it was through the money you loaned us when we were married we got our start, and we owe it to you in honor—I've never liked being in debt to you, but now we'll be square and even. [*then suddenly suspicious*] Wait! What has this got to do with the business his brother is telling Simon? You haven't explained what that business is yet.

DEBORAH [*smilingly evasive*] I'd rather not, Sara, if you don't mind. I know nothing of business, and, anyway, I want you to decide from what Simon tells you about it, purely on its merits as a business opportunity. You will be able to do this without being influenced by your old suspicion of my motives now that you see how I have changed and you know that my only real interest is the chance for a new life, which you can give me whether you and Simon decline his father's offer or not.

SARA But what is the offer? You can tell me that.

DEBORAH [*carelessly*] Why, all I understand about [it] is that my husband realized that Joel hasn't the ability to be the head of a big company, while Simon has proved he has the ability. So my husband suggested that in case of his death Joel and I should offer Simon a controlling interest if he would assume direction of the Company's affairs.

SARA [*her eyes gleaming triumphantly*] My husband to be head of the Harford Company? Ah, if my father—! [*She stops abruptly— then frowning*] But I don't see— If Simon's father wanted that, why didn't he have it in his will?

DEBORAH [*with a mocking smile*] No, no, my husband was much too proud a man for that. He could not publicly admit he had been wrong in disinheriting Simon, or that he needed his help. Not even for the sake of the Company which was his one beloved. [*bitterly*] He preferred to bequeath to me the humiliation of begging— [*hastily*] Of course, you understand, Sara, it is a bargain my husband suggested. He was not the man to give anything for nothing. The Company, I believe, is at present in need of cash, and he knew you—

SARA [*her face hardening*] Ah, so that's it! The gold we've slaved to save! [*curtly*] No, thank you, Mrs. Harford. My husband has his own business, and it's enough. We don't want the Harford Company.

DEBORAH [*shrugs her shoulders indifferently*] Well, that's for you and Simon to decide. I appreciate your viewpoint and I won't blame you if you refuse. But please don't make any decision from what I say. Wait until Simon tells you all the facts. He will know if there is any advantage for you in the offer. Oh, there's another thing I was forgetting. My husband proposed that, in fairness to you, since you would necessarily have to make your home in the city, I make over to you, as part of the bargain, a one-half interest in my house and garden, so that you could live there by right of ownership and not feel under any obligation—

SARA [*her eyes gleaming again*]   The Harford mansion! I know it's one of the finest in the city.

DEBORAH   Yes, it is really a very beautiful and valuable property, Sara. And I need not tell you how delighted I would be. I will be so horribly lost living there alone. In fact I want to double my husband's offer, and deed the whole property over to you so that it will be entirely yours, and you will have the sole management of it. All I ask in return is that you allow me to live there with you—and my grandchildren. [*She adds laughingly.*] Oh, I admit this is shameless bribery on my part, Sara, but I am so alone, and it would mean so much to me—

SARA [*touched and greedy*]   I think it's very generous of you, Mrs. Harford. [*then warily*] But, of course, it depends on what Simon—

DEBORAH   Oh, certainly, but I hope he will find the business part of it advantageous. And now, let us not talk of business anymore. I really know so little— [*eagerly*] Could I see my grandchildren now? Oh, I know they must be asleep. All I wish is a peek at them, so I can begin feeling myself an actual, living, breathing grandmother! [*She laughs gaily.*]

SARA [*smiling—touched*]   Indeed you can. Their grandmother has the right. [*She runs from her chair and Deborah gets up, too.*] Only I better go up alone first and make sure they're asleep. If one of them was awake and saw you he'd be so excited and full of questions—

DEBORAH [*smiling*]   Oh, I know. I remember Simon— [*She stops abruptly, her expression suddenly bitterly resentful.*]

SARA   I'll be right back, Mrs. Harford.

DEBORAH [*throws off her mood—smilingly*]   I would be grateful if you could call me Deborah from now on.

SARA [*with instinctive humility*]   No, that's too familiar— [*then hating herself for this—assertively*] All right, I will, Deborah. [*She goes out, rear.*]

DEBORAH [*stares after her—as if in spite of herself, an expression of triumphant gloating forces itself on her face, and she smiles jeeringly.*]

At least old age has not impaired your talent for acting, Deborah! [*then savagely*] No! You lie! You know you lie! I meant every word sincerely! What if I did misrepresent the business aspect of it? That is nothing to me! That concerns Simon! I only use it! The real issue for me is between Sara and me, and that is decided! And I am grateful to her! I already feel an affection for her! I will make myself love her! She has been kind and generous and understanding! She has given me life again! I feel freed from myself, eager to live! I— [*She stops abruptly and sits down again as the door from the study is opened and Simon enters with Joel. Joel's expression is one of cold, bitter humiliation. Simon is repressing a feeling of gloating satisfaction and excited calculation. He comes and puts a protecting, possessive hand on his mother's shoulder.*]

SIMON [*gently*] Poor Mother. I'm so sorry. [*She gives a quick bitter look up at his face and moves her shoulder away from his hand. He goes on comfortingly.*] But never mind. You mustn't worry anymore. [*in an almost bragging tone*] I think, without flattering myself, I can promise I'll soon win back for you all his stupid folly has lost.

JOEL [*with cold anger*] It is cowardly to insult the dead.

SIMON [*stung—turns on him—bitingly*] Is it an insult to state a fact? He did act like a fool, as Mother will agree—

DEBORAH [*coldly*] I agree with Joel that the dead are, after all, the dead. [*Simon stares at her in resentful surprise. She adds curtly.*] Am I to understand you accept your father's proposal?

SIMON [*resentfully*] Of course. Did you think I would refuse to save you from being ruined and left a pauper?

DEBORAH [*sharply*] No, no! We will have none of such consideration, if you please. I told you it is my wish, as it was your father's, that there be no hypocritical family sentiment in this bargain.

SIMON [*taken back and hurt*] Hypocritical, Mother?

DEBORAH Yes, hypocritical. You hated him and you certainly owe him no obligation. As for you and me, we have not even corresponded in years. We have forgotten each other. Our old relationship of mother and son died, from perfectly natural causes, long ago. In the meanwhile, we have both changed completely in character—

SIMON [*bitterly*] Yes, I begin to see how completely you have changed!

DEBORAH [*indifferently*] Good, I am glad you do. And I see as clearly
the transformation in you. Well, then? Are we to pretend we are
what we were, or are we to be sensible and frankly admit the obvious truth that we are now strangers? Admit it without resentment
as the inevitable result of time and circumstance. I believe it is very
important for us to do that, Simon—here and now—to free each
other from the sentimental duty to remember a past each of us has
forgotten. I think it is extremely necessary, now that conditions
beyond our control, have brought us together again, that we start
our new relationship on a foundation of lasting fact so it may have
the chance to develop into a pact between friends who can rejoice
in each other's successful freedom. [*She pauses—then adds with a
little taunting smile*] Anyway, I warn you frankly that, even if I
tried, I could never play the role of a slavish loving mother convincingly again.

SIMON [*bitterly*] I am glad you admit it was just a role.

DEBORAH [*ignoring this*] So now you ought to appreciate why I must
insist you consider your father's and my proposal purely and simply
as a business deal. Accept, if it strikes you as a profitable opportunity.
If not, decline it. And no more sentimental maundering about poverty. Why should the Company's ruin necessarily condemn me to
rags. I have no doubt you would offer me a home with you. If not,
Joel has—

SIMON Naturally, Mother, I would welcome you—

DEBORAH Well, then, no need, is there, to have pathetic visions of my
begging in the gutter? Besides, I could—or so Nicholas Gadsby
assures me—always marry well again.

JOEL [*repelled—coldly*] I consider it grossly improper of you, Mother,
with Father scarcely cold in his grave, to—

SIMON [*repelled—coldly*] I agree with you, for once, Joel. It is revolting, Mother! [*then with a sneer*] And I would not take Gadsby's
flattery too seriously. It is not so easy to catch a rich husband—even
for a young and beautiful woman.

DEBORAH [*smiling*] That jeer might have hurt my vanity once, Simon,
but now I am a grandmother, I am long past the desire to possess
husbands. [*She laughs.*] Besides, you'll admit I can always have
Nicholas, and he is quite well off.

JOEL [*rebukingly*] Mother! This ill-timed levity is—

DEBORAH Inconsequential—to you, I know. [*She turns to Simon with a return of her cold curtness.*] Well, I hope you are thoroughly convinced now that whatever is arranged must be on a strictly business basis so there can be no possibility of any future misunderstanding about sentimental obligations. I refuse to be indebted—to you—for anything.

SIMON [*stares at her—then brusquely*] Very well, Mother. [*He sits at the table—Joel behind it—curtly*] As I have told Joel, I will accept Father's proposal only on one condition. If you cannot agree to it, there is no more to be said.

DEBORAH [*coldly*] And what is the condition?

JOEL [*with cold anger*] It is preposterous, Mother—an insult to my father's memory!

SIMON [*ignoring him*] There can be no question of my giving up my prosperous business here to take up his bankrupt one. That is absurd. Father, in his blind vanity, grossly overestimated the prestige of his name. I have never needed that prestige. I do not need it now. I have never been his son. I have always been myself. My condition is that I absorb his Company in mine. His Company must cease to exist. There must be only my Company.

JOEL [*angrily*] You see, Mother! Father would rather have faced ruin a thousand times—

DEBORAH [*dryly*] But unfortunately he left me to face it. [*She stares at Simon—with a strange smile*] I see, Simon, what an opportunity this is for you to realize a life-long ambition. [*then briskly*] I accept your condition.

JOEL I protest, Mother! You have let him beat you down like a swindling horse-trader! He sees the tremendous advantage for him in Father's offer. He would accept it unconditionally if you—

DEBORAH [*cuttingly*] Your protest is voted but kindly remember mine is the final decision. [*with a smile*] I want your brother to drive the hardest bargain he can, to be unscrupulous and merciless—

SIMON [*dryly*] Naturally you could expect no mercy in a strictly business deal, Mother. [*then matter-of-factly*] Then the matter is settled—provided, of course, Sara consents, and you may take that for granted.

DEBORAH   Yes, I have talked with Sara and I think you will have no trouble convincing her.

SIMON   [*with resentful curtness*]   I know that, Mother. Sara does as I advise in these matters.

JOEL   [*gets to his feet—stiffly to Simon*]   I bid you good night. I shall go to the city by the morning stage and have the announcement made that you are assuming control of the Company.

SIMON   [*curtly giving orders*]   Yes, see to that if you please. The sooner it is known the better. You never can tell in these days when creditors may grow uneasy, and suspicious.

JOEL   [*stiffly*]   Before I go. I wish to protest again, in Father's name, against what I consider the dishonor of your conduct and of my mother's. You will, of course, wish me to resign from my position.

SIMON   [*indifferently*]   No. You are an excellent head bookkeeper, I know. So why should I? And I shall see that you are given an interest in my Company, commensurate, under the circumstances, with the interest you were left in Father's Company.

JOEL   [*stiffly*]   I shall engage an attorney to protect that interest.

SIMON   [*impatiently*]   Attorney or no attorney, I could easily swindle you out of it, if I liked. But you are too helpless a foe. [*He nods curtly in dismissal.*] Good night.

JOEL   [*stiffly*]   I will keep my position only because I feel it my duty to Father's memory to do all I can—for I warn you that, whatever you do, the Company will always be my father's Company in my eyes.

SIMON   [*irritably*]   I do not care a tinker's damn what it is in your eyes. [*Joel stares at him, is about to say something more, then bows stiffly to Simon, ignoring his mother, and stalks out the door at rear. Simon frowns exasperatedly after him—then suddenly chuckles with amusement, with a change of manner towards Deborah of their one-time intimate sharing of a joke.*] God, he'll never change, will he, Mother? He isn't a man. He's a stuffed moral attitude!

DEBORAH   [*unconsciously falling into the mood of their old affectionate intimacy—laughing maliciously*]   Yes, haven't I always said Joel is God's most successful effort in taxidermy! [*They laugh amusedly together—then stop abruptly and stare at each other. Deborah defensively, Simon resentfully*]

SIMON   I must confess, Mother, after all your explanation, I still do not see why you should suddenly take such an antagonistic attitude toward me as you have. [*hopefully*] Or was that simply for Joel's benefit?

DEBORAH   [*lightly*]   Good heavens, no! Is Joel important? No, it was for your benefit—and mine.

SIMON   One would think I had in some way deeply offended you. Whereas, if either of us has cause to feel injured, it is I! For some time after we last met, I kept writing you and you never deigned to answer.

DEBORAH   Because at that last meeting I realized that our old relationship was quite dead, and there was no good keeping up a pretense for sentiment's sake. You are wrong to think my present feeling is one of antagonism. I have no reason to feel that. No, my feeling is one of indifference. [*Simon looks hurt and startled. She goes on quietly.*] I will be quite frank, Simon. If I had heard of your death— Oh, of course, I would have tried to be dutiful and recapture sentimental, fond motherly memories of what used to be between us, but I am afraid I would have been as indifferent to your death as you have changed to be, as I would be to the death of a stranger, which is what you really are to me now.

SIMON   [*woundedly*]   Mother!

DEBORAH   No, no, please, let us face the truth. You would have felt the same if I had died.

SIMON   No!

DEBORAH   Yes. Why deny it? That is what Time does to us all. We forget and pass on. It is perfectly natural—and necessary. You have your life of a husband to live. You have your children. One can only think of so much. One must forget and eliminate the past. Why not admit that?

SIMON   [*coldly—his face hard*]   Very well. I do admit it.

DEBORAH   Good! There the past is finally buried, and we can start again and learn to become friends. I want to be the friend of Sara's husband, Simon. I want to be proud of what you are, of what you will do to recoup the Harford fortune, of the great success in your chosen career I see before you. I am determined to live with a world that exists, Simon, and accept it as good because it is, and all else is not. I have forgotten my old silly presumptuous cowardly disdain for material success. I hope to live to see you become a Napoleon of finance.

SIMON [*stares at her—bursts out with contemptuous disgust*] It is no lie that you have changed—incredibly! [*then abruptly and eagerly*] But what you say is true. Finance is only one medium for ambition in the country today, through which one can conquer the power where possession alone gives you the liberty to be free! [*He smiles.*] It is a strange coincidence that you should come tonight and say these things. Just before you came I had torn up and burned what I had done on that absurd book—set myself free of the past—

DEBORAH [*quietly*] I congratulate you. You are wise. It was meaningless except as an obstacle in your way—a sentimental memory of a dead self. [*Sara enters from the rear. They turn to her. She looks disturbed for a second at finding them close together, then comes forward smilingly.*]

SARA I'm sorry to keep you waiting so long, Deborah, but our talking here had wakened Jonathan and I had to get him back to sleep. [*glancing from one to the other—with a trace of suspicion*] What are you talking about? Where's Simon's brother?

DEBORAH [*gaily*] Simon was talking over this business—for the last time, I hope.

SIMON Joel just left. I'm sending him to the city by the first stage to announce that we are taking over Father's Company and making it a part of our business. [*with a gloating grin at her*] Do you understand, Sara? His Company ceases to exist. We absorb it. There will be only one Company.

SARA [*her eyes lighting up with a vindictive triumph*] Ah, leave it to you! If my father had only lived to see— [*then with sudden dismay*] Then you decided it all—without waiting to ask me!

SIMON Because I was sure of your consent and I knew Mother had talked to you.

SARA But she didn't—

DEBORAH No, Simon, you know I haven't the knowledge to explain all the business details.

SARA She was begging me—

DEBORAH   Yes, I begged Sara to forget all the bitterness in the past, now your father is dead, and allow me to become her friend. And she promised she would try.

SARA   Yes, I did. But—

SIMON   [*with a strange, resentful air—almost sneeringly*]   It is strange to think of you two as friends.

DEBORAH   [*with a little smile*]   He doesn't believe we can be, Sara.

SARA   [*defensively*]   Why can't we, I'd like to know? I've always felt grateful to her for giving us our start in life.

DEBORAH   Yes, we will prove it to him, won't we? We won't let him discourage us.

SIMON   [*frowning—irritably*]   Discourage you? What a stupid thing to say, Mother! You know very well nothing would please me more.

DEBORAH   [*laughingly*]   There, Sara. Now we have your husband's blessing.

SIMON   [*changing the subject abruptly—to Sara*]   To get back to business: I didn't wait for your consent because I knew you couldn't possibly refuse such a good bargain. [*then almost as if he were showing off his authority before his mother*]   And after all, you know from experience you can trust my judgement.

SARA   [*uneasily again*]   I do know, yes. But—

SIMON   [*enthusiastically now*]   I tell you, Sara, this is the luckiest kind of coincidence—an extraordinary opportunity for us—exactly the chance for expansion and growth we were hoping for. [*with a sly glance at his mother—chuckling complacently*]   And a finer bargain than I would have dreamed possible, thanks to Mother. I was going to be merciful and generous, but she insisted I consider it nothing but a business deal, and drive the hardest bargain I could. So I did, and I don't mind confessing in her presence, now the deal is completed, that we will be getting something for practically nothing.

DEBORAH   [*laughing*]   And so am I. I had nothing and I am getting Sara's friendship and a chance to make a new start in life as a good grandmother. [*She turns to Sara—eagerly*]   But all this talk of business is meaningless to me. What is important— May I go up and see my grandchildren now, Sara?

SIMON   [*frowning—curtly*]   No, they're asleep. You'd only wake them.

SARA [*defending her*] All she wants is to peek at them from the door. Isn't it, Deborah?

DEBORAH Yes. To meet myself as a grandmother by seeing them in the flesh. And you can trust me not to wake them, Simon. [*smilingly*] You forget I've had experience. Many a time I looked in at you and never disturbed you.

SARA [*smiling at him maternally—teasingly*] Oh, him. It's hard to get him to sleep but once he drops off you could fire a cannon and he'd never budge.

DEBORAH Yes, that's the way he used to be when he was little. [*She laughs.*] I can see you have made him your eldest son, as well as your husband, Sara.

SARA [*laughingly*] Oh, he's been that from the day we married. [*teasingly*] Only don't let him hear you, Deborah. I'd offend his dignity.

DEBORAH Well, I hope you notice I am not one bit jealous of you taking my place, Sara—now.

SARA [*stares at her*] Yes, I do notice. I feel it.

DEBORAH I'm so glad you do, Sara, because now there can never be any misunderstanding on that score. And I know you won't be jealous if I can make your children love me. I do want them to love me.

SARA Ah, don't think that of me. I'm not that selfish and greedy. I'll be only too happy— Don't I know how lonely and lost you must have been all those years without love to live for. [*She takes Deborah's arm—gently*] Come along now and see the children. [*They start back, ignoring Simon, who has listened frowningly, feeling completely out of it, his face hardening with resentment.*]

SIMON [*sharply*] Wait! [*as they turn back—injuredly*] You might at least wait until I have finished explaining about the bargain I drove, Sara.

SARA [*humoring him*] Of course, Darling. [*to Deborah, teasingly*] That's the way he is now. Once he gets his mind set on business the devil himself couldn't stop him.

DEBORAH [*seriously*] Well, I'm sure he owes his great success to that power for concentration, and that it will lead him on to greater and greater achievement. So it's really an admirable quality. [*Simon stares at her suspiciously but she appears absolutely sincere.*]

SARA   Oh, I know, and I'm so proud of him, Deborah.

SIMON   So proud you can't even listen while I tell you—

SARA [*placatingly*]   Ah now, don't get angry at me. Darling, can't you take a little teasing without— [*then resentfully herself*] Much good it will do me to listen now after you went ahead and agreed without consulting me at all!

SIMON [*harshly*]   You know very well my asking your consent has never been anything but a formality. What do you really know of business? It is I alone who have the right—

SARA [*suddenly frightened and hurt*]   Simon! You've never said that before! You—

SIMON [*guiltily*]   I'm sorry, Sara. No, and I wouldn't say it now if you'd give me a chance to ask your consent. It isn't too late for you to refuse. Nothing is signed yet. I can still back out, if you wish.

SARA   After you've given your word? [*proudly*] I hope Deborah knows I've too much honor for that!

DEBORAH [*jokingly*]   But can't you see, Sara, all he wants is to prove to you how clever he has been for your sake, and have you say you're proud of him.

SARA [*smiling*]   Oh, he knows that. I'm all the time telling him how proud I am, and making him vain and spoiling him! [*She laughs fondly.*] So go on now and tell me, Darling.

SIMON [*made self-conscious and ill at ease—awkwardly*]   What I wanted to say is— [*Suddenly he stares at his mother—sneeringly*] You a doting old grandmother, Mother? You will forgive me if I cannot picture that transformation! You've never cared about children, except as toys to play with in your garden and beguile your boredom—unless my memory is all wrong!

DEBORAH [*undisturbed—smiling*]   Yes, that is true, more's the pity. But that was an old dead me who was afraid of life. I am not that now. [*to Sara*] He doesn't want to believe that I have changed, Sara.

SIMON [*sneeringly*]   Oh, I'm open to proof. But it will take a lot of proving, Mother.

SARA [*resentful at him—rebukingly*]   Ah now, you shouldn't sneer at your mother like that. It's not kind. You ought to help her and take her word. What do you know of women? But I tell you I feel it in her no matter how she's lied to herself in the past, she's not lying to herself now. [*She glances at Deborah affectionately—smiling*] I'd still feel that, even if I knew she thought she was lying and wanted to lie.

DEBORAH [*gives her a strange grateful look*] Thank you, Sara. I am absolutely sure now we can become great friends.

SARA [*to Simon*] And I'm certain it's going to mean content for her, Simon, if you'll not interfere. [*arrogantly with a touch of brogue*] Sure, do you think I'm that stupid she could fool me? I know the fancy she has for the children already without a sight of them, and once she's seen them she can't help loving them. [*proudly*] Who could? And won't it be a great help for them to grow up fine gentlemen to have a grandmother who's a great lady— [*She stops abruptly—guilty and humiliated*] Never mind. What is it you were going to say about the bargain, Simon? [*without waiting for him to answer*] Maybe you don't know or you couldn't act so unfriendly toward her, that your mother, as part of the bargain, is going to deed over her fine mansion and land in the city to us. She'll only live there as our guest and I'll have the whole management and be the mistress.

SIMON [*his face hardening*] I will not consent to that.

SARA [*defiantly*] But I have consented, and it's only fair you leave me to decide about our home, which is my business, if you want me to agree with what you've decided about the Company.

SIMON I told Joel I did not want even the one-half interest in Mother's home that Father suggested she offer me. We will rent a house first, and later buy our own home. We need be under no obligation to Mother—

DEBORAH [*sharply*] I told you there could be no question of obligations. I made the offer to Sara as part of my bargain with her— [*smilingly*] and, to be frank, I think I am getting all the best of it. I will still have all the privileges of my home and none of the responsibilities of actual ownership. And I will have Sara and my grandchildren for company. No, if there is any obligation, I am obliged to Sara.

SARA [*smiling*] No, Deborah, it's a great bargain for us, too. [*to Simon, a bit impatiently*] Can't you see, Simon, that we'll be getting a fine mansion for nothing at all, with a beautiful, spacious garden for the children to play in.

DEBORAH [*staring at him with a strange mocking little smile—jokingly*] Really, Sara, your husband's attitude is most unflattering. You would think I was some wicked old witch, the way he dreads the thought, living in the same house with me!

SIMON [*resentfully*] Don't be silly, Mother. I—

DEBORAH [*as before*] He seems to feel so antagonistic to me because I didn't answer a few letters. But I know you appreciate my reasons for that, Sara.

SARA I do, and I'm grateful you had the fairness and good sense not to—

SIMON [*bitterly*] So it is I who am antagonistic, Mother? Well, perhaps I am—now—with good reason—but if I am, whose wish was it—? [*then abruptly with cold curtness, shrugging his shoulders—to Sara*] But, as you said, Sara, our home should be your business, and I am willing to abide by your decision. It is really a matter of indifference to me what house I live in. I shall have to concentrate all my attention on reorganizing my Company and for a long time to come I can see I shall have to do practically all my living at my office. [*becoming more and more enthusiastic—eagerly*] You can't realize what an opportunity this is for me, Sara, and what a tremendous bargain I have got! Father became panic-stricken, the coward, the minute he found himself out of his conservative depth. He greatly exaggerated the danger. It will be easy for me—

DEBORAH [*turning to Sara—gaily*] Let's leave our Napoleon to his ambitious destiny and go up to the children, Sara.

SARA [*teasingly*] Yes, let's. He'll be owning the whole world in his mind before you know it. [*They turn towards the door at rear, laughingly.*]

SIMON [*resentful—coldly*] Wait. Although I have agreed to let you decide where we shall make our home, Sara, I would like to utter a word of warning—in Mother's presence, so that everything may be open and above board. [*sneeringly*] You will forgive me if I do not possess the entire confidence in this sudden friendship between you you both appear to have. Oh, I do not doubt you think you feel it now, but it will be a difficult matter when two such opposites as you are have to live together in the same home day after day, with continual friction and conflict of character developing.

SARA [*resentfully*]   You've no right to expect the worst. And if it should happen, we can always change it one way or another, can't we?

DEBORAH [*gaily*]   Yes, you can always dispossess me. You will have the legal right to, you know. But I am sure I will never give you just cause. You trust me not to, don't you, Sara?

SARA   Yes, I do.

DEBORAH [*smiling, with a strange undercurrent*]   I promise to leave you entirely alone, Simon. So you need not worry. As for you thinking Sara and me as hostile opposites, that, I believe, is something which exists only in your mind, because you persist in remembering the dead me who was your mother. But Sara, at heart, sees how I have changed, and that she and I can have much in common, now.

SARA [*stubbornly*]   Yes, I do, Simon.

SIMON [*resentfully*]   All right then. I have nothing more to say. But don't forget I warned you. And remember I have the right to expect a peaceful atmosphere in my home. I will have too many important things on my mind to be distracted by domestic dissensions. So please don't come to me—

DEBORAH [*gaily—but with a strange undercurrent*]   I hereby take a solemn oath never to come to you.

SARA [*staring at him—puzzled and resentful*]   What's come over you, Darling? It is [not] like you to act so grudging and stubborn—I can't see—

DEBORAH [*as before*]   Yes, one would actually think you resented us becoming friendly, Simon. [*to Sara—teasingly*] Men are such vain little boys, Sara. I have an idea he would prefer us to be jealous enemies and fight a duel to the death—

SIMON [*forcing a laugh*]   What a fantastic idea, Mother! And you think you have changed! [*He comes to them—protesting*] You know very well, and Sara knows, it has always been my dearest hope that circumstances would someday present you and Sara with the opportunity really to know each other. I was sure when that happened, you could not help loving each other, and I am delighted that, at last, my hope has been realized. I made the objection I did only because I wanted to convince myself you were sure of each other's good faith. My experience in business has made me over-cautious about contracts entered into in haste, perhaps. But now I admit myself entirely convinced. I congratulate you—and myself on my good fortune. It needed only your reconciliation to complete my happiness and give me absolute confidence in the future. [*He kisses them. Sara's face lights up happily. Deborah's remains teasingly mocking.*]

* * * CURTAIN * * *

Tao House
Oct. 6th '38

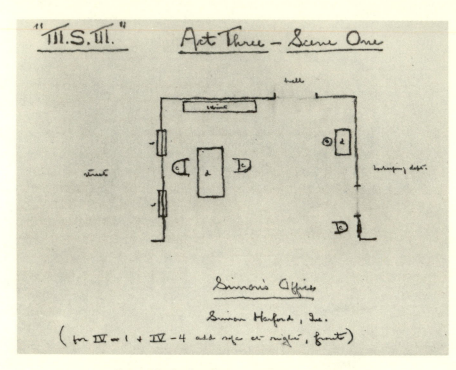

Simon Harford's office—Act Three, Scene One

*Yale Collection of American Literature, Beinecke Rare Book
and Manuscript Library, Yale University*

Act Three, Scene One

SCENE *Simon's private office in the offices of Simon Harford, Inc. in the city four years later. It is an early morning in the late summer, 1840.*

The room is small, well-proportioned, panelled in dark wood. The furniture is old, heavy and conservative. A dark rug is on the floor of polished oak boards. On the walls are pictures of Washington, Hamilton, Daniel Webster, and, incongruously, John C. Calhoun.

In the left wall are two windows looking out on the street. Between the windows is a chair, facing right. Before the chair, a large table with drawers which serves as Simon's desk, with another chair on the other side of it, facing his. In the rear wall right, is a door leading into the hall. At left of this door, a tall cabinet stands against the wall. At right, front, is a door leading into the bookkeeper's office. Farther back against the wall, is a high desk with a tall stool in front of it. At front, right, is another chair facing left.

As the curtain rises, Simon enters at rear and comes to his table. He has changed greatly in the four years and looks older than the thirty-five he is. His body has put on twenty pounds or more of solid flesh, mostly around his chest and shoulders and arms, which gives him a formidably powerful appearance. On the other hand, his face has become thinner, more heavily lined and angular. There are patches of grey over his temples. His expression is that of one habitually tense, with a mind disciplined to function efficiently at a high pitch while suppressing all manifestation of nerves. His manner is curtly dictatorial. He speaks rapidly and incisively. He is dressed conservatively in dark clothes, obviously expensive.

SIMON [*before sitting down, picks up an engagement pad from the table and glances at it*] Nothing of importance—except the railroad directors—that isn't important now—a signing of papers—it is finished—it is mine. [*He tosses the pad on the desk and sits down—stares at the table top a moment*] Mustn't forget Sara's engagement—it is time I did something to take her away from Mother's influence—make her my old Sara again— [*then frowning*] Bah!—better leave well enough alone—I really don't want her here interfering in my business—in which she takes no more interest, anyway—as little as Mother— [*then dismissing it*] Well, let's hope she's early before the others begin trooping in—

[*He picks up the morning mail stacked on his desk and at once becomes concentrated on going through it. The manner in which he does this is characteristic. He goes from one letter to the next with astonishing rapidity, seeming to take in the contents of each at a glance and make an instant decision, setting it on the table at his right, or dropping it in the waste basket.*

The door from the bookkeeper's office at right is opened and Joel Harford enters, closing the door quietly behind him. He stops to glance at his brother, then comes and stands in front of his desk. Joel looks older. The stoop in his shoulders is more pronounced, with a suggestion of weariness and resignation now beneath the uncompromising rigidity of his habitual poise. He stands waiting, staring at Simon with his customary cold disapproval. Simon deliberately ignores Joel's presence—or attempts to, but it immediately gets on his nerves, and at last he exclaims exasperatedly, stopping his work with a nervous jerk.]

SIMON   Well? Don't stare like a frozen codfish! Is this another of your periodical duty-to-the-Company protests against my management? If so, I don't care to listen.
JOEL [*stiffly*] As a stockholder, it is my right—
SIMON [*contemptuously*] Your right has no power, so you have no right. But relieve your conscience, if you must. Only be quick. I have no time— [*tensely explosive again*] Damn you! You have the

stupid effrontery to criticize my leadership in the face of all I've accomplished in four years! I have five mills now, all running profitably, instead of one. I have transformed what was Father's bankrupt business into a marine division of my Company which is a model of its kind. I have—

JOEL [*interrupts coldly*] I do not minimize what you have done in that respect. What I object to is your reckless use of credit which continually leaves the Company in a fundamentally unsound position. You pay off debts only in order to borrow more largely. You go on gambling—

SIMON Don't be a frightened old woman! [*arrogantly*] It is not gambling when I know the dice are loaded in my favor by my ability to turn any possible contingency into a fresh opportunity.

JOEL You think only of further expansion. That is bad enough when you restrict it to your proper sphere, but when you adventure into new fields— [*stiffly*] I refer now to the deal for the railroad you are to conclude this morning. I am unalterably opposed to this folly. You know nothing of railroading.

SIMON Neither do most of those engaged in it. [*arrogantly*] But unlike them I *will* know all there is to know. Anything I choose to make mine, I make mine!

JOEL Finally, I want to warn you again against the growing unscrupulousness of your methods, the ruthlessness with which you take advantage of others' misfortunes. You are making the Company feared and hated.

SIMON [*curtly*] Good! I want it to be feared. As for others, I do to them as they would do to me—if they could! I ask no quarter. Why should they? [*contemptuously*] What a sentimental ass you are, Joel! You would like to apply to business the ethics men and women pretend to observe toward one another in their private lives. That is as stupid as trying to play poker by the rules for chess. The game of Commerce has its own ethics, and they are more frank and honest—and so, more honorable!—truer to the greedy reality of life than our hypocritical personal ones. The only moral law here is that to win is good and to lose is evil. The strong are rewarded, the weak are punished. That is the sole justice which functions in fact.

All else is an idealistic lie about things as they are not and never were—and can never be, men—and women—being what they are. A lie that I would be stupid to permit to get in my way, or in my Company's way.

JOEL [*coldly*] I am thinking of my father's Company, not of you. But I realize I am wasting words. [*He turns toward the door to right.*] I will go back to my work.

SIMON [*with nervous exasperation*] Yes, for God's sake! Now your duty to your conscience is done, get out! [*Then as Joel goes toward the door, suddenly his whole expression and manner change and he speaks in a strange conciliating tone.*] Wait. Sit down a while. [*He indicates the chair at right of his desk. As Joel stares in cold surprise without making any move toward the chair, he bursts out angrily.*] I said sit down! Either you obey me or you look for another job! Don't think because you happen to be my brother, you can presume—! [*Joel's face betrays no emotion. He comes back and sits down stiffly in the chair. Simon's manner abruptly becomes strangely placating.*] I'm sorry, Joel. Didn't mean to fly out at you like that. It has been a strain getting this affair of the railroad settled. My nerves are on edge. [*He pauses. Joel sits staring at him. He goes on and gradually his eyes drop from Joel to his desk, and more and more it seems he is talking to himself.*] It's the usual reaction. I concentrate all my mind and energy to get a thing done. I live with it, think of nothing else, eat with it, take it to bed with me, sleep with it, dream of it—and then suddenly one day it is accomplished—finished, dead!—and I become empty, exhausted, but at the same time restless and aimless and lonely, as if I had lost my meaning to myself—facing the secret that success is its own failure. [*with a wry smile*] A vacation would be in order at such times—relaxation, complete change. But where? How? A voyage to France, say. With Sara. A second honeymoon. But Sara would not leave the children, and to take the children along would mean it would be their vacation with their mother, not mine with my wife. It would be no change for me. I have enough of that atmosphere at home. [*He pauses—then with a sneer*] Perhaps Sara would even insist on taking Mother with us. She might feel lonely without her. They have grown to be such loving friends, drawn to each other by their devotion to the children! [*forcing a joking tone*] I assure you, I am left entirely out of it now—in the lonely cold, so to speak. Sometimes, I feel a stranger in my own house. That is Mother's doing, of course. She imagines she has been very subtle, that I have not seen—Whereas the truth is, I have had too many important Company affairs on my mind to bother. But I promised myself that as soon as I had time, I would put a stop to her greedy scheming, and now the railroad deal is completed— [*He smiles strangely.*] That may be the change in activity I need. I have neglected my interests in my home too long, unwisely entrusted them to others to protect—a sure way to be swindled! [*He pauses—then strangely*] If you ever fall in love, Joel, take my advice and do not marry. Keep love your mistress with no right of ownership except what she earns day by day, what she can make you pay for possession. Love should be a deal forever incomplete, never finally settled, with each party continually raising the bids but neither ever concluding a final sale. [*He laughs mockingly at Joel's coldly disapproving face.*] Yes, my advice to you would be to shun marriage and keep a whore instead!

JOEL [*with cold disgust*]   Such ideas are on a par with your conception of honor in business dealings. [*rebukingly*] I cannot see why you wish to discuss such matters with me.

SIMON [*as if surprised at himself*]   No, for that matter, neither can I—except that my mind is empty and restless, and I can trust you to listen without hearing much. [*again with a conciliating manner*] I wanted to ask you: Why is it you never come to visit Mother? I am sure she would like—

JOEL [*dryly*]   You know she has as little desire to see me as I have to see her.

SIMON [*strangely*]   You should come, if only out of curiosity. You would be astounded at the way she has transformed herself [*sneeringly*] into a doting old grandmother. I think you would not know her now, any more than I know her. But the grandmother phase of her transformation is not the strangest. Although difficult to believe of Mother, it is at least understandable as the whim of a lonely old woman. It is her affection for Sara that is most incredible. I never thought that would last a month before they became enemies again. But it has become even more harmonious and intimate—seemingly. I have watched its development with the greatest curiosity. I think they both knew I was watching, and were determined to prove—Mother, at any rate. The strangest thing has been to notice how she has gradually taken what she needed of Sara into herself. Physically she has steadily grown younger and stronger and fleshier. She looks more like the mother of my children now than their grandmother. Or so she appears to me. That is why I would like you to see her. I want an outside observer to verify my perception of her. I know my suspicions cannot be mere fantasies of my mind, and yet I would like to be sure.

JOEL [*stiffly*] If Mother ever requests me to visit her, I will do so, as is my duty as her son. Otherwise, I will not.

SIMON [*ignoring this*] It is as though she had slowly taken possession of Sara in order to make of my wife a second self through which she could live again—to use Sara as a strong sanctuary in which she could hide from her old cowardly self, so terrified by life. [*with a strange grim smirk*] Or, in another aspect, trick Sara into being an accessory in the murder of that old self, which was once my mother. And so leave me motherless. Which at the same time by becoming Sara, leave me wifeless, for naturally I could not regard— [*He stops abruptly—then goes on with an increasing brooding strangeness.*] It has been difficult to see clearly what she was doing, to discern which of many greedy purposes was her main purpose, what the final achievement is she is working and scheming toward. I have been very confused as I have observed the two of them, and yet I have had flashes of revelation, too. Sometimes the two have appeared to lose their separate identities in my mind's eye. Have seemed, through the subtle power of Mother's fantastic will, to merge and become one woman—a woman in Mother's image, but not her as I have ever known her. No, a strange woman, like a figure of woman in the abstract, spirit of Woman made flesh and flesh of her made spirit, mother and wife in one—to whom I was never anything more than a necessary adjunct of a means to mother-

hood—a son in one case, a husband in the other—but now no longer
needed since the mother by becoming the wife has my four sons
to substitute for me, and the wife having them, no longer needs a
husband to use in begetting—and so I am left alone, an unwanted
son, a discarded lover, an outcast without meaning or function in
my own home but pleasantly tolerated in memory of old service
and as a domestic slave whose greed can be used to bring in money
to support Woman! [*with a calculating vindictive calculation*] Yes,
that is what Mother flatters herself she has accomplished. But she
doesn't realize there are fundamental weaknesses in her plan, that
the past is never dead as long as we live because all we are is the
past. She is going to discover, beginning today, and Sara, too, that
whenever I wish, I take back what belongs to me, no matter— [*He
checks himself with a sudden wary glance at Joel's expressionless
face.*] But all these fanciful speculations are nonsense, of course,
which you mustn't take seriously—the reaction of my mind, left
restless and purposeless after the strain of successfully completing
the railroad deal.

JOEL [*gets up from his chair—coldly*] I have not listened. I have no
interest whatsoever in your private affairs. And I know you were
simply using me to talk aloud to yourself. If you have done, may
I go back to my work.

SIMON [*explodes with tense exasperation*] Yes. Take your idiotic conscience to hell out of here. I will direct the Company as I choose!
And until I ask for your advice, which will be never, kindly keep
your mouth shut! [*Joel turns and goes into the bookkeeper's office
at right, closing the door behind him. Simon looks after him—with
angry self-contempt*] By God, when I begin making a spiritual con-
fidant of him, I should begin, also, to doubt my own sanity! [*Then
he relaxes and falls to brooding again.*] But no. Even that dull fool
realized I was really addressing myself—because I have no one but
myself—because I have been left alone—driven out of all lives but
my own—Mother has seen to that—by God, I was right to ask Sara
to come here this morning!—it's high time I began to take back
what is mine! [*He fights down his anger—with brooding bitterness
again*] Yes, Mother has been clever and subtle—left me with no life

but this one which she always despised—this daily grind of slavery
to an unscrupulous greed for power—the ambition to be a Napoleon
among traders!—I, who once dreamed—! [*abruptly with self-exas-
peration*] Rubbish!—no hypocritical pretenses, if you please— You
have no right— Your old dream was childish idealism—a stupid
boy's misconception of man's true nature—which is that of a hog,
as your experience with him, and with yourself, has already demon-
strated—the possession of power is the only freedom, and your pretended disgust with it is a lie—why, only a week ago you were so
completely absorbed in the winning of the railroad you did not give
a damn for anything else in the world! You were as passionately
enthralled as a lecher gaining a new mistress, as happy as a gambler
who risks everything he possesses on the turn of a card— [*with a
strange satisfied chuckle*] Except, of course, I had stacked the cards
beforehand so I could not lose! [*matter-of-factly*] No, you must
allow for your present state of mind—the reaction of emptiness after
success—you've always felt it— But never so strongly before—there
is a finality in this—as if some long patient tension had snapped—
as if I'd reached the end of a blind alley in my mind where I no
longer have the power to discipline my will to keep myself united—
another self rebels—secedes—as if at last I must become two selves
from now on—division and confusion—a war—a duel to the death—
[*he adds with revengeful bitterness*] Well, let those who are responsible for the challenge beware, for I will make it their duel, too!
I have learned only too well in my life here the strategy of dividing
in order to conquer—of creating strife and rivalry, and waiting until
the two opponents are exhausted destroying each other—then I step
in and take advantage of their weakness to possess them both. [*He
smiles with a gloating revengefulness.*] Yes, Mother and Sara!
Henceforth, I must insist you both sit in this game and take up the
two opposing hands you have dealt me and play them with all your
greed!—I must demand that each of you henceforth takes upon herself her full responsibility for what I have become, to its last final
implication! [*abruptly—impatient*] Bah! What rubbishy fantasies!—
As if I really desired two damned possessive women prying and
interfering in my private business!—and I talk as though I had con-

ceived some elaborate plan of campaign against their alliance—if
I have, it is hidden in my mind—I do not yet see clearly—all I know
is that on an impulse I asked Sara to come here—some confused
feeling that if I get her alone away from Mother's influence, I would
desire her again—it is a long time since I have slept with her—but
at home her body has become repugnant, her beauty ugly—and,
anyway, she is too preoccupied being the children's mother to have
any love to spare—that, also, is part of Mother's scheme to dispossess
me— [*irritably*] Rot! For God's sake, forget your idiotic suspicions
of her! That silly old woman's senile mind is too occupied with pretending contentment as a doting grandmother, to engage in such
elaborate conspiracy—although she is undoubtedly responsible for
much of the indifference—but to return to Sara, hadn't I better think
out more exactly how I shall attack?—no, wait until you feel her
out and see how much of the old greedy Sara still lies behind her
present self of contented, satisfied mother—the ambitious Sara who
used to long to own an Irish-castle-in-Spain, gentleman's estate!—
who was willing to use any means or to pay any price—even her
beautiful body—to get what she wanted—as when, that night at the
cabin before we were married, she made me take her body so I'd
be bound in honor to marry her, and then use me as a first step
in her rising in the world!—as unscrupulous and ruthless as a whore
selling herself!—if that hadn't happened, I might never have married her—the long engagement Mother advised might have opened
my eyes to that common greedy nature hidden behind her beauty—
the lust masquerading as love!—if I possessed the insight into
woman's true nature I have now I would have swindled her into
giving herself by promising marriage—and then having had all I
wanted of her, deserted her—it would have served her right to be
beaten at her own game—I would have forgotten her and returned
to Mother, waiting for me in her garden— [*bitterly*] But she wasn't
waiting for you, you fool!—she had driven you out before you knew
Sara—she wanted to be rid of you, so she could be free—she was
through with you—she no longer wanted or needed your love—she
was just as ruthless and unscrupulous about discarding you as Sara
was in taking you—your happiness didn't count—yes, again it is a

case of Mother being really responsible—I would never have fallen in love with Sara if—and her responsibility began a long time before that, too—I had not felt any really serene happiness in her garden since I was a little boy—she made it plain that I possessed no right to be with her, that I was merely permitted to remain there to amuse her, a toy that her whim tired of and ruthlessly discarded!—that nonsense about her summerhouse—that was her way of showing me—and she took pains to point it out to me by implication that day she deliberately made up the fairy tale about the exiled Prince and the magic door—Yes, I never knew peace or faith in life again from that day— [*angry at himself*] Damnation!—what a sentimental ass, to be digging back in the past to boyhood memories—the pastime of weaklings with no present or future!— [*bitterly*] Nevertheless, it does trace the responsibility—the guilt—to the source—and indicates the line poetic justice should pursue to recompense and punish— In the case of Sara, too—Mother's is the spiritual greed, but the material lust is Sara's—Mother did not drive me to a career in the slave markets of trade where in buying one sells oneself—or sit me at a table in the gambling dive of commerce—she read Byron aloud, and despised business—it was Sara's lust, dreaming of Irish castles in Spain and a landed lady's estate, that has made me a cotton good's Napoleon!—who drove me to make her proud of me at any price— [*He pauses—then with an air of bitter satisfaction*] I begin to see in part the plan of the campaign I must start when she comes—she must be forced, gradually, of course, to take over her full responsibility—to share the burden and the cost—to pay back what is mine—all that I still desire from her, at least! [*He sits staring before him, frowningly concentrated, his expression becoming coldly ruthless and calculating.*]

[*The door from the hall at rear is opened and Sara enters. She has not changed much in appearance in the five years.[1] Has grown a little more matronly, perhaps, but seems no older. Is still exceedingly pretty, strong*

---

1. O'Neill means four, not five, years. It has been four years since the close of act 2 (1836–40). See the synopsis of scenes at the beginning of the play.

and healthy, with the same firm pronouncedly female figure. But she is dressed much better, with discriminating taste and style now, and expensively. In her personality, however, one is at once conscious of a decided change in quality, from her old positive, eagerly-grasping aliveness to a more passive, satisfied contentedness. Her manner has taken on a lot of Deborah's self-assured poise, and her way of speaking copies Deborah, although the rhythm of Irish speech still underlies it. She stands looking at Simon but he is oblivious of her presence. Sara smiles assuredly, a smile that has lost its old passionate tenderness and become maternal, complacent in possessiveness—a smile that takes its proprietorship for granted. Smiling with growing amusement, she tip-toes forward until she stands by his table.]

SARA   You might ask me to sit down, Simon. [*He jumps startledly in his chair.*]

SIMON   [*his frayed nerves exploding angrily—as if he did not recognize her*]   God damn it, what do you mean by sneaking—! [*then confusedly*]   Oh, it's you. I didn't—

SARA   [*taken aback but forcing a smile*]   Well! That's a nice greeting, I must say, after you begged me to come.

SIMON   I apologize, Sara. For a moment, I didn't recognize who it was. [*He springs to his feet—with a forced cordiality, indicating the chair across the table*]   Sit down, do. [*She sits in it and he sits down again.*]

SARA   I had no idea you'd gotten so nervous. You haven't seemed to be at home.

SIMON   [*affecting carelessness*]   Perhaps I control myself better there. Or perhaps, on the other hand, you have been too occupied with family affairs to notice!

SARA   [*smiling*]   If that isn't like you, to put the blame on me, when it's you who come home every night with your head so full of business you might as well be on the moon for all the attention you pay your mother or me. [*with a trace of bitterness*]   Or the children. [*abruptly changing the subject—with a forced interest*]   Speaking of business, tell me about the Company. You've been doing wonders with it, I know. You never mention it anymore to us at home, but everyone tells me you're becoming the young Napoleon of trade here in the city.

SIMON [*pleased but at the same time scornful*] The most flattering comparison the mind of woman can imagine! If men and women had ever admired Christ one-tenth as much as they admire that greedy adventurer, what a success Christianity might have been! [*He laughs sneeringly—then abruptly with a proud boastful air*] Here's a bit of news about my success you haven't heard yet, Sara. I've got the railroad now. You remember I promised myself I would. Well, it's mine!

SARA [*with forced enthusiasm*] Isn't that fine! I congratulate you, Simon.

SIMON [*with a preening satisfaction*] I have a final meeting with the directors this morning. Merely a formality. They've already agreed to my terms. Not easy terms for them to accept, I might add! They are left without a vestige of real power. I become absolute master. But they had no choice. They were on the verge of bankruptcy. I did not strike until I knew they were divided among themselves and weakened by dissension and jealousy and conflicting purposes— which I had secretly encouraged, by the way, to hasten the end. [*enthusiastically*] Wait till you see what I do with the road in a couple of years! I have learned from their mistakes. I'll make no mistakes!

SARA [*her enthusiasm more forced*] I'm sure you won't.

SIMON [*noticing her tone—deflated, and for a second boyishly hurt*] You're not very enthusiastic.

SARA [*hastily*] Oh, I am. [*forcing a smile*] Maybe my feelings are a little hurt. You used to say "us" and "ours" and now everything with you is "I" and "mine."

SIMON [*stares at her sharply—as if he saw with satisfaction some calculation verified*] Ah, you feel that?

SARA [*hastily and defensively*] No. It's selfish of me to talk like that. God knows I've more than enough to content me with a beautiful mansion for my home, and as happy a life as a woman could wish with Deborah and my children, without grudging you what is yours.

SIMON [*dryly*]   Yes, one should never complain of the price one must pay for what one wants from life—or thinks one wants.

SARA [*a bit defiantly*]   I know what I want, and I have it.

SIMON [*ignoring this*]   For example, I might complain with equal reason that you used to speak of our home and our children, while now—

SARA [*in her turn stares at him sharply*]   Ah! You feel that, do you?

SIMON [*carelessly*]   No, I said I might. But I have too many important affairs on my mind to give much thought to—

SARA [*trying to conceal her disappointment*]   I'm glad you're frank about it. After all, it's only natural. You can't give your mind to everything. [*bitterly*] And we've seen for a long time, Deborah and I, that you care more for the Company than anything else in life.

SIMON [*ignoring this last—carelessly but with a taunting undercurrent*]   Anyway, I must confess I cannot believe your possessive adjectives are more than a boast. I always have the feeling at home that, although Mother has relinquished all outward show of ownership and authority, she has managed to keep in possession.

SARA [*resentfully*]   Well, you're wrong. I have the only say about everything, and she's happy to let me have it.

SIMON [*smiling*]   Yes, Mother has always had a subtle talent for contriving it so that others must desire what she desires—and then generously giving them their way!

SARA   She hasn't with me. I'm not such a fool—

SIMON   Not when you're on your guard. But you're so kind and sentimental you never suspect—

SARA   There's nothing to suspect! No woman could be a truer friend than she's been to me! She's more like a sister, or my own mother, than a mother-in-law. And she's been such a good grandmother to the children—even if she does spoil them.

SIMON [*gives her a calculating glance*]   Yes, she is spoiling them. There's no doubt about that.

SARA [*defensively*]   If she does, it's only because she's still a child in her heart, herself, a great part of her, and like one of them. And there's no harm. I can always correct any bad ways she gets them into.

SIMON [*watching her*]   Of course, there's no harm done—if you're sure you haven't let it go too far.

SARA [*angrily*]   I haven't! I can take care of my children, thank you, without any advice— [*accusingly*] Is that your reason for inviting me here—to try and make trouble between your mother and me?

SIMON [*curtly*]   Don't be ridiculous! I'm delighted at the friendship which has developed between you. The more so, because I never dared hope—

SARA [*almost tauntingly*]   We know you didn't. Well, we fooled you!

SIMON   Make trouble? Don't you think I appreciate peace and harmony in my home, if only for selfish reasons.

SARA   You should.

SIMON   Do you imagine I'd prefer to have you at each other's throats?

SARA   No. That'd be crazy. [*then reproachfully*] While we're talking of this, Simon, I want to say something I've meant to for a long time. I know you've kept a secret grudge against her in your heart. But isn't it about time you stopped being so childish, and forgave—

SIMON [*sharply*]   Don't be stupid. There's nothing to forgive. What makes you say I harbor a grudge? Do we ever quarrel? Am I not always pleasant with her?

SARA   Yes, as you'd be to an acquaintance in the street!

SIMON [*impatiently*]   But what's the use of pretending we have anything in common anymore, when we haven't. Just because she happened to bear me into the world! This absurd sentimental sense of obligation between parents and children! Obligation for what? Almost any fool of a woman can have a son, and every fool of a man has had a mother! It's no great achievement on either side, and all the hypocritical values we set on the relationship are stupidity.

SARA [*angrily*]   That's not true! I've my four sons and I know the love I feel for them, and the love they feel for me!

SIMON [*ignoring this*]   And don't tell me Mother minds my indifference. She has learned not to need me.

SARA [*with a trace of vindictive satisfaction*]   That's true enough. She doesn't miss you now she has the children.

SIMON [*bitterly*]   Yes. As you have.

SARA [*stares at him defiantly*]   As I have, yes. [*then with a strange eagerness—teasingly*] Don't tell me you're jealous of the children—with me?

SIMON [*curtly resentful*] I have had too many important matters on my mind to bother about your children. That's your business.

SARA [*bitterly*] No. I know you never give them a thought— [*then forcing a smile—placatingly*] But I hope you didn't ask me here—for the first time in Heaven knows how long—just to quarrel with me. [*She gets up and comes around the table to him.*] I know I didn't come for that. [*She puts a hand on his shoulder.*]

SIMON [*moved*] Forgive me. I'm tired. Worn out and nervy. This railroad deal has been a strain.

SARA [*looks down at him worriedly*] I know, Simon. You haven't looked well for a long time—not like yourself at all.

SIMON [*bitterly*] Then you do notice once in a while.

SARA [*ignoring his tone—smilingly*] Did you think you're the only one can notice anything? Your mother has seen it, too. She pays some attention to you even if you don't to her.

SIMON [*coldly*] Indeed? And what was it you both noticed?

SARA [*pauses—then slowly*] That you've been changing in some queer way inside you. Sometimes at night when you sit in the parlor with us, all of a sudden, it's like a stranger staring at us. It's a frightening feeling, Simon. I think I began to notice it around the time you started sleeping in your own room away from me—

SIMON [*stares at her calculatingly—then with a deliberately provocative coarse sensuality*] Ah, that's it, eh? Your body felt swindled and it made you suspicious, I suppose, that I might have found another woman's body that is more beautiful and desirable to mine than yours? You probably think I must be secretly keeping some beautiful mistress who has stolen your place in bed! [*He smiles tauntingly.*]

SARA [*startled and repelled*] Simon! You know such a nasty thought would never enter my head! It's the last thing I'd ever suspect! And I don't see how it could come to your mind— [*She gives him a look of suspicion, all the jealousy of her passionately possessive nature beginning to flare up.*] Unless you've had the thought yourself—

SIMON [*his face lighting up with satisfaction—provocatively*] No, no. I was only joking.

14

conflicts are but one and the same?

Sara: (looks down at him puzzled and worried - pats his shoulder comfortingly) I know you're tired, Simon.   You haven't looked well for a long time - not like yourself at all.

Simon: (bitterly) And Then you do notice once in a while.

Sara: (ignoring his tone - smilingly) Did you think you're the only one can notice anything? You said you've been watching us. Well, we've been watching you, too.

Simon: We and Mother and Company!

Sara: (defensively) Yes, Your Mother has noticed, too.   She pays some attention to you even if you don't to her.

Simon: (strangely, ignoring this) Parent company through which she attempts to control - (Abruptly) Don't mind my silly jargon, Sara. Go on.   What was it Mother noticed about me?

Sara: (quickly)   I noticed it, too, although she was the first to mention - (She pauses - then slowly) It's hard to tell you.   It seems queer and foolish when you say it.   I know you'll laugh at it. But watching you lately at night when you've sat in the parlour with us for some time now - I think I began to around the time you started sleeping in your own room away from me -

Simon: (with a strange coarse mockery) Why? Did that make you suspicious? Think I might be secretly keeping a mistress in business hours, did you?

Sara: (startled and repelled, takes her hand from his shoulder - resentfully) Simon! Don't say that! You know such a dirty thought would never enter my head!   It's the last thing I'd ever suspect!   And I don't see how it could come to your mind - (She gives him a look of frightened suspicion) Unless you've had the thought yourself -

Simon: (his face lighting up with a pleased satisfaction - provocatively casual) No, no.   I was joking.

Sara: (more uneasy, and jealously angry - with a lapsing into brogue)   It's a queer nasty thing to joke about!   I don't believe you! You must have had the wish - (With a sudden fierce passion she grabs his head and turns his face up to hers) Look at me!   I want the truth! If I thought you ever wanted another women - !

Simon: (looks up at her, putting his arm around her and hugging

Page 14 from typescript—Act Three, Scene One
*Yale Collection of American Literature, Beinecke Rare Book
and Manuscript Library, Yale University*

SARA [*jealously angry—forgetting all ladylike poise*] I don't believe
you! You must have had the wish— [*With a sudden fierce passion
she grabs his head and turns his face up to hers.*] Look at me! If I
thought you wanted another woman—!

SIMON [*puts his arm around her and hugs her to him, his face triumphantly gratified—teasingly*] Well, what would you do?

SARA I'll kill her, that's what I'd do! And you, too! [*then miserably
frightened*] Simon! You don't deny it! Tell me—!

SIMON [*provocatively unconvincing, hugging her again*] No, no. Of
course I would never—

SARA You don't say that as if you meant it! [*struggling to free herself*] Let me go! I don't want you hugging me—when maybe you're
wishing it was another— [*Furious at the thought, she grabs his
shoulders and shakes him fiercely.*] Tell me the truth, I'm saying! Is
that the real reason you began sleeping alone—that you'd found
someone prettier, and grown tired of me? Is it to confess that you
had me come here? Are you going to ask me to set you free to be
hers? [*savagely*] If you are, you can hold your prate! I'll see her in
hell first! If any woman thinks she can take you, she'll find I'll fight
to the death! I'd tear her to pieces, first! And you! And myself! I'd
do anything! [*She sits down on the arm of his chair and hugs him
to her with passionate possessiveness.*] You're mine till death, and
beyond death, and I'll never let you go, do you hear! [*She kisses
him passionately on the lips.*]

SIMON [*his face happy now with confident possession and aroused desire*] So you really are jealous?

SARA [*fiercely*] Of course I'm jealous! Am I flesh and blood? Don't I
love you more than all the world?

SIMON Do you? I thought the children—

SARA [*almost contemptuously*] Ah, the children! [*hastily*] Not that I
don't love them with all my heart. But they're not my lover and
husband! You come first!

SIMON Do I? I shouldn't say from your actions for a long time—

SARA My actions! Are you trying to say I'm to blame? Why, there's
nights when you stare as if you were wondering who I was and
what was my business there. You sit with us deep in your thoughts,

as if I was dead. Or you converse with us so pleasant and polite, like a gentleman guest come in to spend the evening.

SIMON   Perhaps I do feel like a dispossessed intruder. You know I never approved of our living with Mother.

SARA [*impatiently*]   Ah, don't blame her. She's as sweet as can be to us. [*then going on*] And behind all your pleasant talk to us, you mean something else, and when you're thinking it isn't about business deals alone you're scheming . . . [*confusedly*] I don't know how to say it, Darling, but it's as though the minute you came home I felt everything begin to change until nothing is what it seems to be, and we all get suspicious of each other.

SIMON [*stares at her fixedly*]   What? Even you and Mother?

SARA [*reluctantly*]   Yes. [*hastily*] No, I meant it might if we weren't careful. It's like a spell that tries to come between us. [*defiantly*] But we don't let it.

SIMON [*ignoring this last*]   Ah. That is strange. I thought you had both entirely forgotten your old jealous animosity, that you lived in a perfect harmonious unity of interests and desires now. Why, sometimes as I watch you I become so intensely conscious of your unity that you appear as one woman to me. I cannot distinguish my wife from— It is a bewildering confusion in which I myself seem to lose my separateness, to dissolve, to have no life except within— [*with strange bitter intensity*] Suffocating! Devouring! I have to fight with all my will! [*catching himself and hastily forcing a casual tone*] But that's absurd nonsense, of course—a fanciful flight of imagination. My mind has been under such a strain lately, it's gotten out of control.

SARA [*strangely*]   Is that when you stare at us as though you hated us? [*then forcing a smile*] That's a queer crazy notion for you to have, Simon—that you can't tell your own wife from—her. [*with strange resentment*] But I think I know the kind of feeling that you mean. I've felt myself at times that she'd like me to have no wish but her wish, and no life that wasn't ruled by her life.

SIMON [*watching her*]   Yes, Mother has always been extremely greedy for others' lives. You have to be constantly on guard—

SARA [*defiantly*]   But she knows I'm too strong— [*abruptly shame-*

faced] Ah, what am I saying! It's mean and wrong of me to suspect her. It's only that she's been so lonely all her life, poor woman. I won't hear a word against her! [*accusingly with rising jealous anger*] And don't think I don't see you've changed the subject to her so you wouldn't have to answer me about having a mistress. [*She suddenly breaks—miserably*] Tell me you haven't, Simon! I couldn't bear— [*She starts to sob.*]

SIMON [*springs up and hugs her to him—passionately*] Of course I haven't, Sweetheart! What a mad idea! Here! Look at me! [*He lifts her face to his.*] I swear on my honor—!

SARA [*relieved—joyously*] Oh, Darling. I know I'm foolish—but I love you so! [*She kisses him and he responds, hugging her with a passionate desire. She breaks away, stirred and happy, but modestly embarrassed—with a soft laugh*] We mustn't. Supposing someone came in. It's a long time since you've kissed me—like that—Darling.

SIMON A long time since you've given me the chance!

SARA [*teasing tenderly*] I like that! When I've been hoping every night! You'll say next it was I that wanted you to sleep alone. [*sadly*] You don't know how you hurt me when you did that, Simon. I tried to believe your excuse that you didn't want to keep me awake when you couldn't sleep because your mind kept making plans for the Company. But I couldn't help fearing the real reason was you didn't want me.

SIMON [*passionately*] You know I want you now, don't you?

SARA [*desirously but embarrassed*] Oh, here—now—yes— But at home—

SIMON Yes, at home everything changes, as you said.

SARA You're different there. Here, you're my old Simon. It's like old times.

SIMON That's why I asked you to come. Because I want to be your old Simon and want you again. Because I want you to want me as you used to. But at home there is always Mother coming between us.

SARA [*frowns*] Yes, it's true you feel her always there, watching— [*Simon gives her a sharp calculating glance. She adds hastily, defensive and guilty*] But you mustn't blame her. She doesn't mean to interfere. She can't help being there. And I'm sure she doesn't bother her head about what we do. You only imagine that, Darling, because you think of her as the kind of woman she used to be. The trouble is you've paid so little attention to her for years you haven't noticed the change in her. You don't know the nice, kind contented old grandmother she is now.

SIMON [*sneeringly*]   Mother was always an accomplished actress. [*then quickly and calculatingly, pretending to give in*] Well, perhaps you're right. I must admit she seems sincere in her affection for your children.

SARA [*eagerly*]   Oh, she is, Simon! She loves them dearly and they love her.

SIMON   From their talk, they must spend a great deal of their time in her garden.

SARA [*Resentment shows in her face.*]   Yes, they do. But now they'll be away at school a lot of the day. [*then defensively*] It's good for them to be with her. She's a great lady and her influence helps train them to grow up gentlemen.

SIMON   Well, of course, if you don't mind—

SARA [*defensively*]   Why should I mind?

SIMON   I'd say there can be such a thing as too much of her influence for their good. You see, I remember my experience with her maternal possessiveness. If I hadn't got away from her, before it was too late, she'd have made me entirely dependent upon her for life— a tenth-rate poet—a day-dreaming romantic fool, wasting my days lazily lolling in her garden, without the ambition or courage to be free, contentedly enslaved to her fantastic whims!— [*He checks himself—hurriedly*] So you can understand why I am worried about her influence over our children. After all, they are my sons, too, Dear, and although you don't give me credit for it, I do have their futures constantly in mind.

SARA [*gratefully*]   I'm so happy to know you think of them. It hurt me to feel you didn't—because they're you and me together—our love—you in me— [*She hugs him to her and kisses him—then pushes back from him bashfully.*] I ought to be ashamed. I don't know what makes me so brazen. [*hastily*] About her and the children. I'd never mention it if you hadn't, that I don't think it's good her reading poetry at them all the time, especially Byron. I hate him because I remember my father, reciting it to himself before the mirror and putting on the airs of a lord, or a Napoleon, and him sponging on my mother for life, without a dollar to his name!

SIMON [*frowning*] Yes, Mother is very romantic. She used to read Byron to me. [*He recites sneeringly.*] "This makes the madmen who have made men mad by their contagion—all unquiet things which stir too strongly the soul's secret springs, and are themselves the fools to those they fool."

SARA [*tenderly proud*] Ah, it's different when you recite it! I love it! [*She hugs him.*] You're a big boy still with the old touch of the poet in you, and I love you for it!

SIMON [*frowns—curtly*] Nonsense. That is dead in me. [*boastfully*] You forget I am the president of a railroad, too, now—or soon will be. [*He smiles at her.*] The railroad I promised you.

SARA [*happily*] That does sound like my old Simon. I'd like to feel again that what is yours is mine, too.

SIMON [*hugging her*] Then you can begin thinking of yourself as my partner again from this moment on. [*with strange boyish enthusiasm*] I have our new partnership all planned, Sara. Wait till you hear. [*then quickly and calculatingly*] But first, let's get this matter of Mother and the children settled. I agree that it's bad to have her muddling their brains with romantic dreams. We want them trained to live with reality so when the time comes they will be capable of serving our Company as we decided long ago they could best serve it—Ethan as manager of our marine division, Wolfe to direct the banking branch which we will own before long, Jonathan as our railroad executive, and Honey our representative in politics.[2]

SARA [smiling happily] Ah, you have great dreams for them, haven't you? And I thought you'd forgotten— Forgive me, Darling.

SIMON [*smiling*] No, I have never forgotten our plans for their lives.

---

2. In an interview O'Neill told Elizabeth Shepley Sergeant (see Introduction, n. 1) that Honey's character was modeled upon Kennedy ancestor John Francis Fitzgerald, mayor of Boston from 1906 to 1907, father to Rose Kennedy, and grandfather to John F. Kennedy. Fitzgerald's nickname was "Honey Fitz." His political and social behavior matches Honey's lifestyle in the cycle plays that followed *MSM*.

And I am confident they will have the brains and ability, provided we don't permit Mother to poison their minds with nonsense.

SARA [*resentfully now*] She's always telling them stuff about how they must do what they want, and be free.

SIMON [*sneeringly*] Good God, does she still harp on that stupid dream? As if man born of woman could hope to be free. The freer he is of outside things, the more abject slave he becomes to himself! [*sharply*] It's our duty to the children to put a stop to her interfering before it's too late, Sara.

SARA   Yes. [*hesitantly*] I could ask her not to— [*then guiltily*] No, I'd be ashamed. It would be like breaking my part of a bargain I'd made in honor to trust her.

SIMON [*dryly*] It was no part of the bargain, was it, that she should steal your children and make them her children?

SARA [*defensively*] Ah now, that's going too far. She's never tried— [*resentfully*] Anyway, they know who their mother is and who they love best.

SIMON [*dryly provocative*] Do they? I have the idea they are becoming as confused between you as I. [*quickly*] I mean as I am at home. Here, you yourself, my wife, my partner—my mistress, too, I hope. [*He hugs her desirously.*]

SARA [*responding passionately*] Yes, let me be that above all, Darling! Don't ever dream of having another!

SIMON [*abruptly with a strange, brisk business-like tone*] We've allowed things to get in a confused muddle at home. I've been too preoccupied with the Company's affairs, and you've been too busy housekeeping for Mother and acting as nurse girl while she's left free to play she's their mother to them.

SARA [*with a flash of resentful anger*] Ah, I'd like to see her try—! I'm glad you had me come here today. I feel different here with you. I begin to see a lot of things I've been blind to. I begin to remember times when I've made myself not suspect her! Maybe I have been too trusting taking her at her word as I would my own mother that's gone. Maybe I've given in to her too much, and let her put her thoughts in my mind until I mistook them for my thoughts, and was obeying her without knowing it, and letting her make a slave of me. [*stung at the thought—threateningly*] But she'll not make a fool of me anymore!

SIMON It's very true that Mother works in peculiar ways to steal what she desires. You must bear in mind that she has never been quite normal. She's always been different from all other women, whimsical and perversely fanciful, not to be judged by normal standards. My father always considered her entirely irresponsible. Even her best friends have put her down as more than a little queer ever since she was a girl. Yes, we might as well be frank, Sara. There is an unbalanced imaginative streak in her that one must continually guard against.

SARA [*uneasily*] You mean she's insane? [*reacting against this*] Ah no, that's crazy, Simon. I won't let you say such wicked things. The poor woman!

SIMON [*sharply*] I didn't say insane. Of course, she's not insane. I meant she has no sense of the right to freedom of others. [*then with a smile*] I don't see why you should be so indignant. I know in the old days you suspected her of being a little crazy.

SARA [*guiltily defensive*] Maybe I did—the way she was. And didn't she tell me herself she'd got to the point where she didn't dare go in that summerhouse of hers for fear she'd never come out again. That's crazy, isn't it?

SIMON [*strangely*] Who knows? It all depends— Do you know if she ever goes in the summerhouse now?

SARA No. She always keeps it locked. The children used to plague her to open it but she never would. [*uneasily*] Why do you ask?

SIMON [*evasively*] Well, it shows she's not as changed within herself as she pretends, doesn't it? [*again in a brisk, business-like tone*] Then you agree. The children must be forbidden to go to her garden or her rooms in future. She can see quite enough of them, when you and I are present. And you stay away from her garden, too.

SARA I hardly ever go. I've always had a feeling she didn't want me there.

SIMON [*briskly*] Then you'll give orders to the children.

SARA Yes. [*then guiltily*] But who will tell her?

SIMON Why you, of course.

SARA   It'll break her heart. She's been so good— I promised her— When I think of how sweet she's been to me— I hate hurting her.

SIMON   [*avoiding her eyes—calculatingly, with feigned reluctance*] Well, I suppose I could tell her, if you want to be spared.

SARA   [*relieved—eagerly*] Would you? But promise me you won't be cruel to her, Simon. If you'll put yourself out to be kind, and make up with her, she won't feel so lonely at losing the children.

SIMON   [*concealing his satisfaction—matter-of-factly*] Don't be foolish, Dear. You can rely on me to treat Mother considerately, if only for selfish reasons. I want peace in my home. I know her erratic unstable mind, and that a sudden shock to her vanity might have dangerous consequences. So I shall call on my memories of the past and humor her as I would a fanciful child. I'll drop in at her garden on my way home this evening. [*with a strange happy satisfied air*] There. That puts Mother in her place—back where she belongs. Let's forget her now and think only of us. [*He gives her a loving, possessive hug.*] As we did in the old days.

SARA   [*happily*] I'm only too glad to, Darling. Tell me the plans you've made for our new partnership.

SIMON   Just what I want to do. I have grown very lonely, Sara. Achievement no longer means what it once did because I have no one to share it. In the old days what made it significant was that it was for you. I knew it was what you desired from me and it was my delight to give you your desire, and prove I had not failed you and that your love could justly be proud of me.

SARA   [*protesting a bit guiltily*] And do you think I'm not still proud? But I am, Darling.

SIMON   Here, now, alone with me again, you mean? Yes, I can believe that. And I want to propose to you that we should start our old life together again.

SARA   I want that as much as you, Darling. If you knew how unhappy and ugly I've felt since you started sleeping alone—and even before that when you'd lie beside me as if I wasn't there.

SIMON   I never felt we were alone—there, in Mother's house. That's why I had you come here. I want to ask you to help me create a new life of opportunity and ambition and boundless desire for our love, distinct and separate from our life as husband and wife at home—a life completely free from the influence of Mother and the children, in which we can be lovers again. [*He presses her to him passionately.*]

SARA [*sensually aroused—kissing his hair*] Darling! You know I'd love nothing better! I'll do whatever you want.

SIMON Good! I knew Mother couldn't have entirely destroyed in you my old Sara who desired so passionately to take what she wanted from life, no matter what the cost.

SARA [*resentfully*] Destroyed me? She knows better than to try! And don't talk as though I'd ever stopped wanting you. It's you who got so all you wanted was the Company. You even took it to bed with you in your thoughts. It wouldn't let you sleep.

SIMON [*ignoring this, goes on with a smile at her of a strange, perverse, insinuating lechery*] I want the old Sara, whose beautiful body was so greedily hungry for lust and possession, whose will was as devoid of scruple, as ruthlessly determined to devour and live as the spirit of life itself! [*He hugs her.*] The Sara who came to my cabin on that night long ago, before we were married, with her mind made up to use her beautiful body to keep anyone from taking what she regarded as hers, to make sure of a husband—

SARA [*guiltily*] Ah, don't say— [*reproachfully*] You'd never have known I had that in mind if my honor and my love hadn't confessed it to you! And you were proud I wanted you that much! You loved me for it! So you shouldn't remember it against me.

SIMON [*passionately*] Against you? How can you think that? I tell you I desired her more than anything in life! And now I desire her to come back more than anything in life! She was the inspiration for my career. I owe her all my success. She is the cause of the Company, the spirit of its ambition! Now I need her again to inspire me and it! I want her to come back to me here, as she came to me that night, willing to gamble with the highest possible stake, all she has, to win by any possible means, to sell her dearly.

SARA [*half pleased and flattered and half guiltily defensive*] Ah, don't talk of it that way—as if I was some low street girl who came that night to sell herself. I was bound I'd have you because I loved you so much. [*flusteredly*] But I don't want you to remember it. I never think of it but I'm ashamed I could have been so bold and brazen. [*then proudly*] But, all the same, I'm always proud of it, too.

SIMON [*amorously playful*] Well then, I know you will be willing to become your old true self again for me. It is she I need and want to possess me now, and be as bold and brazen about it as of old—and as beautiful and as desirable! I must confess, Sweetheart, that I have become as bored with the meek, contented, passionless, ambitionless, commonplace, woman, the virtuous good wife and mother that Mother's influence has made you at home, as you must be yourself in your secret heart.

SARA [*impulsively*] Yes. That's true when—

SIMON Ha! I knew it! [*He hugs her.*] But [for] the old passionate greedy Sara, I would give all I possess again.

SARA [*teasingly—but with a strange undercurrent of boastfulness*] Well, look out then. I could be her, for I love you just as much now. But, maybe, you'd better let her sleep. She might be bolder than ever and want more! [*She kisses him—then suddenly embarrassed and shy, pushes back from him.*] But what a way for me to act! Here in your office, of all places! [*then strangely*] But it's strange, I feel in a way it's being here with you makes me feel—there's a queer thing in the air here that makes you—and I'd stayed at home so long I'd forgotten— [*confusedly*] But I don't know what I mean— [*She hugs him passionately again.*] Except I love you now with all of me and all my strength, and there's no one else in the world, and I'm yours and you're mine, and I don't care how shameless I am! [*She kisses him.*]

SIMON Sweetheart! That fits in exactly with my plans for our future here. I hoped you would feel as you do. You ought, because the Company is you. Your nature is its nature. It derived its life from your life. You are its mother. It was born of your—just as my life in it was born of you, and is your life which you must claim for your own again.

SARA [*moved but at the same time puzzled*] Darling! But you're taking it too deep for me and getting me confused. Tell me plainly what your plan is.

SIMON [*with a brisk, business-like air now*] This: The children will be away most of the day at school from now on. You'll be free. Well, I want you to work with me here in the Company as my secretary and secret partner.

SARA [*amazed and joyous—her face lighting up eagerly*] Darling! Do you really mean—?

SIMON Then you'll do it?

SARA [*excitedly*] Will I? It's too good to be true! It's what I always used to want, don't you know that? Even in the old days, before we lived with your mother, I felt shut out from this part of your life, with you away from me in it all day. [*She kisses him.*] Oh, you make me so happy, Darling, when you prove you want me that much!

SIMON [*teasing with a suggestive lecherous air*] Wait! There's a condition. Nothing for nothing, is the rule here, you know. You'll have to pay for this opportunity.

SARA [*smiling*] Stop teasing now and tell me. I'll do anything you want.

SIMON [*teasing as before*] What! Do you mean to tell me a virtuous wife and mother like you will agree to become my mistress?

SARA [*shocked, embarrassed, and at the same time amused and curiously fascinated and delighted*] So— Then I'm the mistress you were wishing for! Well, God be thanked, you weren't dreaming of any other!

SIMON [*teasing as before*] No, you are the one. I don't know of anyone else who would be more desirable. And I can make you a most favorable offer.

SARA [*protestingly, but curiously pleased*] To hear you you'd think I was a wicked fancy woman you were offering to buy. That's a nice way to talk to a decent wife! [*teasingly*] But let's hear your offer. Maybe it's not enough. I value myself highly, I'll have you know!

SIMON [*teasingly as before*] I'll agree to pay with all my worldly goods. You can get the whole Company from me for your own— that is, of course, piece by piece, as you earn it! I put no limit whatever on the wages you may demand for your love.

SARA [*greedily*] The whole Company to be mine! [*forcing a joking tone*] Well, I'm flattered you set so high a price on me. It proves I still must be beautiful to you, for you to want me that much. [*She kisses him suddenly with passionate gratitude.*] Oh, Darling, and I was so afraid I'd become ugly to you and you were sick of me.

SIMON   Then you will take the place?

SARA   You know I will. [*She hides her face on his shoulder shame-facedly—then suddenly lifts it and bursts out*] But don't be talking of wages. Aren't I always yours just for the taking for love of you!

SIMON [*smiling playfully*]   No, no! Forget that! I have no rights whatever except what you choose to sell me. This is a new secret life for us, remember, which concerns the Company's life, since it will be lived here in it. So it must be strictly a business partnership, a deal for profit on both our parts. A double life of amorous intrigue for each of us, too, if it pleases our fancy to think of it that way. You will be revenging yourself on your husband who has grown bored with his virtuous wife, by selling yourself to a lover. And I think the husband will be keeping a beautiful mistress to take my wife's place. [*He laughs with an undercurrent of taunting.*] Come, confess now, doesn't this prospect of a sinful double life with me give something in you a proud feeling of new life and freedom.

SARA [*fascinatedly*]   Yes. [*then hugging him, with a little lustful, tender laugh*] Aren't you the big boy, still making up games! But I'll play any game with you you like, as being as you think I'm beautiful and you want me. [*She laughs again—this time with a touch of warm boldness.*] And it will be fun playing I'm a wicked, lustful, wanton creature and making you a slave to my pleasure and beauty. [*with a strange undercurrent of gloating contempt*] All the same, I think you're a fool to let me cheat you into buying what you own already! [*Suddenly shocked at herself she stops guiltily and stares at him bewilderedly.*] God forgive me, what makes me talk like— Darling, you know I don't mean— [*jokingly but resentfully and suspiciously, too*] I think it's your teasing. You're leading me on to talk before I think— [*confusedly*] No, I don't mean to say that, either.

SIMON [*teasingly*]   Well, we needn't go into the meaning of what you mean now, Beautiful Mistress. I am sure that will all become clear to you as you go on. It's enough now to know you've agreed and that's all settled. I am glad it was so simple. I was afraid you might raise objections.

SARA [*tenderly now*]   Objections? When you want me and I want you?

SIMON   Well, Mother won't approve of my taking you away, as well as the children.

SARA [*resentfully*]   It's none of her business.

SIMON [*with a strange gloating air*]   Poor Mother. She will be very lonely again. I think she will welcome visits even from me in her garden. [*quickly*] All I'm afraid of now, Sara, is that when you get home with her she will make you change your mind.

SARA [*resentfully*]   Make me? I'd like to see her. She knows better. She knows who's the stronger. But don't make me think of her now. [*She kisses him.*] All I want to think of now is that you want me again.

SIMON [*hugs her—passionately*]   I do! I have never wanted you so much! No, not even in the days before we were married! Your body is beautiful, Sweetheart!

SARA [*kisses him passionately*]   Darling! [*Then she breaks away—with a soft happy laugh*] Aren't we the shameless ones! [*then suddenly staring at him uneasily and sadly*] But I wish—even if you're still joking—you wouldn't talk as if my body was all I meant to you. Love is more than—

SIMON [*ignores this—slowly*]   Yes, you will have to learn to be shameless here. That is to say, to free yourself from false shame and be what you are. In your new life and work, in order to be successful, you will have to deal daily with the greedy fact of life as it really lives and devours itself, and forget all the sentimental lies and moral hypocrisies with which its ugliness is hidden. You will have to strip life naked, and face it. And accept it as truth. And strip yourself naked and accept yourself as you are in the greedy mind and flesh. Then you can go on—successfully—with a clear vision—without false scruples—on to demand and take what you want—as I have done! [*then in a more matter-of-fact tone*] But you will discover all this for yourself. You will be successful. You have the natural talent.

And I know you will find the game I play here in the Company as fascinating a gamble as I find it. [*strangely now—as if he were talking aloud to himself*] A fascinating game. Resembling love, I think a woman will find. A game of secret cunning stratagems, in which only the fools who are fated to lose reveal their true aims or motives—even to themselves. You have to become a gambler where face is a mask. But one grows lonely and haunted. One finally gets a sense of confusion in the meaning of the game, so that one's winnings have the semblance of losses. The adversary across the table in whose eyes one can read no betraying emotion beyond an identical lust—this familiar stranger to whom with a trustful smile one passes the cards one has marked, or the dice one has loaded, at the moment he accepts them trustfully becomes oneself.

SARA [*protests uneasily*]   Now, Darling, please don't be mixing everything up in my mind. I don't know what you mean by that queer talk of marked cards and loaded dice.

SIMON [*smilingly, but with a threat underneath*]   Oh, you will someday. I promise you you will. [*then as she stares at him uneasily—abruptly briskly business-like*] Well, I think we've settled everything. [*He glances at his watch.*] I'll have to ask you to go now. The railroad directors will be here in a few minutes. You will start your work here tomorrow morning.

SARA [*has gotten off the arm of his chair—jokingly bobs him a curtsy*]   Yes, Sir. At your service. But you haven't told me my secretary duties yet. Remember I've no experience. You'll have to train me.

SIMON [*curtly now*]   I will. By my example. You'll learn quicker that way. At first, all I wish you to do is sit and watch how I deal with everything. As though you were an understudy learning to play my part. As you learn, I will let you act in my stead now and then until finally you will find yourself capable of taking my place—if ever the need arises.

SARA [*excitedly*]   Me! Oh Simon, it sounds too grand!

SIMON   In your spare time, when I am away, I want you to draw plans for the country estate with the great mansion you used to dream about where we are going to retire when we have enough. [*She looks startled and embarrassed. He smiles strangely.*] What's the matter? Is it that the idea of my ever retiring hasn't occurred to you for a long time? I was just to go on and on—while you remained contentedly at home with Mother and your children?

SARA [*guiltily defensive*] I thought that was what you wanted. [*hurriedly and a bit confusedly*] But I never forgot my dream of the estate, never fear! How could I forget I was born on my father's great estate, in a castle, with a great park and stables and— [*hastily*] But I haven't felt I ought to want—I have your mother's house, as beautiful a mansion as there is in the city, and I was content. I mean, I felt I oughtn't to be greedy for more.

SIMON Well, from now on, remember you cannot want too much! No price is too high for me to pay my mistress for her love, eh? [*He pats her cheek playfully.*]

SARA [*repelled—pulling away*] Darling, I wish you wouldn't talk as if love—

SIMON [*ignoring this*] You shall have your estate. Of course, it wouldn't do to withdraw that much capital from the Company now. There is so much to be accomplished before the Company can be free and independent and self-sufficient. But as soon as we have enough. Meanwhile, if you get it actually planned to the last detail, then you will have everything all ready when the time comes.

SARA [*excitedly and greedily now*] Yes! Oh, that will be fun! And I've got every bit of it clear in my mind—or I used to have—

SIMON You can afford to make bigger, more ambitious plans now, in view of the Company's progress since you last dreamed of it.

SARA [*greedily*] Oh, I can always dream bigger dreams, and I'll be only too delighted to make plans— [*then checking herself, guiltily*] Well, I'd better go now, and not be in your way. [*She kisses him—tenderly.*] Goodbye, my Darling! You've made me so happy. You're the sweetest dearest husband— [*then with shy passion*] No, I'm forgetting. It's love again now, isn't it? And I'm your wicked, evil mistress! [*She laughs devilishly.*] And don't you forget I'm your mistress now, and start wanting some other woman! [*She kisses him again—then breaks from his arms and opens the door.*]

SIMON Wait! Mother will be curious about your visit here but don't tell her anything. Leave that to me. I can make the meaning clearer to her I think.

SARA [*pityingly but at same time scornfully*] Ah, poor woman. I'm not anxious to tell her— [*then with a sudden, maliciously gloating smile*] She'll be so suspicious, trying to lead me on to tell, and yet pretending to herself to be too high and mighty a lady to lower her pride to ask me! Well, it'll do her good! She's gotten to think she owns me! [*She stops abruptly, guilty and ashamed.*] Ah, I ought to be ashamed! What makes me feel like that here? [*She looks around the office almost frightenedly—then hastily*] I'll go now. [*She goes out and closes the door.*]

SIMON [*looks after her and smiles strangely—ironically*] Well, that half of my responsibility sharing scheme is launched successfully— Sara is not very clever at bargains—too trustful of promises—not a good judge of real values—or prices—but she will learn by experience—I will see to it she learns—in a year she will not know herself. [*He walks back to his desk.*] Yes, that part of it will work itself out according to plan. [*He suddenly frowns resentfully—impatient*] Plan?—what plan?—you'd think this was some intricate intrigue you were starting, whereas it is very simple—you want Sara—all right, you take her, and that's all there is to it—as for Mother, she has interfered and carried on an intrigue to isolate you—she must be taught to confine her activities to their proper sphere—to remain back where she belongs—very well, put her in her place this afternoon—and that will settle her half of it. [*He sits down at his desk— with a strange smile of anticipation*] But it won't be so easy to deceive her—she peers suspiciously behind face values—she knows the real price is always concealed—I shall have to force her mind back into the past where her ambitions belong—where I once belonged with her— [*He pauses. His expression becomes relaxed and dreamy. His voice sinks to a low nostalgic musing tone, hardly above a whisper.*] It will be pleasant to find myself in her garden again after all these years—it will be a relief to leave this damned slave pen and talk with someone whose mind is not crucified on this insane wheel—whose greed, at least, is of the spirit—I remember it used to be so restful in her garden—life existed only as a rumor of War beyond a high wall, a distant, drowsy din, a muffled squelching of feet in a trough—far-off, dim, unreal, divorced and separate, with no sense of a confusing union— [*He stops. A pause. There is a knock on the door at right. At once Simon becomes the formidable, ruthless head of the Company. He calls curtly.*] Come in. [*Joel enters.*]

JOEL   The directors are in the outer office. I thought I should pay them the courtesy of announcing them myself, considering their importance.

SIMON [*acidly*]   They have no importance. They had it when they had power. But I took it from them. So now they have none. They are ruined and worthless. They have nothing! And your courtesy is meaningless and a cruel joke which mocks at their plight. If I was one of them, I would knock you down. [*sharply*] Tell them to come in. [*Joel stares at him—then goes out.*]

* * * CURTAIN * * *

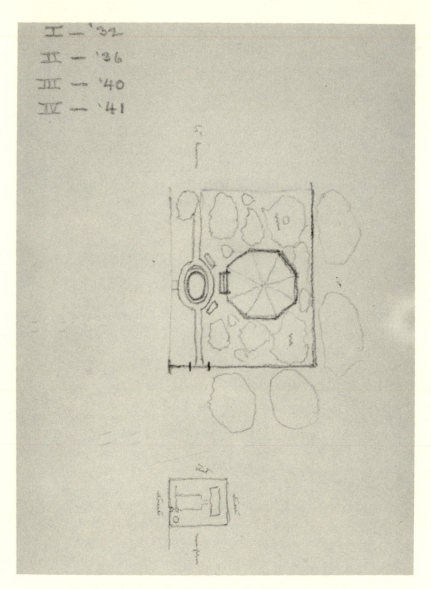

Garden, skyview showing pool—Act Three, Scene Two
*Yale Collection of American Literature, Beinecke Rare Book
and Manuscript Library, Yale University*

Act Three, Scene Two

SCENE *Same as Scene One of Act Two, the corner of the Harford garden with the octagonal Chinese summerhouse. Late afternoon sunlight from beyond the wall at right, falls on the pointed roof and the upper part of the arched lacquer-red door and ivy covered walls of the summerhouse. The shrubs, clipped as before in arbitrary geometrical designs, and the trees along the brick wall at rear glow in different shades of green. The wall at right casts a long shadow. The lawn is a bright green, setting off the deeper green of shrubbery and trees. The water in the small oval pool before the summerhouse is still another shade of green. The garden has the same appearance as before of everything being meticulously tended and trimmed. This effect is a morbid oppressive one of artificiality, and perverse childish fantasy, of nature distorted and humiliated by a deliberately mocking, petulant arrogance.*

Deborah is sitting on the steps leading up to the summerhouse door, dressed all in white. She appears greatly changed from the previous Act. Where she had seemed a prematurely-old, middle-aged woman then, she now has the look of a surprisingly youthful grandmother. Actually, she appears much younger now at fifty-three than she had then at forty-nine. Her body and face have filled out a little. There is something of repose and contentment in her expression, something of an inner security and harmony. But her beautiful dark eyes and her smile still retain their old imaginative, ironical aloofness and detachment.

Her four grandchildren, the sons of Simon and Sara, are grouped about the pool in front of her. Ethan, the eldest, in his twelfth year, is sitting on the stone bench at rear of pool on her right. Wolfe Tone, a year younger, is sprawled on his back on the narrow coping of the pool at front, his folded hands supporting his head, staring up at the sky.

Jonathan, a year and a half younger than Wolfe, and Owen Roe ("Honey"), the youngest, who is seven and a half, are sitting sideways, facing each other, on the stone bench on Deborah's left, playing a game of casino with the bench as table.

Ethan is tall and heavily built for his age, broad-shouldered and muscular. His face is strong, broad, good-looking in a rugged, rough-hewn mould. There is a resemblance to Deborah about his forehead and deep-set dark eyes. He has his mother's straight black hair, and obstinate, passionate mouth. But his nose and chin and swarthy complexion are his father's. His manner is groping and awkwardly self-conscious, but stubbornly, almost sullenly, determined.

Wolfe is an opposite type, of medium height for his age, slender and wiry. His face is handsome and aristocratic, pale, with light brown hair and hazel eyes. The resemblance to Sara's father, Cornelius Melody, is marked and there is also much that reveals Deborah in his face and expression. Added to this is a cold immobility about the cut of his features as a whole that immediately brings to mind his uncle, Joel Harford. He does not resemble his father or his mother. His manner is politely pleasant and compliant, but it is the distant amiability of indifference.

Jonathan is undersized with a big head too large for his body. He is also thin but one gets no impression of frailty or weakness from him but of an exhaustless energy. The general facial resemblance to his father is so striking one does not notice any other. His hair is brown, his complexion swarthy, his eyes grey-blue. His manner is quick, self-assured, observant and shrewd. "Honey" takes after his mother's side of the family. He is an obvious Irish type with a clear skin, rosy and white complexion, blue eyes and curly black hair. A chubby, roly-poly youngster. He is lazy, laughing and good tempered, full of health and animal spirits, his eyes bright with a sly humor, his smile infectious and charmingly ingratiating.

From all four boys one gets the impression of an underlying natural boyishness—a feeling that each is in one way or another too old for his years.

Deborah is reading aloud from Byron's "Childe Harold." Ethan listens with absorbed interest, his eyes fixed on her face. Wolfe stares at the sky, his expression emotionless. One cannot tell whether he is listening or not. Jonathan's and Honey's attention appears to be wholly concentrated on their game.

DEBORAH [*reads—and one feels that for the moment she has forgotten her audience and is reading aloud to herself*]

But Quiet to quick bosoms is a Hell,
And there hath been thy bane; there is a fire
And motion of the Soul which will not dwell
In its own narrow being, but aspire
Beyond the fitting medium of desire;
And, but once kindled, quenchless evermore,
Preys upon high adventure, nor can tire
Of aught but rest; a fever at the core,
Fatal to him who bears, to all who ever bore.

This makes the madmen who have made men mad
By their contagion; Conquerors and Kings,
Founders of Sects and Systems, to whom add
Sophists, Bards, Statesmen, all unquiet things
Which stir too strongly the soul's secret springs,
And are themselves the fools to those they fool;
Envied, yet how unenviable! What stings
Are theirs! One breast laid open were a school
Which would unteach Mankind the lust to shine or rule:
Their breath is agitation, and their life
A storm whereon they ride, to sink at last,
And yet so nursed and bigoted to strife,
That should their days surviving perils past,
Melt to calm twilight, they feel overcast

With sorrow and supineness, and so die;
Even as a flame unfed, which runs to waste
With its own flickering, or a sword laid by,
Which eats into itself, and rusts ingloriously.

[*She stops and stares before her.*]

ETHAN [*starts from his concentrated attention—with an affectionate, understanding smile*] You were reading that to yourself, too, weren't you, Grandmother?

DEBORAH [*starts—then smiles affectionately*] Perhaps, Ethan. There is a lesson in it—a warning for each of us—such as— [*with a strange note of self-mockery*] well, to be suitably grateful for a calm twilight, for example. But, of course, that is not the lesson youth should learn from it.

ETHAN [*scowling*] I hate lessons. I don't see any lesson in it.

WOLFE [*speaks up quietly without moving*] I do.

DEBORAH [*stares at him—strangely*] Yes. I'm afraid you may, Wolfe. But perhaps it's the wrong lesson. [*Wolfe stirs uneasily but continues staring at the sky.*]

ETHAN [*jealously*] Oh, him! He sees everything, to hear him tell it!

DEBORAH [*smiling*] I think he does see too much.

ETHAN He only pretends to, so he can pretend he's too good for anything, and doesn't want what he knows he can't get.

JONATHAN [*without looking up from the cards—grinning*] That's right, Ethan.

DEBORAH Another country heard from! I didn't know you were listening, Jonathan.

JONATHAN [*self-assuredly*] Oh, I can mind the game and keep track of what's going on at the same time. And win, too. [*He plays a card.*] There. Big casino. That beats you, Honey.

HONEY [*grins with ungrudging admiration*] You always beat me. But you can't beat Wolfe.

JONATHAN I would if he wasn't so darned lucky. I play better. It's just his luck.

WOLFE It is not. It's because I don't care whether I win or not. You only like winning. That's why you make mistakes.

DEBORAH [*smiling*] A profound observation, Wolfe. You will grow up to be a philosopher, I think.

WOLFE [*distrustfully*] What's a philosopher? [*then with a quick indifference*] I don't care what I grow up to be.

JONATHAN I'm going to own a railroad. Father wants me to.

HONEY I'm going to be a gentleman and 'lected President of America, like Mother wants me.

DEBORAH [*smiling*] I'm afraid you can't be both nowadays, Honey.

HONEY [*For a moment his grin vanishes and he gives her a scornful, defiant look.*] Mother says I can. [*smiling again, to Jonathan*] Come on. Let's play 'nother. This time I'll show you.

ETHAN [*jealously*] Aw, don't talk to those crazy kids, Grandmother. Read some poetry.

JONATHAN [*dealing—jeeringly*] We know what Ethan's going to do— to hear him talk big! He won't do what Father and Mother want! Oh, no!

HONEY [*joins in jeeringly*] He won't go to Harvard! He won't be a gentleman!

ETHAN [*with sullen doggedness*] Well, I won't. Wait and see.

JONATHAN He's going to run away to sea and be a sailor!

ETHAN I will, too.

WOLFE [*indifferently*] Well, why don't you, then? Who cares what you do?

ETHAN [*turns to glance at him*] Shut up, you! Mother and Father care. And Grandmother.

DEBORAH [*gently*] Indeed I do care, Ethan.

WOLFE [*goes on indifferently*] Why anyone with sense would want to be a sailor working like a nigger slave—

JONATHAN They don't get hardly any pay either. Ethan 'll never get rich.

WOLFE [*ignoring this*] On a dirty, smelly ship—

ETHAN [*stung—angrily*] That's a lie! Ships aren't dirty. They're the prettiest things in the world! And I love the sea! [*more angrily, stares at his feet threateningly*] You take that back or I'll—

DEBORAH   Now, now. Giving Wolfe a bloody nose wouldn't convince him that ships and the sea are beautiful, would it?

WOLFE   [*calmly*]   He won't hit me. He knows he can lick me, and Ethan's not a coward.

ETHAN   [*abashed*]   No. 'Course I won't. Only don't you say—

WOLFE   [*indifferently*]   All right. Ships are beautiful then. Who cares?

ETHAN   [*glances at him again—then sits down, abruptly changing the subject*]   Please read some more, Grandmother—that part about the ocean. That shows how Lord Byron loved the sea.

WOLFE   Who cares about him? Except I'd like to have been born a lord.

DEBORAH   [*smiling—assuredly*]   Yes, that would entitle you to any amount of disdainful indifference, wouldn't it? [*then to Ethan*] You must know that part by heart, Ethan.

ETHAN   I do. But it's better when you read it, Mother— [*hastily—embarrassed*] 'Scuse me, I mean, Grandmother.

DEBORAH   [*gives him a tender look*]   You needn't apologize. I like you to call me Mother.

WOLFE   [*turns his head to stare at her—enviously*]   You like it when I get mixed up, too. Why do you?

DEBORAH   [*starts, forcing a smile*]   Why, I suppose because I'm so fond of your mother I'd like to be her. And, of course, because I love you, too. [*He stares, then turns abruptly to gaze up at the sky again. Deborah begins to read.*]

> There is a pleasure in the pathless woods,
> There is a rapture on the lonely shore,
> There is society, where none intrudes,
> By the deep Sea, and music in its roar:
> I love not Man the less, but Nature more,
> From these our interviews, in which I steal
> From all I may be, or have been before,
> To mingle with the Universe, and feel
> What I can ne'er express—yet cannot all conceal.
>
> Roll on, thou deep and dark blue Ocean—roll!
> Ten thousand fleets sweep over thee in vain;

Man marks the earth with ruin—his control
Stops with the shore;—upon the watery plain
The wrecks are all thy deed, nor doth remain
A shadow of man's ravage, save his own,
When, for a moment, like a drop of rain,
He sinks into thy depths with bubbling groan—
Without a grave—unknelled, uncoffined, and unknown.

JONATHAN [*suddenly speaks without looking up from his game*] Sinks
with bubbling groan—no better than a drop of rain—unknown.
That'll be you if you don't watch out, Ethan. [*He adds with a curt,
contemptuous, practical finality that recalls his father*] And that's
foolishness.

HONEY [*echoing him*] Yes, Ethan's a fool.

ETHAN [*who had been listening with dreamy intensity—recoiling*]
Shut up, you! [*to Deborah—eagerly*] Now skip to the one that begins: "And I have loved thee, Ocean."

WOLFE [*interrupts impatiently*] No! That's enough for Ethan, Grandmother. He's had his share. Read my part—the one you say you used
to like so much, and don't anymore. [*As she hesitates, strangely re-
luctant, he turns his head to stare at her—insistently*] Go on. Why
don't you ever want to read that?

DEBORAH [*starts—evasively*] Why, no particular reason, except that I
no longer believe it. And it hardly strikes the right note of inspiration for a future banker. But if you insist— [*She recites without
looking at the book, a note of personal arrogance growing more
marked in her voice as she goes on, staring straight before her.*]

I have not loved the World, nor the World me;
I have not flattered its rank breath, nor bowed
To its idolatries a patient knee,
Nor coined my cheek to smiles,—nor cried aloud
In worship of an echo: in the crowd
They could not deem me one of such—I stood
Among them, but not of them—in a shroud

Of thoughts which were not their thoughts, and still could,
Had I not filed my mind, which thus itself subdued.

I have not loved the World, nor the World me,—
But let us part fair foes; I do believe,
Though I have found them not, that there may be
Words which are things,—hopes which will not deceive,
And Virtues which are merciful, nor weave
Snares for the failing: I would also deem
O'er others' griefs that some sincerely grieve—
That two, or one, are almost what they seem,—
That Goodness is no name—and Happiness no dream.[1]

WOLFE [*staring at her—strangely*]   And you don't agree with that any-more?

DEBORAH [*starts—forcing a smile, carelessly*]   No, it is much too bitter and disdainful a dream for a contented grandmother.

WOLFE [*stares at her curiously*]   You spoke it then as if you still meant it.

DEBORAH [*forcing a joking manner*]   Oh, I'm an accomplished actress, as your father could tell you. [*He stares at her—then turns his head to look up at the sky again. Honey gives a sly, laughing chuckle over something in the card game.*]

WOLFE [*without looking*]   Watch out, Jonathan. Honey's cheating. I can tell by his laugh.

JONATHAN [*half turns his head to reply—as he does so Honey transfers cards from his pocket to his hand. Jonathan says laughingly.*]   Don't I know! He can't help giving himself away. But he's always so tickled with himself he never sees that as soon as he starts cheating I cheat back to show I can win at that game, too. [*He turns back to the game—suddenly he grabs Honey's hand.*] Hey! That's too much! Look, Wolfe! Look! Ethan! See what he's up to now! He's been putting extra cards in his hand! [*He laughs—to Honey*] You ninny! Don't you think I'd notice you have too many cards? How'd you expect—?

---

1. Con Melody recites lines from this poem in the second and third acts of *TP*.

HONEY [*choking with merriment*]   But that makes it funnier if I did fool you! [*He laughs unrestrainedly, a merry entirely shameless and droll guffaw. Looking at him the others, Deborah included, cannot help joining in.*]

ETHAN [*disgusted with himself for laughing—scowls*]   It's all right to laugh but if Mother knew, wouldn't she take you over her knee! You know she's always telling us about honor.

HONEY [*still chuckling—confidently*]   She won't know.

DEBORAH   No, we promised we'd never tell on each other, didn't we?

HONEY   And I did it playing with her the other night, anyway, and she couldn't help laughing.

DEBORAH [*smiles at him*]   Well, Honey, all I can say is, if you hope to be President you'll have to learn to be more skillful. [*She laughs— then stops suddenly, listening to something beyond the wall at right.*] There's your father coming home.

WOLFE [*staring at her wonderingly*]   You can always tell his walk from anyone's, can't you?

DEBORAH [*smilingly—with a sneer beneath*]   That's easy now, Wolfe. He walks with the proud tread of a conquering Napoleon. [*Suddenly, listening, her expression changes to one of alarmed surprise and she stares at the door in the wall with dread—tensely*] He has stopped— [*For a moment there is a tense silence in which the boys, conscious of the change in her, regard her puzzledly. Then there is a sharp rap of the knocker on the door and Deborah quivers frightenedly.*]

JONATHAN [*starts for the door*]   I'll let him in—

DEBORAH [*in a panic*]   No! [*Then she stammers confusedly.*] I must be mistaken. It cannot—be your father. He has never dared—I mean, he would never come unless I invited him, and I would never—

WOLFE [*staring at her*]   What are you so frightened about, Grandmother?

DEBORAH [*fighting to control herself*]   I'm superstitious. I'm afraid—like your mother. I don't like strangers attempting to intrude— [*then with swift urgency*] Run to the house and get your mother, Ethan! Tell her she should come here at once! [*But, as he starts to obey, frowning and puzzled, there is a louder knock on the door and Si-*

mon's voice calls sharply: "It's I, Mother. Open the door!" *Again Deborah's expression changes completely. All fear vanishes from her face; she seems in a flash to become arrogantly self-confident. A little smile of gloating scorn comes to her lips and she murmurs softly.*] Well, it is not I who wish— [*with abrupt impatience*] Well, Jonathan? Don't you hear your father? Open the door. [*He stares at her puzzledly—then goes and opens the door. Simon comes in and Jonathan closes the door after him. Simon approaches his mother, giving a quick glance around, his face set in a coldly pleasant smile.*]

SIMON   Good evening, Mother.

DEBORAH [*coldly pleasant in her tone*]   This is an unexpected pleasure, Simon.

SIMON   Evidently. Such whispering I heard, cooling my heels before the sacred portals. I trust I have not intruded on any secret conspiracy.

DEBORAH [*startled—stares at him*]   Conspiracy? [*coldly pleasant again*] Naturally we were surprised. We could not believe our good fortune.

SIMON [*turning to his sons*]   You boys go to the house. I have to talk to your grandmother.

DEBORAH [*uneasily*]   I would like them to remain in the garden, if you don't mind.

SIMON [*coldly domineering*]   As it happens, I do mind, Mother. [*For a moment, angered, she stares at him defiantly. Then she shrugs her shoulders with assumed indifference and looks away. He turns to the boys who are standing hesitantly, glancing puzzledly from his face to hers—sharply*] You heard what I said. [*They start, reply obediently,* "Yes, Father," *and hurry off down the path at right. He turns back to Deborah—curtly*] I happen to know their mother is waiting for this chance to see them alone. [*She gives him a quick suspicious glance. He bows with dry formality.*] If I may sit down, Mother?

DEBORAH [*coldly*]   Of course. This is your property. Pray do so. [*She sits on the steps again.*]

SIMON   Sara's property. [*He sits on the stone bench on her left.*]

DEBORAH [*with a trace of mockery*]   But what is hers is yours. Or so I felt you thought.

SIMON [*pleasantly*]   Yes, that is quite true. [*He pauses, glancing around the garden. She glances quickly at him again, her expression set in indifference, but her eyes suspicious and curious. He remarks casually.*] Sara has probably told you of her visit to my office this morning.

DEBORAH   No.

SIMON [*wondering*]   She hasn't?

DEBORAH   No. I am not curious. She told me before she left you had asked her to come there.

SIMON [*feigning surprise*]   That I had asked her? [*She glances at him sharply. He goes on carelessly.*] Well, it is of no importance who asked whom, I suppose. You say she has not mentioned our interview in any way?

DEBORAH [*with forced indifference*]   No. I imagine it concerned property of yours—her name and papers you wished her to sign. She knows I would not be interested in that.

SIMON   Her purpose in coming had nothing to do with papers. Although, of course, it did concern property. [*He adds with a sneering smile.*] You know Sara.

DEBORAH [*as if caught off guard, starts to sneer herself*]   Yes, you may be sure I— [*She catches herself and looks at him defensively.*]

SIMON   As you'll see, Sara suspects—and with good reason, I think— that she is being secretly swindled of what is rightfully hers.

DEBORAH [*startled—with feigned indifference*]   I cannot believe Sara imagines that. What is the nature of the plot you claim she suspects, if I may ask? [*She sneers.*] Not that her husband is defrauding of his love, I trust?

SIMON [*smilingly*]   As a matter of fact, that was one of the matters she wished to discuss with me.

DEBORAH   Indeed? It is silly of her to wish to keep what she no longer needs.

SIMON [*ignoring this*]   Not that she holds me responsible for her loss. She very shrewdly suspects whose hidden influence is really to blame.

DEBORAH [*stares at him—then coldly scornful*]   I am not interested in all this mysterious insinuation. I do not believe Sara ever—

SIMON [*interrupts as if he hadn't heard*]   I was very glad she came. It gave me a chance to talk over with her a new arrangement at the office I have been contemplating for some time. I had to obtain her consent—which she was only too willing to give, as it turned out. I find it advisable, from many standpoints, to add a private confidential secretary to my employ.

DEBORAH [*scornfully*] And you had to have Sara's consent for that?

SIMON [*smilingly*] You will understand why when I tell you the one person who possesses the qualifications I desire is a very young and beautiful woman.

DEBORAH [*starts—her first instinctive reaction one of vindictive satisfaction and gloating pity*] Ah! Poor Sara! So this is what your great romantic love comes to in the end! I always knew— [*Abruptly and guiltily her reaction changes to one of overstressed moral indignation.*] How dare you mention such filth to your mother! Have you become so utterly coarse and debased, so lost to all sense of decency, that you feel no shame but actually boast you are deliberately planning to dishonor yourself and disgrace your family? [*then with disdain*] But I don't know why I should be surprised. After all, this is an inevitable step in the corruption of your character that I have had to watch for years, until I could hardly recognize my son in the unscrupulous greedy trader, whose soul was dead, whose one dream was material gain! Now, after this final degradation, I cannot recognize my son in you at all! He is dead and you are a repulsive stranger I will not allow myself to know!

SIMON [*has been watching her with a gloating satisfaction—mockingly*] Yet if I am not mistaken, Mother, you were not altogether displeased to see Sara's husband become so worthy, in your mind, of being her husband.

DEBORAH It's a lie! That you can have such a vile suspicion proves to what depths your mind—!

SIMON May I point out that you have been jumping too eagerly to conclusions, Mother. I have not said my secretary was to be anything more intimate than my secretary. [*Deborah looks guilty and discomfited. He adds with a mocking smile.*] I am afraid the good grandmother you have become has not entirely forgotten the French Eighteenth Century Memoirs in which she once lived, or such an improper suspicion could never enter her mind.

DEBORAH [*stares at him strickenly—pleadingly*] Simon! It is not kind to make me remember— [*with dread*] Oh, why did you come here? What—?

SIMON [*ignoring this*] And I don't see how you can think Sara would ever consent—unless you secretly believe her true nature is so greedy that she would sell anything if offered the right price.

DEBORAH [*stares at him fascinatedly—with a strange eagerness*] So that's it! You offered— [*with a strange taunting laugh*] Then you have been made a fool of. She has swindled you by selling rights to property she no longer needs or wants!

SIMON Ah! And you think it was you who brought that about?

DEBORAH [*distractedly*] No! No! How dare you think I could concern myself with your low greeds! [*violently*] And I will not think such ignoble things about Sara's motives! I will not have you put such thoughts in my mind about a woman to whom I owe an eternal debt of gratitude, who is the sweetest, kindest, most generous-hearted—

SIMON I am sorry to have to disillusion you, Mother, but I think you will discover before our interview is over that Sara has not been as blind as you hoped, nor as unsuspectingly trustful as you imagined. [*Deborah starts and stares at him uneasily. He goes on in a pleasant matter-of-fact tone like one disinterestedly stating facts.*] You made the mistake of underestimating your adversary. Your vanity made you overconfident in your superior subtlety of mind. It does not do to hold one's enemy in the battle for supremacy in too much contempt—

DEBORAH I will not have you talk as though Sara and I were engaged in some fantastic duel—as though our home were a battleground! It is insane of you. I bitterly resent your intruding here without my consent and attempting to create suspicion and jealousy between Sara and me. You cannot! We have reached too deep an understanding. We have built up too close a friendship through our mutual love for the children! Through love of them we have learned to love each other! I trust her and I know she trusts me! It would take more than your obviously malicious insinuations to shake my faith in her!

SIMON [*coldly domineering*] We will deal with the facts, if you please, Mother, not with sentimental posing.

DEBORAH [*staring at him with a fascinated dread—stammers*] Simon! Why are you saying such things? What are you trying to do? I feel behind this—I know this is some insane plot to revenge yourself on me!

SIMON [*with a cold smile*] Plots and intrigues! You must be still dreaming of eighteenth-century romance, Mother! Revenge on you? That is a mad idea, Mother, coming from you who have seemingly grown so sane. Revenge for what? As far as I remember, there was never a serious quarrel between us—merely a difference in philosophical outlook between you whose true nature is to hide from life in dreams and I whose inner compulsion is to deal solely in reality and the facts of things. I thought even that trifling quarrel of the past had vanished in indifference and been forgotten long ago.

DEBORAH I have forgotten it. But I know you—

SIMON [*as if she hadn't spoken*] I know I have forgotten it. [*Suddenly his tone changes to a bitter smouldering resentment.*] Revenge for what, I ask you? It was I who long ago, after I graduated from Harvard, decided of my own free will it was high time I began to live in my own life and not in your life! I then freed myself from your influence, which would have kept me always a tenth-rate versifier, scribbling imitations of Byron's romantic doggerel, wasting my mind humoring your fantastic whims and playing roles of childish make-believe here in your garden with you, lost in dreams, while love escaped and life passed down the street beyond the wall, forgetful we were hidden here. [*He pauses, staring around the garden. His tone has taken a strange quality of nostalgic yearning. He murmurs as if to himself.*] It is so restful here. I had forgotten how restful it was. [*Deborah stares at him. Her expression has lost its bitter resentment, has suddenly lighted up with a gloating, triumphant perception.*]

DEBORAH [*with a little smile—carelessly*] So you have never forgotten that old quarrel? As you say, it was childish of us. I remember now I used to be of the opinion it was I who made you leave, who forced you out into your own life. So that I might be free.

SIMON [*curtly*] Yes, you consoled your pride with that lie. But the truth was, if I had wished, I could have remained here with you forever. You are honest enough to confess that now, I hope?

DEBORAH [*still watching him—smilingly*] Yes, if you wish. I appreciate that a Napoleon of affairs must believe implicitly in his own star. [*She laughs softly—teasingly*] You are still such a strange greedy boy, do you know it, Dear?

SIMON [*again glancing around the garden—with again the tone of nostalgic yearning*] Yes, I had forgotten the quiet and the peace here. Nothing has changed. The past is the present.[2] [*Suddenly he turns on her—harshly accusing*] You are the only jarring discordant note. Because you are not the same. You are a stranger here. This garden of your old self disowns the doting old granny you have made yourself pretend to be.

DEBORAH [*watching him, her eyes gleam with a secret gloating—quietly*] I do not feel alien here. Perhaps it is you whom my garden disowns, in hurt pride, because you long ago disowned it.

SIMON [*with sullen boyish boastfulness*] Yes, I did. I'm glad you admit it. [*then justifying himself—placatingly*] Well, it could hardly expect me to stay buried alive forever.

DEBORAH [*quietly, her eyes gleaming*] No, I suppose not. [*She pauses, probing under a casual tone.*] I am sorry you do not believe in my sincerity as a good grandmother.

SIMON [*sneering resentfully*] Oh, you were always able to play a part so convincingly that you fooled even yourself!

DEBORAH [*with a soft teasing laugh*] Don't tell me you are jealous of your children, too!

SIMON [*curtly*] Too? I don't know what you mean. Jealous? Don't be absurd, Mother. Beyond observing your obvious campaign to obtain control of the children, and pitying Sara for what I mistakenly thought was her blind trustfulness, I have regarded the matter as none of my business.

DEBORAH [*starts to protest angrily—checks herself and changes the subject—quietly casual*] Speaking of business, how are the Company's affairs these days? I am sure you must be becoming richer and more powerful all the time.

---

2. There is an obvious similarity here between Simon's line and Mary Tyrone's line in *LDJ:* "The past is the present, isn't it? It's the future, too" (Yale edn., p. 87).

SIMON [*in a boastful tone*]   Yes, I am, Mother. I concluded a deal today which adds a railroad to the Company's properties.

DEBORAH [*flatteringly but with underlying sarcasm*]   How splendid!
My congratulations, Dear.

SIMON [*pleased*]   Thank you, Mother. [*then in his brisk, business-like
tone*] Oh, it's nothing in itself. But it has significance as another step
forward. It's an added link in the chain in which my ships bring
cotton to my mills to be made into my cloth and shipped on my
railroad. [*frowning impatiently*] But there is a lot to be done before
the chain is completed.

DEBORAH [*with a little mocking smile*]   Yes, I perceive it is not enough.

SIMON [*deadly serious*]   Far from it. The next step must be to acquire
my own bank. Then I can control and manipulate all the Company's
financing.

DEBORAH   I see. And you will want your own stores here in the city to
sell your goods.

SIMON   Yes. I have that in mind.

DEBORAH   And at the other end of your chain you should possess plantations in the South and own your own nigger slaves, imported in
your own slave ships.

SIMON [*staring before him, tense and concentrated, his expression hard
and ruthless—eagerly*]   Yes. Of course. I had not considered that
but it is obviously the logical final step at that end. [*She stares at
him and gives a little uneasy shrinking movement. He turns to her
with an affectionate teasing smile.*] You are wonderfully shrewd and
farsighted, Mother, for a beautiful lady who has always affected
superior disdain for greedy traders like my father and me.

DEBORAH [*impulsively—with a trace of seductive coquetry*]   You find
me still a little beautiful? I fear you are merely flattering a poor ugly
old woman.

SIMON [*ignores this*]   I am glad to find you changed in that one respect, Mother. You now have the courage to face some of the things
that have reality. You don't have to cower behind romantic ideal-
isms from every ugliness of truth. [*He stares at her strangely.*] The
ugliness of life you would learn, if you possessed it as long as I have
now, can become identical with beauty.

DEBORAH [*uneasily*]   I do not understand you.

SIMON [*strangely*]   Well, as I admitted to you, I do not understand all the implications of the duel of duality myself—not yet—but I will in the end, I promise you! [*She looks away from him, as frightened as if this were a threat. He speaks casually.*] Yes, I am glad you appreciate what I am achieving through the Company. I see now that behind your old pose of lofty spiritual contempt, you were proud of Father's ability in trade. I will make you prouder of me than you ever were of him, Mother.

DEBORAH [*her eyes gleaming again—softly*]   Ah. But I am already, Dear.

SIMON [*boastfully*]   He had scruples. I have none. He disguised his greed with Sabbath potions of God-fearing unction at the First Congregationalist Church. Else he had feared to swallow it. I fear no God but myself! I will conquer every obstacle. I will let nothing stand between me and my goal!

DEBORAH [*uneasily again*]   What goal, Simon?

SIMON [*turns to her in surprise*]   But I thought you saw that, Mother. My goal is to make the Company entirely self-sufficient. It must not be dependent upon anything outside itself for anything. It must need nothing but what it contains within itself. It must attain the all-embracing security of complete self-possession—the might which is the sole right not to be a slave! Do you see?

DEBORAH [*strangely moved*]   I see, Dear—that you have gone very far away from me—and become lost in yourself and very lonely.

SIMON [*vaguely*]   Lost? Oh no, don't imagine I have lost. I always win. My destiny is victory at any cost, by any means. [*abruptly boyishly boastful again*]   Wait and see, Mother! I'll prove to you I can lead the Company to glorious, final triumph—complete independence and freedom within itself! [*He pauses and looks around the garden, then he sighs wearily—strangely*]   But sometimes lately, Mother, alone in my office, I have felt so weary of the game—of watching suspiciously each card I led to myself from across the table—even though I had marked them all—watching my winnings pile up and becoming confused with losses—feeling my swindler's victorious gloating die into boredom and discontent—the flame of ambition smoulder into a chill dismay—as though that opponent within had spat an extinguishing poison of disdain—

DEBORAH [*strangely, tenderly sympathetic*]   Oh, I know! I know, Dear!

I used to know so well! [*tensely*] I tell you I had once reached a point where I had grown so lost, I had not even a dream left I could dream without screaming scornful laughter at myself. I would sit locked in the summerhouse here, so no one could come between and protect me from myself, in the dark, squatting on folded legs in mockery of mystic meditation—sit there for hours in wisdom-ridiculing contemplation of myself, and spit in my mind, and spit in my heart, like a village idiot in a country store spitting at the belly of a stove—cursing the day I was born, the day I indifferently conceived, the day I bore— [*with a terrible intensity*] Until I swear to you, I felt I could by just one tiny further wish, one little effort more of will, push open the door to madness where I could at least believe in a dream again! And how I longed for that final escape! [*She suddenly turns and stares at him with hatred.*] Ah! And you wonder why I hate you! [*abruptly overcome by a panic of dread, starting to her feet*] Simon! What are you trying to do! Leave me alone! Leave the past in its forgotten grave! [*trying to control herself and be indifferent*] But that is foolish. You are simply being childishly morbid and silly. Frankly, I am bored with listening to your nonsense. I will go in the house now. Sara must be wondering what is keeping me, now the sun is setting. [*She starts for the path off left. As she does so, Simon, without looking at her begins to speak again in his tone of nostalgic yearning. As he speaks she stops, makes herself go on, stops again, tries to go on, finally stops and turns to stare at him.*]

SIMON   Then I began to remember lately—and long for this garden—and you, as you used to be and are no longer—and I as I was then before I became a wife's husband and a children's father and a Company's President—that old harmonious union in the spirit of you and me—here in the freedom of a dream—hiding from the slave market of life—in this safe haven, where we could repose our souls in fantasy, in happy masquerades and fairy tales and the sustaining bravadoes of romantic verse—evade, escape, forget, rest in peace! [*He sighs wearily.*] I regret I have lost that paradise in which you were the good, kind, beloved, beautiful Queen. I have become so weary of what they call life beyond the wall, Mother.

DEBORAH   [*moved and fascinated, takes a step toward him—tenderly*] I see you have, my son. [*then diffidently but at the same time putting forth all her charm coquettishly and playfully*] But perhaps—who knows?—your loss is not irrevocable, Dear. We—you and I—in partnership in a new company of the spirit, might reorganize your bankruptcy—if I may put it in terms you understand. [*She smiles teasingly.*]

SIMON [*with a passionate eagerness*] Yes! [*He grabs her hand.*]

DEBORAH [*as if the touch of his hand alarmed her—shrinks back, turning away from him—guiltily stammers*] No! I swore to her—I would never interfere. I cannot! Unless you offer me more proof I cannot believe she has been guilty of the treachery to me that would set me free to welcome this opportunity— [*with sudden fierce passion*] Ah! If she only would be guilty I could be myself! I could be free to dream again! [*horrified at herself*] No! I am content. I have all I desire. [*She turns to Simon—resentfully and derisively*] My dear boy, your childish fancies are ridiculous. Do be sensible. We do not really wish such nonsense. And if we did, it would be impossible, we have both changed so much. [*carelessly taunting*] But, if you care to drop in here once in a while on your return from work I know the children would be pleased to see you. You could boast to them of your heroic exploits as the Company's victorious little Napoleon.

SIMON [*stiffens, stares at her with hatred for a second—then coldly, in a curt business-like tone*] I'm glad you mentioned the children. It reminds me of my real purpose in coming here. I must inform you that Sara and I have decided you are having a very bad influence on our children—

DEBORAH [*startled—resentful and uneasy*] That is ridiculous. Why, I have been at pains not to influence them at all! I teach them to rely on themselves, to own their own lives and be what they want to be, to have the courage to preserve their independence and freedom!

SIMON I remember only too well your ideal of freedom for others, Mother—that they must not be the slave of anyone but you!

DEBORAH [*with a strange eagerness*] You say Sara decided—? [*guiltily*] No! I won't believe you!

SIMON Sara decided that henceforth the children must be forbidden to see you except in the house when either she or I are present to protect them.

DEBORAH [*strickenly—with increasing desperateness*] You mean they are to be taken from me? I am to be left entirely alone again—with no life but the memory of the past— Ah! You can't be so cruel! I have made myself love them! I have created a new life in which I am resigned to age and ugliness and death out of that unselfish devotion to them and to their mother— [*abruptly, her face hardening with an eager hatred*] And you say Sara decided this? [*desperately*] No! I won't believe—

SIMON [*curtly*] I would hardly lie about something you can confirm as soon as you see her.

DEBORAH [*fighting a battle within herself—eagerly*] No, that would be too stupid. It must be true.

SIMON You'll find she is giving them their orders in the house right now.

DEBORAH [*with an almost joyous vindictiveness*] Ah, if she has betrayed me and broken all her pledges! That releases me! I am under no further obligation! I owe her nothing but— [*fighting herself again but more weakly*] No! I still cannot believe! I know her too well! I know she loves and trusts me! She would never suspect me—

SIMON [*curtly*] Nonsense, Mother. You know there is nothing strange about her being jealous of your stealing her children. You used to be jealous of her—

DEBORAH [*arrogantly*] I? Jealous of that common, vulgar biddy? [*then eagerly—with a vindictive satisfaction*] So she is jealous of me? Well, perhaps she has cause to be!

SIMON Naturally, she is afraid—

DEBORAH [*gratified*] So she is afraid of me? [*with a vindictive laugh*] But her fear is too late. I already have Ethan and Wolfe. They can never forget me! The other two still have too much of her in them— [*again fighting herself desperately*] But I know it wasn't Sara who decided this! It was you! But you never think of the children. It must have been she! Yes, yes! You are right! I have been a fool! I should have known! And I *have* known deep down inside me! I have never entirely trusted her! I have always suspected her of hy-

pocrisy! I have resented her interference and possessiveness. I have
hated the intolerable debt of daily gratitude! [*then brokenly*] But
how could she do this to me! She knows how much the children
have meant to me! She knows without them, I shall be lost again!

SIMON [*pleasantly, almost teasingly*] Come now, Mother. Let's have
done with posing. You are not really as exercised by the loss of the
children as you pretend. I think that you are honestly relieved, and
feel liberated from an irksome duty that was becoming a bore.

DEBORAH [*fiercely*] No! I love— [*abruptly with eagerness again*] Well,
perhaps you are right, Dear.

SIMON You were never intended for the job of Sara's unpaid nurse-
maid. Nor for the role of doting grandmother. You are still too
young and beautiful—

DEBORAH [*flattered*] No, I know I am not. But I love your thinking so,
Dear. [*with a wry, bitter smile*] You are deceived by that false, fleet-
ing Indian summer glow, the mocking presage of impending winter.

SIMON [*as if he hadn't heard*] I will confess now, Mother, I have
watched with anxiety the corrupting effect of the hypocritical life
you have been leading on your character—the gradual loss of your
former aristocratic distinction, your old fanciful charm, the quality
you once had of being unique and unlike all other women. I have
seen you fall completely under Sara's influence and become merely
a female, common, vulgar, a greedy home-owner, dreamless and
contented!

DEBORAH [*angrily*] You are talking nonsense! I have told you it is I
who have influenced her! Deliberately! As part of my scheme!
[*hastily*] No! What made me say that? I had no scheme. I simply
wished—

SIMON I have watched her dispossess you from yourself and take
possession. [*with a resentful intensity*] By God, there have been
times when, as I watched you together in the house at night, she
would seem to steal all identity from you and absorb you! Until
there was but one woman—her!

DEBORAH [*with a strange exultant satisfaction*] Ah, you felt that, did
you? That we were one, united against— That is what I wished to
do! [*gloatingly*] Poor boy, I can appreciate how frightened— [*then*

angrily] But you are blind or you would have seen it was I who took possession of her in order to— [*She checks herself—hastily*] But, as you say, it is very confusing. One cannot see clearly what or why— [*frightenedly*] And I do not care to see. Why do you put such morbid nonsense in my mind? Besides, it does not matter now that you have shown me clearly, Dear, I do not need her to take back what is mine. I mean, naturally, after the treacherous way she has betrayed my trust in her, there can be no question of any further friendship between us. Although, of course, I shall go on pretending. I will not give her the satisfaction of letting her see how she has hurt— And, anyway, I know I have won and I am already revenged.

SIMON [*staring before him—strangely*] Yes, Mother, I rely on you to help me keep her in her rightful place hereafter.

DEBORAH [*regards him calculatingly—then with a caressingly gentle air*] And my place? What place do you intend me to have now, Dear?

SIMON [*with a queer, hesitating embarrassment*] Why, here in your garden, of course, as always in the past.

DEBORAH [*softly insinuating*] Alone? I was not always alone in the past, if you will remember. [*She pats his hair with maternal tenderness as if he were a boy—with a teasing laugh*] What? Have you no hope to offer your poor lonely mother?

SIMON [*awkwardly stiff and formal to cover his strange embarrassment*] I do not wish you to be too lonely, Mother. I will be happy to consider any suggestion you—

DEBORAH [*with a teasing laugh, ruffling his hair playfully*] Ah! I see! Still Napoleon! Still so proud! It must be I! I must know my new place and beg! Very well. I will play your humble slave, Sire. Will you deign to visit me here and comfort my exile?

SIMON [*stiffly*] I wish you would not speak so fancifully, Mother. Please remember we are dealing with reality now and not with romantic dreams. [*then eagerly under his awkward formality*] In reply to your request, I shall be delighted to drop in and keep you company here for a while each afternoon on my way home.

DEBORAH [*gloatingly tender*] Good! Now that is off your mind, Dear. You have won that victory and can rest on your laurels for a while. [*She laughs and kisses him playfully on the forehead, and sits on *the steps again. A pause. He looks round the garden and she regards him with an amused motherly smile.*]

SIMON [*again with the yearning note*] Yes, it is very restful here. A little rest here each day will restore the soul. [*He sees the volume of Byron on the steps. He picks it up—with a forced casual air.*] What's this? Ah, Byron. Sara bitterly resents your poisoning her children's minds with such romantic rubbish. She wants them to be inspired by practical ideals. Her dread is that any of them should resemble her father and shame her pride. I have had to be so careful never to shame her pride. [*He examines the volume—with pleased boyish surprise*] I thought this looked familiar. It is the same, isn't it, Mother—the one I gave you for your birthday long ago. [*turning over the pages*] Yes, here's the inscription. "To my beloved Mother." [*to her, with a boyish, grateful smile*] This makes me happy, Mother. I thought, of course, you must have burned this— [*abruptly with a taunting, challenging air*] I mean after I decided to leave you and begin my own life.

DEBORAH [*smiles amusedly—softly*] Oh, I agree now it was you who left me and not I who sent you away. And I did want to burn your gift, I was so furious with you, but I could not.

SIMON [*satisfied, turning over the pages—eagerly*] Yes, here are the parts I marked, and the parts you marked, and the parts we marked together. [*again in his tone of yearning nostalgia*] Do you remember, Mother, we would be sitting here just as we are now, and I'd ask you to read aloud to me—

DEBORAH [*softly*] I remember, Dear, as clearly as if it were yesterday. Or, even, as though it were now.

SIMON [*intent on the book*] Remember this? We both marked it. [*He reads.*]

> . . . there is a fire
> And motion of the Soul which will not dwell
> In its own narrow being, but aspire
> Beyond the fitting medium of desire;

[*He stops and stares around the garden—strangely*] It is a long time since I have thought of the soul. Out there in the gutters called

streets beyond the wall it appears to be a weak sentimental supposi-
tion, a superstitious superfluity—but here in this garden— [*He
checks himself as he meets her eyes staring at him with a tender
gloating fixity. He reads again.*] "And, but once kindled, quenchless evermore." [*He pauses, giving the pause a tense significance—
thoughtfully*] "Evermore." Yes, it is, I think, the most cowardly and
convenient of all man's evasions, that he forgets the present is merely
the last moment of the past, and the delusion of his hope he calls
the future is but the past returning to demand payment of its debt.

DEBORAH [*uneasily, with a little shiver*] I do not like that thought,
Dear.

SIMON [*does not seem to hear her—reads again*]

> Preys upon high adventure, nor can tire
> Of aught but rest;

[*He smiles at her—teasingly*] I have observed for some time how
tired you were with rest, Mother. [*He reads again.*]

> . . . a fever at the core
> Fatal to him who bears, to all who ever bore

[*He smiles.*] Well, there is no zest in living unless one preys upon
high adventure by gambling with danger. I have discovered that as
leader of the Company. As for it being fatal, that's a coward's
thought, eh, Mother? Remember what Frederick the Great said to
his Grenadiers who hesitated to be slaughtered for his greed and
glory: "You damned stupid blackguards, do you want to live forever?" [*He laughs.*]

DEBORAH [*forcing a laugh*] Yes, so stupid of them, wasn't it?

SIMON [*turns the pages—with a return to boyish enthusiasm*] Ah!
This was our favorite. I don't have to look at the book. I still know
it by heart. I could never forget—I'll bet you can guess what it is,
Mother.

DEBORAH [*smiling fondly—teasingly*] Why, how excited you are, Dear.
What a romantic boy you still are at heart! Yes, I'm sure I can
guess— [*She recites—with growing arrogance*]

I have not loved the World, nor the World me;
I have not flattered its rank breath,—

SIMON [*breaks in and takes it up, taking on her tone of arrogant disdain*]
. . . nor bowed
To its idolatries a patient knee,
Nor coined my cheek to smiles,—

DEBORAH [*with a scornful hauteur*]
. . . nor cried aloud
In worship of an echo:

SIMON . . . in the crowd
They could not deem me one of such—

DEBORAH . . . I stood
Among them but not of them—

[*He joins in here and they both finish together.*]
. . . in a shroud
Of thoughts which were not their thoughts,—

[*They stop abruptly and stare at each other—then they both burst out laughing merrily, and Deborah claps her hands.*]
SIMON I remember so well now, Mother!
DEBORAH Yes, that was just as it used to be, wasn't it? [*From the house off left Sara's voice is heard calling in a tone of repressed uneasiness:* "Simon, are you in the garden?" *The two both start resentfully. Deborah gives him a hostile contemptuous look.*] She wants her husband. You had better go.
SIMON [*angrily, as if aloud to himself*] God, can I never know a moment's freedom! [*He calls curtly, almost insultingly.*] I am here with Mother. What do you want now? [*Sara's voice answers with an attempt at carelessness, but betraying hurt and anxiety at his tone:* "Nothing, Darling. I simply wanted to be sure." *A door is heard closing. Simon says with a chuckle*] She wants to be sure. I thought she sounded a little uneasy, didn't you, Mother?

DEBORAH [*with a malicious smile*] Yes, now you mention it—even a little frightened perhaps.

SIMON [*frowning—with his curt authoritative air*] Never mind, Mother, I will not permit such an intrusion on our privacy to occur again. I have already ordered her never to come here. [*then eagerly insistent*] Now let's forget her existence. We had a moment ago. We were back in the past before she lived in us.

DEBORAH [*tenderly*] I am only too happy, Dear. [*She takes his hand— with a seductive playfulness.*] Take my hand so you will not get lost.

SIMON [*kisses her hand with a shy boyish impulsiveness*] Oh, don't be afraid, I will never leave you again, Mother. [*He pauses—still holding her hand, staring before him with a tender, reminiscent smile*] Do you know what had come into my mind as we laughed together? A memory that goes back long before our Byron days, when I was still at the fairy tale age, and you would read them aloud to me, here. Or, what I liked better, you would make up your own tales. They seemed so much more real than the book ones I couldn't help believing in them.

DEBORAH [*uneasily, forcing a laugh*] Good Heavens, you are going far back! I had forgotten—

SIMON [*insistently*] You can't have forgotten the one I just remembered. It was your favorite. And mine. It comes back so clearly. I can see you sitting there, as you are now, dressed all in white, so beautiful and so unreal, more like a character in your story than a flesh and blood mother, so familiar and yet so strange, so near and yet so far away— [*He suddenly stares at her—a bitter accusation in his voice*] You always took such care to preserve your pose of remaining disdainfully aloof from life! One would have thought you were afraid that even your own child was a greedy interloper who was plotting to steal you from your dreams!

DEBORAH [*uneasily and guiltily—forcing a laugh*] Why, what a mean suspicious thought for you to have had about your poor mother, Dear!

SIMON [*as if he hadn't heard this last—staring before him into the past again*] You would be sitting there before the summerhouse like a sentry guarding the door. [*Again he turns on her resentfully.*] Why did you make that silly rule that no one was ever allowed to go in the summerhouse but you? You wouldn't even permit me— Why did you make such a mysterious hocus pocus about it? [*He glances at the summerhouse contemptuously.*] After all, it's ordinary enough. There are similar ones in many gardens. The way you acted gave the impression it was some secret temple of which you were high priestess! [*He laughs sneeringly.*] No one would have cared a damn about going in there, anyway!

DEBORAH [*with a strange, taunting smile*] Oh, but you know that isn't true, Dear. You used to plead and beg by the hour—

SIMON Only because you made such a mystery of it. Naturally, that made me curious.

DEBORAH Yes, you were a dreadfully inquisitive, prying little boy, always asking questions— You would never learn to mind your own business.

SIMON Well, when you forbid a boy to go anywhere, without giving him any sensible reason—

DEBORAH [*a bit sharply, as if he were still the boy*] But I did. I explained over and over again that I felt all the rooms in the house, even my bedroom, were your father's property. And this garden I shared with you. I naturally desired one place, no matter how tiny, that would be mine alone, where I could be free to dream and possess my own soul and mind. It's just that you stubbornly refused to believe that. You were such a vain little boy. [*teasingly*] You didn't want to admit I could live, even for a moment, without you, did you, Dear? [*then abruptly*] But you have no cause to complain now. I have not opened the door for years and I will never again set foot in it. As you may guess from what I told you of my last experience alone in there. [*She gives a little shudder.*]

SIMON [*stares at her with a strange fixity*] You mean when you laughed and spat in your heart until you longed to open any door of escape?

DEBORAH [*with a shiver—hurriedly*] Yes, yes! Why do you remember that so well? Let us change the subject, if you please.

SIMON [*insistently*] Why haven't you had it torn down, and not let it remain as a constant reminder.

DEBORAH [*defensively*] Because its outside reminds me of nothing. It is part of the garden. It belongs here, that is all. I do not notice it. [*pleadingly*] I asked you to talk of something else, Dear. You were starting to remember a fairy tale.

SIMON [*eagerly*] Yes, I want to tell you, Mother. But the strange part is that there is a connection with the summerhouse.

DEBORAH [*startled*] Ah! Then I do not care to hear—

SIMON Oh, not in your story. The connection was in my imagination, because of the silly mystery you made of the damned place, I suppose. [*He begins to tell the story, staring before him as if he visualized it.*] The story was this, Mother. I'll tell it without attempting to reproduce the fantastic romanticism with which you delighted to embellish your dreams. There was once upon a time, long ago in the past, a young King of a happy and peaceful land, who through the evil magic of a beautiful enchantress had been dispossessed of his realm, and banished to wander over the world, a homeless, unhappy outcast. Now the enchantress, it appeared, had in a last moment of remorse, when he was being sent into exile, revealed to him that there was a way in which he might regain his lost kingdom. He must search the world for a certain magic door.

DEBORAH [*with a start*] Ah.

SIMON She told him there was no special characteristic to mark this door from other doors. It might be any door, but if he wished to find it with all his heart, he would recognize it when he came to it, and know that on the other side was his lost kingdom. And so he set forth and searched for many years, and after enduring bitter trials, and numberless disappointments, he at last found himself before a door and the wish in his heart told him his quest was ended. But just as he was about to open it, confident that he had but to cross the threshold to re-enter his kingdom, where all had been happiness and beauty and love and peace, he heard the voice of the enchantress speaking from the other side, for she was there awaiting his coming. She called to him mockingly: "Wait. Before you open I must warn you to remember how evil I can be, and that it is probable I maliciously lied and gave you a false hope. If you dare to open the door you may discover this is no longer your old happy realm but has been changed by me into a barren desert, where it is always night, haunted by terrible ghosts, and ruled over by a hideous old witch, who wishes to destroy your claim to her realm, and the moment you cross the threshold she will tear you to pieces and devour you."

DEBORAH [*with a little shudder—forcing a laugh*] Oh, come now, Dear. I am sure I never— It is you who are adding silly embellishments of fantastic evil. I remember the story as an ironically humorous tale.

SIMON [*goes on as if she had not interrupted*] "So you had better be sure of your courage," the enchantress called warningly, "and remember that as long as you stay where you are you will run no risk of anything worse than your present unhappy exile befalling you." Then he heard her laugh. And that was all. She did not speak again, although he knew she remained there, and would always remain, waiting to see if he would dare open the door. [*with a strange bitterness*] But he never did, you said. He could not make up his mind. He felt she was lying to test his courage. Yet, at the same time, he felt she was not lying, and he was afraid. He wanted to turn his back on the door and go far away, but it held him in a spell and he could never leave it. So he remained for the rest of his life standing before the door, and became a beggar, whining for alms from all who passed by, until at last he died. [*He turns to stare at her—forcing a smile, resentfully.*] That, I suppose, constitutes the humorous irony you remembered?

DEBORAH [*laughingly, a strange gloating in her face and an undercurrent of taunting satisfaction in her voice*] Yes, I remember that ending now, and I must confess I still think it shows an amusing insight into the self-betraying timidities that exist in most of us. [*teasingly*] I remember how resentful you were at the ending. You used to insist I imagine a new ending in which the wicked enchantress had reformed and become a good fairy and opened the door and welcomed him home and they were both happy ever after. [*She laughs.*]

SIMON And you would laugh at me. [*He stares at her—with a strange challenging look*] I would still like to discover if you could possibly imagine a happy ending to that tale.

DEBORAH [*uneasily, meeting his stare*] Why? [*then hastily turning *away and forcing a laugh*] But what silly nonsense, Simon. What a child you are! Fairy tales, indeed! What a preoccupation for a Napoleon of facts!

SIMON [*smiles pleasantly*] Yes, absurd, I admit. It must be the atmosphere of this garden. But the point I was getting at is that I was very impressionable then and your story was very real to me and I connected it with real things. The door of the tale became identified in my mind with the door there [*He looks at the summerhouse door.*] to your forbidden summerhouse. I used to boast to myself that if I were the King I would not be afraid, I would gamble recklessly on the chance— [*Suddenly, moved by a strange urgency, he springs to his feet and goes past her up the steps to the door— harshly*] Let's have done with the mystery right now! (*He seizes the knob.*]

DEBORAH [*starts to her feet in a panic of dread and grabs his other arm.*] No, Simon! No! [*Then her panic is strangely transformed into an outraged, arrogant fury—glaring at him with hatred and repulsion, in a quivering passion, commandingly*] Come away! Obey me this instant! How dare you! Have you lost all decency? Will your vulgar greed leave me nothing I can call my own? Is no solitude sacred to you?

SIMON [*overcome by this outburst, moves back down the steps obediently like a cowed boy*] I'm sorry Mother. I—I didn't think you'd mind now—

DEBORAH [*relieved and a bit guilty*] I can't help minding. Forgive me for losing my temper, Dear. I don't know what I said—or what I meant— The truth is I have become superstitious—remembering the last time I was in there—and I was afraid—and lost.

SIMON [*has recovered his poise as she has weakened—curtly*] That is damned nonsense, Mother. There's nothing there, of course.

DEBORAH [*with a little shiver*] You think not? But I remember I am there.

SIMON Rot! That's insanity, Mother.

DEBORAH [*slowly—with dread*] Yes, I know that is what it is. [*hurriedly*] I suppose it's very ridiculous. There is nothing in there but dark and dust and spider webs—and the silence of dead dreams.

SIMON [*smiling*] Well, anyway, it would not be a happy ending, would it, for me to go in alone? No, someday, I will give you the courage to open the door yourself and we will go together. [*He takes her hand, gently—pretending to joke but with an underlying seriousness*] I think I could be absolutely sure then that the beautiful evil enchantress had reformed and become a good fairy and my happy kingdom of peace was here. Surely, you couldn't forbid me that happy dream, Mother?

DEBORAH [*fascinatedly*] No—perhaps, together—I might not be afraid— there may come a time when I might even welcome—now that she is conspiring to take life from me again— [*with a strange gloating smile*] Yes, she would have only herself to blame if— [*then with a shiver of dread*] No! I don't know what I mean! [*turning on him with forced scorn*] You are being absurd, Simon. It is grotesque for a grown man to act so childishly. I forbid you ever to mention this subject again. It is only on that condition I can agree to welcome you in my garden, you have the same rights here you had in the past but no more. [*pleadingly*] Surely that is enough for your happiness, Dear.

SIMON [*with a mocking gallantry, kissing her hand*] Your wish is my law, Madame. I shall be, as in the past, a slave to your every whim.

DEBORAH [*abruptly changing to a gay, seductive coquetry*] That is as should be, Monsieur. [*laughingly*] I am happy to see that vulgar peasant slut has not made you forget all the old gallantry and gracious manners I taught you, Dear. [*From the house off left comes Sara's voice, and now the uneasiness and suspicion in it are obvious behind the casual words. She calls:* "Simon, are you still in the garden?"]

SIMON [*starts—calls out angrily*] Yes! Of course, I'm here! Why? What do you want of me now? [*A pause. Then Sara's voice comes, hurt and a little forlorn:* "Nothing, Darling. It's getting near supper time, that's all." *Her voice suddenly takes on a resentful commanding tone:* "It's time you came in, do you hear me?"]

DEBORAH [*staring at him—with a bitter, jealous derisiveness*] Your slut commands you now, it seems! As the weak slave of her every greedy whim you had better obey! [*Then as, stung, he starts to make an angry reply, Deborah anticipates him and calls with an undertone of gloating mockery.*] Don't worry, Sara. I'll bring him back to you. [*A pause. Then Sara calls, back, uneasily with a forced carelessness:* "Oh, you needn't bother, Deborah. His hunger would drive him here soon, anyway." *A door is heard closing as she goes back in the house. Deborah gives a malicious laugh.*] A little forced in its self-confidence, that last, didn't you think, Dear? More than a little frightened! [*She gets up. He also rises. She speaks with a cruel eagerness.*] Let us go in now, Dear—together. I am eager to see her. I want to see how frightened she is. [*She takes his arm—tenderly*] Oh, I am so happy—so very happy, Dear!—to have my son again!

SIMON [*tenderly*]   Not half so happy as I am to have my mother again! [*They start to go off, left. Abruptly he stops—in a tone of warning advice made more effective by a provocative hint of taunting behind it*] I want to warn you again, Mother, not to underestimate your enemy. It is all very well to be confident of your possessive power, which I would be the last to deny. But remember she is strong, too. She can match your superiority of mind and spirit with her over-powering physical greed for things as they are, your dreams with her facts, your evasions with her eager acceptances. Where you are sickly and over-refined and timidly superstitious, she is healthy and would break down any door that stood between her and ownership. So take care that the moment you see her you do not surrender to her influence again and let her cunning trick you into confusing what is yours with what is hers and identifying your self with her self. You must jealously defend your separate, unique individuality, your right to freedom, or— And I know you do not want her laughing at you up her sleeve anymore, as she has been doing.

DEBORAH [*has been listening with growing anger—blurts out*]   Laughing at me! The stupid vulgar fool! If she only knew! And you are equally stupid or you could not say such idiotic things! [*arrogantly boastful*] I tell you it is I who have been laughing in my mind at her! It is I who have made a ridiculous trusting gull of her! Swindled her with lies into feeling affection and friendship so I could steal her children. How simple and blind you are, Simon, despite all your experience in marking cards and loading dice to play successfully the game of dispossession! Who made her feel that she was I, and whose will was it that made her no longer need you but banish you into lonely exile in your separate room? I tell you I have secretly intrigued from the first day you came here, schemed and deceived and hypocritically played the doting grandmother. To what end? [*She smiles gloatingly.*] Why, you should see that clearly, at least. You are here, are you not?—my son who can never wish again to leave his mother! [*She laughs with a coquettish taunting and taps his cheek playfully.*] It is singular that such a conquering Napoleon cannot recognize a complete victory and a crushing defeat when he sees them!

SIMON [*stares at her with a curious, objectively appraising look—then with a satisfied objectively approving nod*] Yes, make yourself believe that, Mother, and you can safely defy her. After all, there is a great deal of truth in that aspect of it, as I have suspected. Your truth, of course. Not Sara's. Nor mine. And not even the whole of your truth. But you and I can wait to discover what that is later on. [*He smiles with pleasant casualness.*] Just now I think we had better go in to supper.

DEBORAH [*pulling away, stares at him with a puzzled frightened dread*] Simon! What—? [*Then conquering her fear and suddenly gloating takes his arm again—eagerly*] Yes! Let us go in. I can't wait to tell her you are going to be with me each evening, that you are now my own dear son again!

SIMON [*sharply commanding*] No! Not until I give you permission to speak. I will choose the most effective time. [*coldly and curtly*] You will kindly not forget, Mother, all this reorganization of my home is my affair and must be carried out exactly as I have calculated. You had better not interfere if you expect me ever to keep you company. [*brusquely*] Come. It is getting late. [*She is again looking at him with bewildered dread, has shrunk back, taking her hand from his arm. But he ignores this and grasps her arm and makes her walk off beside him up the path to the house.*]

* * * CURTAIN * * *

Tao House
Nov. 26th '38

Parlor of the Harford mansion—Act Three, Scene Three
*Yale Collection of American Literature, Beinecke Rare Book
and Manuscript Library, Yale University*

Act Three, Scene Three

SCENE *Parlor of the Harford mansion—a high-ceilinged, finely-proportioned room such as one finds in the Massachusetts houses designed by Bulfinch or McIntire[1] and built in the late 1790s. The walls and ceiling are white. A rug covers most of the floor of waxed dark wood. A crystal chandelier hangs from the middle of the ceiling at center, toward front. At extreme left-front a small table against the wall, facing right, then a door leading to the entrance hall, another chair, and farther back, a table. In the middle of the rear wall is the door to Simon's study. On either side of it, a chair facing front. Against the right wall, toward rear, another table. Farther forward, a high window looking out on the street, then a chair, and finally, at right-front, a fireplace. At left, rear of the fireplace, is a long sofa with a small table and reading lamp by its left end. Toward front, at left, is an oval table with another lamp. A chair is by right rear of this table, facing right-front. Another chair is at left-front of this table, facing directly front. It is around nine o'clock at night of the same day.*

Sara, Simon, and Deborah are discovered—Sara in the chair at left-front of the table, Simon across the table from her in the chair at rear-right of it, Deborah on the left end of the sofa by the lamp. Sara is pretending to work on a piece of needle-point but she is obviously preoccupied with her thoughts. Deborah has a book in her hands but she stares over it, as preoccupied as Sara. Simon also holds a book and keeps

---

1. Charles Bulfinch (1763–1844) was a prominent Boston architect. Among the many buildings he designed and/or refurbished were the Beacon Hill monument, the New North Church, the New South Church, Faneuil Hall, the Massachusetts State House, and the Massachusetts General Hospital. He was also appointed by President Monroe to work on the U.S. Capitol in Washington, D.C. Samuel McIntire (1757–1811), a Salem resident, designed many of the colonial mansions there. He was noted for his mantels and cornices and designed the bas-reliefs for the gates to the Boston Common.

his eyes fixed on it but his eyes do not move and his mind is very evidently elsewhere. All have changed their clothes. The two women wear semi-formal evening gowns, Deborah's all white, Sara's a blue that matches the color of her eyes. Simon is dressed in black.

For a moment after the curtain rises there is an atmosphere of tense quiet in the room, an eavesdropping silence that waits, holding its breath and straining its ears. Then, as though the meaning of the silence were becoming audible, their thoughts are heard.

SARA [*thinking*]   Thank God, there's a moment's peace where I can think—ever since they came in, the three of us conversing so pleasant—as if nothing had happened—she's a good one at hiding her feelings—you'd think, taking the children away meant nothing to her—maybe it doesn't—maybe, like he claims, she was only pretending—no, I know she loved them—it's her great-lady pride won't give me the satisfaction to know she's hurt—and there's something more behind it—I thought they'd never come in—I heard them laughing once—and when they came in she looked as gay as you please—something about him, too—sly—like there was a secret between them—I was a fool to let him go to her crazy garden— [*vindictively*] Well, I know he hasn't told her yet I'm going to work with him—I'll tell her the mistress part of it—let her try to smile when she knows that! [*impatiently with a side glance at Simon*] Why doesn't he tell her and get it over—if he doesn't soon, I will!—

DEBORAH [*thinking*]   In the garden, at the end, I was so sure of him—but he changed when he saw her—something in his eyes of her old physical power over him—a reflection of her common, vulgar prettiness—a change in her, too—I felt her warm greedy femaleness deliberately exuding lust in a brazen enticement—she was not half as frightened as I hoped—still, she was uneasy—she couldn't hide her suspicion—and when he tells her he is coming to my garden every evening she will realize her crude animalism is of no avail now—that he is my son again— [*impatiently, with a side glance at Simon*] Why does he wait?—does he shrink from hurting her?—well, remembering her base betrayal of my trust, I will not shrink!

SARA [*reassuring herself—thinking*]   Ah, I'm a fool to waste a thought on her—hasn't he kept his word about the children?—and don't I remember at the office how much he wanted me—even the part of him that belongs to the Company will be mine now—all of him— and my children, too, will be all mine!—there'll be no more sharing with her—this is my home!—she'll be no better than a strange guest, living on charity—let her keep to her garden where she'll harm no one but herself—let her dream herself into a madhouse, if she likes, as long as she leaves me and mine alone!—it'd serve her right for her lies and meanness, trying to steal my children when I trusted her!—

DEBORAH [*thinking—self-reassuringly and then gloatingly*]   She is only pretending to work on her needle-point—thinking—yes, quite as frightened in her thoughts, I think, as Simon and I had hoped—it's merely my imagination that reads desire for her in his eyes—I re- member how tender he became in the garden—how loving—how much he needed me—my beloved son!—never to be taken from me again—every evening in the garden I will encourage him to live with me in the past before he knew her—before he ever thought of women—to be my little boy again—I will bind him to me so he can never reject me and escape again—she will become no more than the empty name of wife, a housekeeper, a mother of children, our Irish biddy nurse girl and servant!—

SIMON [*staring at his book—thinks with gloating satisfaction as though his mind guessed their thoughts*]   I have good reason to congratu- late myself, I think—all goes in accord with my plan—everything moves back into its proper place—they are divided and separate again—they do not sit together on the sofa as has been their wont— I am where I belong between them—there will be no further con- fusion in my mind—no devouring merging of identities—no more losing myself in their confusion—henceforth all is distinct and clearly defined—two women—opposites—whose only relation de- rives from the relationship of each to me—whose lives have mean- ing and purpose only in so far as they live within my living—hence- forth this is my home and I own my own mind again!—I am a free slave-owner! [*He smiles to himself gloatingly and begins to read. As if their minds had partly sensed the tenor of his thought, the two women turn to stare at him with a stirring of suspicion and resentment. They both look quickly away.*]

SARA [*thinking*]   He isn't reading—just pretending to—smiling to himself—sly—

DEBORAH [*her thoughts in the same key as Sara's*]   What is he thinking, I wonder?—of the Company and this secretary-mistress he boasted?—I hate that smug, lustful, greedy trader's smile of his!—

SARA [*thinking resentfully*]   I know that smile—when he's managed a foxy deal for the Company and cheated someone—he spoke at the office as though he was driving a bargain for a mistress—I hope he doesn't think he'll cheat me—I was a fool to let him see I wanted him so much!—

DEBORAH [*thinking resentfully*]   It was unwise to agree so soon to his pleading—I remember, even when he was little, he realized how his begging made me weak, and he used it to get his own way—well, he will discover again, if he has forgotten, that I have ways of getting my way, too!

SARA [*thinks self-reassuringly and a bit contemptuously*]   Ah, I mustn't be uneasy—didn't he show he wanted me as much as I want him?—or maybe more, if I'd tried—so why should I worry my mind?—I'll attend to my needle-point and not let these foolish thoughts disturb me— [*She begins to work determinedly.*]

DEBORAH [*thinks self-reassuringly*]   This is senseless and stupid!—to make myself uneasy and resentful—after he's proved so conclusively—it's unfair to him—I'll be sensible and read my book— [*She begins to read determinedly. There is a pause of silence. It is Simon who stops attempting to distract his mind first. His eyes cease reading and stare at the book preoccupiedly.*]

SIMON [*thinking*]   Yes, I think I can foresee every move of my present campaign here—not even Napoleon planning Austerlitz—Good God, what an insane comparison!—Mother's romantic influence!—nevertheless, I can prophesy exactly every possible development in this battle—but will this one victory insure a peace of perpetual conquest?—who knows?—the immediate future is all I can foretell clearly—my plan doesn't go beyond—I don't even know yet what I wish the final outcome to be, or what is the exact nature of the final peace I want to impose— [*with forced self-reassurance*] Bah! I will cross those bridges when I come to them—sufficient for the day that I control the game now and can have it played as I wish—make them think that each may win—deal the marked cards to give each in turn the semblance of winning so each may mistake losses for gains— [*frowning again—uneasily*] But it means I must always remain in the game myself—be as careful and watchful now outside the office as in it—never relax my vigilance—there is always the danger of failure—bankruptcy and ruin—alliance of devouring enemies—an unceasing duel to the death with life!— [*He makes an unconscious shrinking movement of dread—determinedly self-scornful*] Bah! What nonsense! You would think I saw myself as the victor's spoils—when it is I who will be the victor— [*He tries to read again but at once gives up the attempt.*] I cannot concentrate on this damned book—I read a paragraph and do not remember the sense or find any meaning—

DEBORAH [*has ceased reading and is staring over her book—thinking resentfully*] I cannot read—my eyes follow words but that is all— I feel a restless dread—I cannot help remembering the past—he has awakened so much I had hoped was dead—it is a dangerous price to pay—

SARA [*has stopped sewing—thinks irritably*] It's no good!—I can't put my mind on sewing—I feel something is staring over my shoulder— watching my thoughts pushing and crowding in my brain like a lot of mad sheep something has frightened, and I'm not able to stop them—it's strange here tonight—it's not the house it's been—not home at all—there's no peace— [*unconsciously she sighs regretfully*] It's so changed from the contented way we've been here nights for so long—she and I would be sitting together on the sofa laughing and telling each other about the children—he'd sit alone, thinking out schemes for his Company—minding his own business and not bothering us—

DEBORAH [*with a little shudder*] Yes, a frightening price to demand of me—to release the forgotten Deborah who was his mother from the tomb of the past—how silly he acted about the summerhouse—a grown man—nothing is sacred or secret to him—how tense the quiet is in this house tonight—as though a bomb were concealed in the room with a fuse slowly sputtering toward—and the silence waits—holding its breath—hands clapped over its ears—a strange haunted house—so changed from what it was last night—and every night for years—she would sit here by my side—we would laugh together, thinking of the children—I had forgotten him sitting alone there—he might have been a million miles away—he was buried in the past—I did not need him—

SIMON [*thinking—uneasily*] Perhaps I should have waited—until I had determined the true nature of the final conquest I desire more clearly—I am more cautious with my campaigns for the Company—I calculate first exactly what I want to win—am sure the game is worth the candle—the unceasing vigilance it will demand of me is going to prove an added strain—it begins already—my home is becoming a battlefield—so different from other nights—there was peace here, of a kind—at least an atmosphere in which I could be indifferent to their existence and concentrate on my ambitions for the Company—a man's work in a man's world of fact and reality— [*irritably*] What made their petty sentimental women's world of lies and trivial greeds assume such a false importance?—why did I have to meddle in their contemptible ambitions and let them involve me in a domestic squabble about the ownership of children?—I, the leader of a great Company, a figure of first importance in the life of a great city, a man men fear and envy—

SARA [*regretfully*] Much as I ought to hate her now for the sneak he showed her to be, I can't help wishing he'd never told me—he's a fool to think she could ever have taken my children—I can keep what's mine from the devil himself—it may be weak of me but I wish I could have kept on thinking she was my friend and trusting her—feeling proud of having helped her—

DEBORAH [*regretfully*] Much as I detest her treachery, I find something in me wishing he had not unmasked her—is there any one of us whose soul, stripped naked, is not ugly with meanness?—life is at best a polite pretending not to see one another—a game in which we tacitly agree to make believe we are not what we are—a covenant not to watch one's friends too clearly, for the sake of friendship—

and I have grown to lean upon her health and strength—as one leans
against a tree, deep rooted in the common earth—and what if she
had taken the children?—if she had done it herself, I would have
understood her jealousy—I have been a loving mother, too—I would
have forgiven her, remembering my own greed—

SARA [*as though responding to Deborah's thoughts, gives Simon a resentful look*] If only he hadn't interfered—why did he take the
sudden notion to start minding our business?—

SIMON [*frowning—thinks self-exasperatedly*] What stupid impulse
drove me to start taking a hand in their measly woman's game—
now, of all times, when I've just assumed the added responsibility
of the railroad!—what the devil possessed me to ask Sara to come
to the office?—now I won't have a separate man's life free of woman
even there!

SARA [*thinking resentfully*] If I hadn't gone to his office—I had a feeling I shouldn't—that he was up to some scheme—

SIMON [*thinking*] What bosh to tell her I needed a secretary!—she'll
only be in my way—and I'll have no privacy—she'll pry greedily
into everything—

SARA [*thinking*] As if I hadn't enough to do taking care of my home
and my children without his making me slave for his Company!
[*scornfully*] Is he that weak he can't even manage his own man's
business without my—?

SIMON [*thinking*] My ridiculous proposal to make her my mistress!—
if I wanted one I could buy girls by the dozen—young and pretty—
fresh and not yet possessed—not a body I already own—which possession has made worthless to me—if she hopes she can ever again
make me the greedy slave to it I once was— [*He turns to stare at
her with a vindictive hostility.*]

SARA [*thinking not noticing he is looking at her*] If he thinks his asking me to be his mistress pleased me—treating his wife as if she was
a whore he'd pick up on the street and ask her price—and he ought
to know I was through wanting him—content he'd left me free to
sleep by myself in peace—I was a fool to let him hug and kiss me
like he did at the office and make me remember—make me like a
beast in heat that's a slave to her need and can't help herself—but

I'll show him it will be the other way round this time, and I'll be the one to keep free! [*She turns to stare at him with revengeful hostility, then as they meet each other's eyes, each turns away guiltily. Forcing a casual tone—speaks to him.*] Yes, Simon? You were going to speak to me?

SIMON [*in a like casual tone*]   I? No. I thought you—

SARA   No.

SIMON   I was preoccupied with my thoughts.

SARA   So was I.

SIMON [*a taunt coming into his tone*]   I was thinking of Mother, as it happens.

SARA [*casually*]   That's strange. So was I. [*Neither of them looks at her. A pause*]

DEBORAH [*thinking—resentfully*]   He lied—he said that to hurt her— much as I ought to hate her, I pity her when I see him deliberately trying to humiliate—and if he was thinking of me, it is against my wishes—just as his coming to my garden this afternoon—forcing his way in—one would think a man of his birth and breeding would have more delicacy—would not desire to come where he knows he is unwelcome—

SIMON [*thinking—resentfully*]   By that lie I've put Mother back in my mind—what impelled me to visit her garden again—mysterious summerhouse—all that insane nonsense— Good God, I'll be playing with toys next, and begging her to tell me a fairy tale!—so damned weak of me to offer to visit her each evening—I have no time to waste humoring her senile whims and pretending to take her crazy dreams of romance seriously— [*He stares at her with vindictive hostility.*]

DEBORAH [*thinking with bitter hostility*]   His proposal to visit me each evening—as if he were doing me a favor, forsooth!—I do not want him intruding on my life—I never even wanted him to be conceived—I was glad to be rid of him when he was born—he had made my beauty grotesquely ugly by his presence, bloated and misshapen, disgusting to myself—and then the compulsion to love him after he was born—like a fate forced on me from without, in spite of myself, not of my own will, making me helpless and weak—love like an enslaving curse laid on my heart—my life made dependent on another's living, my happiness at the mercy of another's selfish whims— [*She turns to stare at him with vindictive hostility. Then, as each meets the other's eyes, each turns away guiltily.*]

SIMON [*speaks to her forcing a casual tone*]   Yes, Mother? You wanted to speak to me?

DEBORAH [*echoing his tone*]   No, Simon. I thought you—

SIMON   No. [*Then with a taunt in his tone*]   I was not thinking of you, but of Sara.

DEBORAH [*carelessly*]   That is strange, I was thinking of her, too. [*Neither of them look at her. A pause*]

SARA [*thinking—resentfully*]   He lied to her—it's little thought he ever gives me anymore except when his lust wants something—he said that to hurt her—he's sneering at her—poor woman!—I find it hard to hate her—there's too much pity in my heart—she can't read her book—she's too upset—she's thinking how she'll miss the children—alone all day—I won't be here to keep her company—he'll have me at the office—alone in the past, where she'll have nothing but her old mad dreams to turn to for comfort—he'll have her in an asylum in the end, if he's not careful!—it's a terrible thing he can hate his own mother so!—I didn't even hate my father that much—and if I did hate him, it was on account of my poor mother—the way he sneered at her—Simon sneers at his mother—and Deborah has been like a mother to me—I was proud of having a second mother who's a great lady of a fine Yankee family, who doesn't talk in ignorant brogue like my poor mother did, and is too proud to let love for any man make a fool and a slave of her—who has always kept herself free and independent— [*bewilderedly*] Ah, what makes me remember the past and get the dead mixed up with the living in my mind—like he said he's confused Deborah and me in his mind—his mind, that's just it—it's he that brings confusion to us!

DEBORAH [*thinking bitterly*]   This is all his doing—the malicious plot of a greedy, evil, morbidly jealous child—I know he has lied to me—that he drove her to betray my trust—she would never of her own will—she had begun to look upon me as a second mother—to come to me for advice—to look up to me—and I was happy to regard her as my daughter—because in her affectionate trust I felt safe from myself—because her strength and health and acceptance of life gave me a faith in my own living—a support—and now he dares to take that security away from me!—to offer me in exchange an insane confusion—ghosts from the past to haunt me—with the insolence of one doing a favor or bearing a gift!—

SARA [thinking] Why do I let him?—I'm not helpless—I'm not a thought he moves around in his mind to suit his pleasure—I ought to go to her now and talk with her truthfully—get her to be truthful with me—I'll forgive her if she'll forgive me—and between us we can soon put an end to his tricks!—

DEBORAH [thinking] What fools we are to allow him to do this to us!—if she'd sit with me here as on other nights, we'd understand and forgive each other—with her strength and health beside me, I can defend myself against his greedy dreams—I have only to call her over— [They both speak to each other simultaneously— "Sara" "Deborah." They bend forward so they can see each other past him and they smile at each other with a relieved understanding. Deborah speaks with a strange gentleness.] Yes, Daughter. I ought to have known you guessed my thoughts.

SARA [getting up—with a gentle smile] Maybe I did Mother—and I hope you guessed mine. May I come and sit with you?

DEBORAH I was going to ask you to. Of course you may, Dear. [Sara goes around the table and passes behind Simon, ignoring him, and goes to the sofa. Deborah pats the sofa on her left, smiling an affectionate welcome.] This is your place, you know, beside me.

SARA [bends impulsively and gives her a daughterly kiss on the cheek] I know, Mother. [She sits down, close beside her, so their arms touch.]

SIMON [who has been pretending to read—with contemptuous relief] Ah, so they have decided to forget and forgive—well, I confess I feel relieved—this hate was becoming a living presence in the room—and in my mind—I felt hopelessly involved in it—through my own fault, too—I was stupid to meddle—but now we will be back where we were on other nights and my mind is free to mind its own business— [A sudden sly malicious look comes to his face.] Meanwhile, keeping an eye on them to make sure this sentimental reunion is not too successful—but each is lying and acting, of course—playing the hypocrite in the hope of gaining some advantage—it will be amusing to watch—

SARA [*turns to Deborah with impulsive frankness*] I want to beg your forgiveness, Mother—about the children. It was mean of me to let myself be made jealous, and not to trust you.

DEBORAH [*takes her hand—gently*] I understand. One cannot help being jealous. It is part of the curse of love.

SARA [*with a quick resentful look at Simon*] Yes, you do feel cursed by it when it's too greedy.

DEBORAH [*patting Sara's hand*] Thank goodness, we've understood each other and what might have developed into a stupid quarrel is all forgotten now, isn't it?

SARA Yes, and I'm happy to be here beside you again, feeling your trust and friendship—

DEBORAH [*presses her hand and keeps it in hers*] And I'm so happy to have you back, Dear. I had begun to feel so weak and at the mercy of the past.

SARA [*gently*] Ah now, don't think of what's past. [*with bullying affection*] Shame on you and you with four handsome grandchildren to love, and everything in life to live for.

DEBORAH [*eagerly*] Then I may have the children back?

SARA Indeed you may! And remember I wasn't really the one who took them away from you. [*She casts a resentful look at Simon.*]

DEBORAH [*deeply moved*] You are so kind and generous, Dear! I hate myself for having permitted my mind to be tempted— [*She gives Simon a bitter hostile look.*] But that's over. We have beaten him. [*A pause. The two women sit with clasped hands, staring defiantly at Simon.*]

SIMON [*moves restlessly, his eyes fixed on the book—thinking with a forced, uneasy derision*] Is it possible, after all that has happened between us today, that they actually hope to re-establish their selfish, greedy union—which denied me and shut me out and left me alone— [*bitterly vindictive*] Then I'll soon prove to them—Mother forgets I haven't told Sara yet about my plan to visit her every evening from now on—and Sara forgets Mother doesn't know yet she is to be the mistress I—I have hesitated to tell them so far because— because what?—because I know that then the die will be cast irrevocably, and there can be no possible turning back?—because something in me is afraid?— [*forcing a self-scornful tone*] afraid?— nonsense!—it is for them to be afraid—but I wish I could see the exact nature of the final plan I desire more clearly before I—

SARA [*as if influenced by his thought, gives him a quick resentful look— slowly*] All the same, Deborah, I know how unhappy you felt, sitting alone here. I was miserable myself over there with him between us.

DEBORAH [*glancing at Simon resentfully—lowering her voice to a whisper*] Yes. That's just it, Sara. We must never again allow him to come between—

SARA [*in a whisper*] Ah! It was he who made me believe you were trying to steal my children's love from me. [*They bend closer to each other until their heads are about touching, and all during the following scene talk in whispers, their eyes fixed on Simon.*]

DEBORAH I am sure he did. Just as he tried to make me believe you had gone to his office with the deliberate purpose of betraying me.

SARA [*stares at Simon with bitter hostility*] So that's what he told you, is it? It's a lie. It was all his scheming. He asked me to come there.

DEBORAH Yes, I see that clearly now.

SARA I wonder what mad trick he's up to. Why can't he leave us in peace? What more can he want of us? Haven't we given him all of our time he's any right to? [*bitterly*] But men are the devil's own children! They're never content. They must always grab for more.

DEBORAH [*bitterly*] It's true. You bear them and hope you are free, but it's only the beginning of a new slavery, for they start with their first cry to accuse you and complain of their fate like weaklings and demand your life as if it were their right to possess you!

SARA It's seeing us content with our children without him. He can't bear the thought—

DEBORAH [*beginning to smile with vindictive satisfaction*] Yes. He was always a greedy jealous boy. That's where we may have him at our mercy, I think, Sara. His jealousy drives him to need us. But we already have four sons—

SARA [*beginning to smile, too*] And so we don't have to need him. [*She laughs softly and jeeringly and Deborah laughs with her. Simon stirs uneasily and his eyes cease to follow the lines and stare at the page.*]

DEBORAH Yes, the more I consider it, Sara, the more confident I feel that it is really he who is helpless and lonely and lost—who begs for love and is completely at our mercy!

SARA [*threateningly*] Then let him look out how he plays scheming tricks to destroy our peace! We might lose patience with his greediness and he'd find himself driven out in the night without—to sleep in his office with his Company for a mistress!

SIMON [*his eyes staring on his book now—thinking with a tense dread*] I still feel hatred like a living presence in this room—stronger—drawing closer—surrounding—threatening—me— [*fighting himself*] But that's absurd—they hate each other now— [*frightenedly*] But it seems to have gotten very cold in this room—nonsense!—you know it is an extremely warm night—but it has become dark in here and the room is unfamiliar—nonsense!—it's the same old parlor in the house where you were born and the lamps burn brightly—but surely it cannot be my imagination that Mother and Sara have vanished—as on so many nights before—Mother took her hand and led her back—as if she opened a door into the past in whose darkness they vanished to reappear as one woman—a woman recalling Mother as I knew her long ago—but not her—a stranger woman—unreal, a ghost inhumanely removed from living, beautiful and coldly remote and arrogant and proud—with eyes deliberately blind—with a smile deliberately amused by its own indifference—because she no longer wants me—has taken all she needed—I have served my purpose—she has ruthlessly got rid of me—she is free—and I am left lost in myself, with nothing! [*He has dropped the book in his lap and straightened himself tensely, gripping the arms of his chair, staring before him frightenedly. As his thoughts have progressed, the expressions on the two women's faces have mirrored his description as though, subconsciously, their mood was created by his mind. They become proudly arrogant and coldly indifferent to him. He goes on thinking with increasing dread.*] But it is different now—that is what she was on other nights—her nature has changed—not indifferent now—she stares at me with hate—she is revengeful and evil—a cannibal witch whose greed will devour! [*Their expressions have changed to revengeful gloating cruelty and they stare at him with hate. He starts forward in his chair as if he were about to fly in horror from the room.*]

DEBORAH [*smiling gloatingly*]   See, Sara, he is not even pretending to read now. He is thinking. He must have heard what we were whispering; he looks so uneasy and defeated.

SARA [*smiling gloatingly*]   As scared as if he saw a ghost!

DEBORAH [*her tone becoming contemptuously pitying*]   So like a little boy who is lost.

SARA [*contemptuously pitying*]   Yes, that's like him. There's so much of that weakness in him. Maybe that's what I've loved most in him.

DEBORAH   Because it makes him need you so terribly! Oh, I know! I know so well! I remember— [*Her expression softens to a condescending maternal tenderness.*] Perhaps we are being too hard on him. After all, what he has tried to do has been so obviously childish and futile.

SARA   It's because he's jealous, and that proves how much he loves us.

DEBORAH   Yes, I think instead of being angry, we should merely be amused, as we would be at the mischief of a bad sulky boy.

SARA [*smilingly—complacently maternal*]   And forgive him if he promises not to do it again.

DEBORAH [*smiling like Sara*]   He won't, I know, as soon as he is compelled to realize he can't gain anything by being wicked—except to be severely punished. [*She speaks to Simon with an amused, teasing smile.*] Wake up, Dear! [*He starts and turns to stare at them bewilderedly.*] Why do you stare as if we were strangers?

SARA [*teasingly*]   It's like he always is lately. His mind is so full of grand schemes for the Company we might as well be in another world! [*laughingly*] You might be more polite to your ladies, Darling.

SIMON [*as if suddenly emerging from a spell—with an impulsive grateful relief*]   Ah! Thank God, each of you is here again! [*He checks himself abruptly and looks away from them hastily and hurries on in a confused, evasive, explanatory tone.*] I beg your pardon. I had forgotten you were here. I was thinking of the Company's affairs. I must have dozed off and dreamed—

DEBORAH [*turns to Sara—with gloating amusement*] He must have dreamed we no longer loved him. [*She smiles at Simon with a tender, scornful pity*] My poor boy! Do tell us what you dreamed. [*He ignores her. She laughs teasingly.*] He won't do it, Sara. He was always stubbornly secretive about his dreams, even as a little boy. And so greedily inquisitive about mine. That was the unfair part. He thought I had no right to have any secrets from him. [*She calls teasingly.*] Simon. Why don't you answer me? What was it you dreamed just now that made you so afraid? [*He doesn't seem to hear. She laughs softly.*] No, it's no good, Sara. He is pretending to be quite oblivious to our existence again, to be too deeply absorbed in his great schemes of manly ambition, inspired by the career of Napoleon! But we know he is very uneasy now, not sure of himself at all, wondering what we will decide to do about him.

SARA [*with a little laugh*] Yes, he has a guilty conscience and he knows he ought to be punished.

SIMON [*as if he hadn't heard them, but confusedly apologetic and almost humbly placating and apprehensive, avoiding their eyes*] I—I am afraid I interrupted a private discussion between you. I remember now you were whispering together. Pray continue. I am interested in this book and you need not mind my presence. You can dismiss me from your minds entirely—for the present. I will even regard it as a favor if you do, because, to be truthful, your thinking of me intrudes on my thoughts and confuses me—at a time when it is imperative I concentrate my mind on defining the exact nature of the final goal of my ambition, precisely what peace I desire to impose after—

SARA [*contemptuously*] Ah, he's off at the head of his Company again, Deborah, prancing on a great white thoroughbred Arab stallion around and around his mind, like old Boney himself! [*with a strange boastfulness*] But don't forget, Darling, I'm my father's daughter and wasn't he an officer and a gentleman who helped the Duke drive old Boney out of Spain, and took all he'd gained from him!

DEBORAH [*smiling teasingly*] Yes, I agree with you that whatever plans he makes now concern us in making our plans. If he didn't want us to mind him, he shouldn't have minded our business, should he? [*She laughs softly, teasing and Sara laughs with her. Simon ignores them, staring at his book, pretending to read but his eyes are motionless. Deborah goes on*] But, of course, if by not mind he means not take too seriously, we agree, don't we? We mustn't mind him. We must make allowances and not judge him too harshly. He has always been a romantic boy in whose backward imagination everything became confused—real life with fairy tales—facts with poetic fancies— common summerhouses with enchanted palaces—and heaven knows what other incredible, presumptuous nonsense! Everyone who ever knew him in the old days considered him a queer, erratic boy, subject to spells in which he was irresponsible and impracticable—a little crazy, to be frank. His own father never thought him strictly dependable. Even I have been afraid at times he has inherited a stupid folly of grandeur hallucination—from my father, who, as I have confessed to you, Sara, was a weak minister who in dreams confused Napoleon with himself and with God. [*Her tone has become strange, and bitterly sneering, and she stares before her, smiling with a taunting scorn. Abruptly she checks herself and turns to Sara with a change to a tone of growing, condescending pity.*] So we must be fair and not punish his naughtiness too severely, poor boy.

SARA [*with condescending pity*] Ah no, we know he loves us and means no harm, poor darling.

DEBORAH [*a threat in her tone now*] But we better make it clear to him right now we will not tolerate any more of his malicious meddling in our affairs. [*She turns to Simon.*] Listen, Simon. When you interrupted us we were discussing your stupid attempt to ruin the peace and harmony of your home and destroy with your morbid jealousy the trust and loving friendship that exists between your wife and mother—

SARA [*bitterly*] Yes, wouldn't it divert him from worrying about the Company to have us fight a duel to the death to see which of us he'd deign to give his love to!

DEBORAH [*coldly*] Unfortunately, Simon, while you may be extremely successful in swindling men at their childish gambling for material possessions, you are far too transparent to cheat us with your obviously marked cards and clumsily loaded dice when you venture to play for the possession of love.

SARA Yes, we're more than a match for you there. So you'd better stop right now, for your own good.

DEBORAH [*smiles at him now, cajolingly affectionate*] But we have agreed to forgive you, Dear—just because you are such a silly jealous boy.

SARA Because you've proved, Darling, how dearly you love us.

DEBORAH And because, now that we know how much you need our love, we cannot blame you for feeling bitter because we let the children take your place so completely. We admit that was very wrong of us. But, you see, Dear, we had misunderstood your seeming preoccupation with the Company's affairs. You should have told us you couldn't be happy without our love. We were completely taken in by your pretending. [*to Sara—tenderly mocking*] He appeared to be so free; didn't he, Sara?

SARA [*smiles teasingly*] He did. As independent as you please!

DEBORAH [*teasingly penitent*] We are sorry, Dear. We humbly beg your forgiveness.

SARA [*with the same air*] We promise it won't happen again, Darling. We'll never let you out of our love again.

DEBORAH You will be our first born and best beloved again. [*teasing with a coquettish, enticing air*] So now won't you forget and make up with us, Dear? [*Simon continues to stare at the book as if he did not hear them.*]

SARA [*cajolingly*] Come over here and sit with us now, that's a good lad. You look so lost over there alone. [*She moves over and pats the sofa between her and Deborah—enticingly*] Look, you can sit here and have love all around you. What man could ask more of life? [*mockingly*] You'll be between us, as you've been trying to be.

DEBORAH [*laughingly*] Yes, I do not think there is any danger in that now, Sara. [*She pats the sofa invitingly.*] Come, Dear. [*He does not seem to hear. Deborah laughs softly.*] What? Still so vain and stubborn? [*to Sara*] Well, since the mountain is too proud to come to

Mahomet— [*She takes Sara's hand and they rise to their feet. Their arms around each other's waists, they advance on Simon with mocking, enticing smiles. They are like two mothers who, confident of their charm, take a possessive gratification in teasing a young, bashful son. But there is something more behind this—the calculating coquetry of two prostitutes trying to entice a man.*] We must humor his manly pride, Sara. Anything to keep peace in our home! [*She laughs.*]

SARA [*laughingly*] Yes. Anything to give him his way, as long as it's our way! [*They have come to Simon who stares as if he did not notice their approach, and yet instinctively shrinks back in his chair. They group together in back of him, Deborah at left-rear and Sara at right-rear of his chair. They bend over, each with an arm about the other, until their faces touch the side of his head. Their other arms go around him so that their hands touch on his chest.*]

DEBORAH [*teasing tenderly*] Now don't shrink back into yourself, Dear. Why are you so afraid?

SARA [*teasing tenderly*] We're not going to eat you, Darling, if you are that sweet. [*Their arms hug him, tenderly possessive.*]

SIMON [*tensely, his eyes in a fixed stare on the page of his book, thinking with a mingling of fascinated dread and an anguished yearning*] I cannot keep them separate—they will not remain divided—they unite in spite of me—they are too strong here in their home—the stronghold of woman, the possessor of children—it is a mistake in strategy to attack them here—they unite against the invader—they hate as one— [*more confusedly*] But I must remember they only seem to become one—it is due to the confusion of my thoughts—it exists only in my mind—an hallucination, a dream, not a fact of reality—but I feel her arms around me—they are real—and she is good now, not evil—she loves me—she does not hate me because she loves me, as she always did before—I need not fear her revenge—that she is waiting for an opportunity to get rid of me—no, I can trust her now at last—she is mine and so I can surrender and be hers, as I have always desired— [*He relaxes with a dreamy smile of content in their arms and murmurs drowsily in gentle wonder.*] Why, I see clearly now that this is the final conquest and peace I

must have had in mind when I planned my campaign—and I have
won the deciding victory over them already! [*He gives a strange
chuckle of satisfaction, and closes his eyes.*]

DEBORAH [*smiles, maternally gloating and tenderly possessive*] You see,
Sara. There was no cause for us to be afraid. [*with a strange contemptuous arrogance*] I can always, whenever I wish, make him my
little boy again. [*She kisses him on the cheek.*] Can't I, Dear?

SARA [*gives her a quick resentful jealous look*] I wasn't the one who
was afraid. Don't I know whenever I want, I can make him my
lover again, who'd give anything he has for me! [*She kisses his
other cheek.*] Can't I, Darling? [*She and Deborah suddenly turn
and stare at each other with defiant, jealous enmity over his head,
pulling their hands away so they no longer touch on his chest, but
each still holds him. Simon starts and stiffens in his chair.*]

DEBORAH [*fighting with herself*] Sara—forgive me—I didn't mean—
it's what he did in the garden made me forget— [*pleadingly*] But
we mustn't let ourselves forget, Sara. We must remember what he
has tried to do! We must keep united and defend the peace of our
home as one woman or—

SARA [*penitently*] I know—I shouldn't have said—it's what he did to
me at the office—but I won't forget again. [*Their hands touch around
Simon again but now he strains forward against them.*]

SIMON [*thinking bitterly*] Fool! To allow myself to be swindled by
that mad dream again! Your final victory and peace, eh? Are you
insane? She loves none but herself, I tell you! She is greedy and
evil! Trust her and you will only find yourself again driven out beyond a wall, with nothing, with the door slammed shut forever behind you, and the sound of her mocking arrogant laughter—left
alone to marry the first unscrupulous schemer with a beautiful body
you meet who wishes to sell herself and fulfill her greedy ambition
to own a slave and use him to acquire children and wealth and a
nouveau-riche estate!— No! [*He jerks forward to his feet from their
arms. They each give a frightened pleading cry. He turns to stare
from one to the other for a moment in a dazed awakening confusion—stammering*] Ah! You are both there. I thought—I beg your
pardon—I must have dozed off again and dreamed— [*then with in-*

creasing hostility and derision] But no, it couldn't have been all a dream, for I remember your coming over to me. I remember watching you with amusement and saying to myself: What damned hypocrites they are! By God, if I didn't know each of them so well I would be swindled into believing in their sincerity! Each has learned tricks of deceit from the other! Mother has made Sara almost as convincing an actress as she is, while she has stolen from Sara a false appearance of honest frankness which lends a common natural air to her romantic artificiality! [*then curtly and rudely*] Well, now that the little farce is over, if you will permit me to sit down and return where you belong— [*The two women's faces grow cold and hostile and defiant. But they are also full of dread.*]

DEBORAH [*ignoring him, takes Sara's hand*] Come, Sara. [*They pass behind him to sit on the sofa side by side, as before, clasping each other's hand. They stare at Simon defiantly and apprehensively. He sits in his chair and stares at his book again, pretending to ignore them.*]

SIMON [*thinking uneasily*] I feel their hate again—there is no doubt now it is against me—it was a stupid blunder to attack them openly in the woman's home where they have made themselves so strong— my attack has only served to unite them— [*calculatingly*] But one learns by one's mistakes—in future, I shall wait until I have each alone—at the office—the garden—at night here, I shall remain apart— lock myself in my study, if need be, for greater safety—safety?— what nonsense!—what have I to fear?—it is I who deal the cards and control the game—who cannot lose— [*calculating more confidently and gloatingly now*] Yes, if I am not here they must turn upon each other—they cannot keep up this pretense—which is all for my benefit— [*He gives them a quick glance—then, as his eyes meet their hostility, he hastily brings them back to his work—uneasily*] How they stare—their hatred for me is obvious now—I shall be glad to be alone in my study—I can think of something more important than this damned, petty domestic war—I almost regret now I ever should have considered it important enough to make its confusion a decisive issue— [*He suddenly looks up but avoids their eyes— with a forced angry resentment*] For God's sake, why do you stare like that? Have you no business of your own to mind, or no thought of your own to think? [*He snaps his book shut and springs to his feet—angrily to conceal his apprehension*] Can I never have a moment's privacy in my own home in which I can think clearly? I work like a slave all day to stuff your insatiable maws with luxury and wealth and gross security for the rearing of children! Is it too much to ask in return that I be permitted a little peace of mind at night here, and not have my thoughts constantly invaded and distracted? [*with an attempt at assertive dictatorial authority that rings hollow*] You force me to remind you of a fact you have chosen to ignore, that I am the man of this household and the master. I will not tolerate any more of your interference! If you persist in it, I will be compelled to force either one or the other of you to leave my home—and my life!—forever! That is my final warning! [*He turns toward the door at left, avoiding their eyes. His domineering tone becomes even less convincing.*] I'm going to my study. Hereafter, I shall spend my evenings there alone, and you may do as you please. Tear this house apart, destroy it, devour each other in your jealous rage and hatred, if you must, until only one of you survives! After all, that would be one solution of— But leave me alone! I will not let you involve me and attempt to tear me in half between you! It will be useless for you to try to hound me in my study, for I shall lock myself in! [*He strides to the study door and opens it—then turns, avoiding their eyes, and murmurs in strange, confused, weakly apologetic tones.*] I—I beg your pardon for being rude—I am worn out—have worked too hard on this railroad deal—and now I have it, I seem to have nothing—in victory I feel defeated—the winnings seem like disguised losses—that naturally confuses my mind— [*He pauses. Suddenly he has the beaten quality of one begging for pity. But they remain staring as one at him, their eyes hard and unforgiving. He stammers appealingly.*] You—you know how much I love each of you—it is only when you unite to dispossess me that you compel me to defend my right to what is mine—all I ask is that each of you keep your proper place in my mind—do not trespass or infringe on the other's property— [*Abruptly his tone becomes slyly taunting.*] But I am forgetting I arranged all that today. I will leave you now to inform each other of the secret you are each so cunningly concealing. I think, when you have, the issue will be quite clear and free of confusion. [*He smiles sneeringly but is afraid to meet their eyes. He turns quickly, goes in his study, and locks the door. They stare at the door. There is a moment's silence.*]

DEBORAH [*slowly, hardly above a whisper, but with a taunting, threatening scorn in her tone*] He has locked the door. [*She smiles faintly.*] I have a suspicion, Sara, that our big jealous boy has become very frightened and wishes now he hadn't been so wicked—now, when it's too late.

SARA [*smiling faintly*] I have the same suspicion myself, Deborah.

DEBORAH [*uneasily*] Too late for him, I mean. We have seen through him. We know what he is trying to do. We know what he really is now, in his heart. How vindictive and evil—and mad! I do not recognize him now as the son I gave life to—and once loved. And I am sure you do not recognize in this strange evil man, embittered and hateful—

SARA [*bitterly*] No, he's not the man I loved and gave myself to. I never would have—to this man.

DEBORAH [*urgent and a little desperate*] But we mustn't let him make it too late for us—to continue to be as we have been to each other. We have proved now that as long as we constantly remember that this is something his mind is trying to do to our minds—to make them as evil and vindictive—and mad!—as his—to poison them with his hatred—we can successfully defend our home from ruin and remain united in trust and friendship and love, and keep him outside us where he is powerless, and in the end force him to surrender and submit rather than have us drive him from his home! Promise me you will never forget this, Sara. I swear to you I will not!

SARA And I swear it to you, Deborah! I know it's all the poison in his mind trying to make our minds the slave of his, so he can own us body and soul. Do you think I could ever hate you the way I did when you came in with him from the garden, if he hadn't poisoned my mind with the past at his office?

DEBORAH [*slowly*] Yes, he is very clever at poisoning with the past. [*She shudders—then urgently*] But we have sworn to each other! We will remember it is he and not us!

SARA Yes.

DEBORAH [*hesitates uneasily—then trying desperately to be confidently matter-of-fact, and forcing a smile*] Then I think we can now safely tell each other what the arrangements he spoke of are. As far as I am concerned, I was hiding mine from you only because he said he wished to tell you and made me promise I wouldn't.

SARA He did the same with me. [*with a sudden underlying hostility*] I was only too eager to let you know. [*then guiltily*] I mean—

DEBORAH [*stiffening*] Yes, I can imagine you were. But I think not any more eager than I was— [*She checks herself. In silence, the two women fight together within themselves to conquer this hostility. Then Deborah says gently.*] Tell me your secret, Daughter. Whatever it is, I will remember it is his doing, and I will understand.

SARA [*gratefully*] Thank you, Mother. And I'll understand when you tell me— [*She blurts out hastily with an undercurrent of guilty defiance.*] It's nothing much. He got me to agree to work with him at his office from now on. I'm to start tomorrow—

DEBORAH [*her expression startled and unable to conceal an uprush of jealous hate*] Ah! Then you are the woman he boasted he was living with as a— [*Instinctively she withdraws her hand from Sara's.*]

SARA [*bitterly*] You said you'd understand!

DEBORAH [*contritely—grabbing her hand again*] I will! I do!

SARA [*hurriedly and guiltily evasive*] I'm to be his secretary and a secret partner. He seemed so nervous and tired out and distracted, and he asked me wouldn't I please help him with his work and share— It's something I always used to want to do. I used to feel I was shut out of that part of his life. [*appealingly*] You can understand that, Deborah?

DEBORAH [*sneeringly*] I can. I know only too well how greedy— [*fighting this back—guiltily*] I mean, it is your right. Of course I understand, Sara.

SARA [*reacting to the sneer—defensively*] It's my right, surely. I'm glad you admit that. [*A gloating boast comes into her tone.*] He said he was so lonely. He said he missed me so much and wouldn't I let him have a life just with me again away from home. He said I was still so beautiful to him and how much he wanted me, and I knew he was telling the truth, so I was only too happy to give my consent.

DEBORAH [*angrily*]   Ah! [*She again jerks her hand away.*]

SARA [*guiltily*]   I'm sorry. I didn't mean to boast. [*She reaches for Deborah's hand again.*] But that isn't all of it. Wait till you hear the rest and you won't be angry. I could feel the change in him as he is now in his office—that he's grown so greedy and unscrupulous and used to having his own way as head of the Company, that if I re- fused him, he'd only buy another woman to take my place and I'd lose him. [*pleadingly*] So you see he had the power to make me con- sent. You can understand that, can't you? You're a woman, too.

DEBORAH [*tensely*]   I am making myself understand. Besides, this has nothing to do with me. It is entirely your business.

SARA [*bitterly*]   Yes, business. That's the way he talked. You'd think he was making a deal for his Company. If you think I liked him in- sulting his wife and acting as if I was a street whore he'd picked up and was asking her price—

DEBORAH [*tensely*]   Why should I think of it, Sara? It's entirely your affair. [*She pauses—then strangely with an increasingly bitter vin- dictiveness.*] But—you appealed to me as a woman, didn't you? You mean forget he is anything to me. I can. I have forgotten him sev- eral times before in my life. Completely as if he had never been born. That is what he has never forgiven. If I were in your place I would hate him, and I would revenge myself by becoming what he wished me to be! I would become it so ruthlessly that, in the end, he would feel cursed by having what he wanted! I would make him pay for me until I had taken everything he possessed! I would make all his power my power! Until I had stripped him bare and utterly ruined him! Until I had made him a weak slave with no ambition left but his greed for me! And when he had no more to pay me, I would drive him out of my life to beg outside my door! And I would laugh at him and never permit him to return—! [*She stops abruptly— guiltily*] But it is really none of my business, Sara. I do not mean to interfere between husband and wife or presume to advise you. [*confusedly*] I—I don't see how I can have such vile, disgusting dreams—unless he is still thinking of us in his study, his mind still deliberately willing to poison mine. [*with a flash of renewed vindic- tiveness*] And as a woman I still say it would be poetic justice if you destroyed him by giving him his desire! And as a woman, my pride will glory in your revenge— [*then hastily and guiltily*] I hope you understand, Sara, and do not think I am a cruel, evil mother.

SARA [*with a vindictive smile—strangely*]   I understand well enough. If you think there isn't a woman in me who felt exactly like that the moment I guessed what he was up to, you don't know me! And he doesn't! But he'll find out— [*then guiltily*] I don't know how I can think such wickedness—except it's what you said that he's still poisoning us. [*abruptly changing the subject*] But now tell me what he made you agree to that you've been hiding. I'll understand, whatever it is, that he did it.

DEBORAH [*with a strange vengeful gleam in her eye*]   Yes, we have been forgetting my part of it, haven't we? Well, it's merely this, Sara, that he begged me to give him a life alone with me again away from his office and his home.

SARA [*stares at her suspiciously*]   What do you mean? [*Instinctively she starts to pull her hand away from Deborah.*]

DEBORAH [*with a trace of mockery*]   Now, now. You promised to understand. [*Sara controls herself. Deborah goes on matter-of-factly.*] He begged me to let him keep me company in my garden every evening from now on. [*Sara stiffens with hostility and then fights it back.*] And, as I know how lonely I would be in the future without the children—

SARA [*eagerly*]   But I've told you you'll have them back. You asked me if you could.

DEBORAH [*with a taunt underlying her cool persuasive tone*]   Yes, but I had forgotten then— No, Sara, you are very generous and I am most grateful, but I really will not need them, now that I have my own son again.

SARA [*gives way to a flash of jealous, uneasy anger*]   Ah, and so that's what it is! I knew I shouldn't have let him go to you! I've always known if you were ever given the chance—! [*She jerks her hand from Deborah's.*]

DEBORAH [*pleading now frightenedly, grabbing Sara's hand*]   Sara! You promised to remember! But it's my fault. I'm afraid I sounded as if I were taunting you. Forgive me. I really didn't mean— The truth

is—I didn't want him in my garden ever again. I hated him for forcing his way in. But then he lied and made me hate you. He tricked
me into remembering the past with him. He made himself appear
like a little boy again, so forlorn and confused and lost in himself—
needing my love so terribly! So I couldn't help but consent. Surely,
as a mother, you can understand that, Sara!

SARA [*has controlled herself—tensely*] I do, Deborah. I've sons of my
own and I know how I'll long to have them back after they've left
me.

DEBORAH [*with a sort of taunting satisfaction*] Then you have no objection, Sara?

SARA [*defensively*] Why should I? You're his mother. You've a right.
And I'll have my own sons all to myself now. I'll have him all day
at the office. No, you're entirely welcome. [*with a strange bitter vindictiveness*] And when I think of the way he swindled me into letting him go to your garden—and of all he's done today to make us
hate each other—I tell you, as woman to woman, I hate him [so
much] that if I was in your place I'd give him his wish, and I'd let
him go back and back into the past until he gets so lost in his dreams
he'd be no more a man at all, but a timid little boy hiding from life
behind my skirts! Or, better still, no more than a nursing baby with
no life or hunger of his own outside me! And I'd dandle him on my
lap and laugh at his mad cries for liberty! [*then abruptly ashamed
and uneasy*] But those are evil thoughts he's putting in my mind.
I'd never think them myself.

DEBORAH [*with a strange bold manner*] There is no need to be ashamed
before me, Sara. I admit that has occurred to my mind, too—in the
garden when I hated him for intruding— After all, if he will insist
on trespassing in the past—! [*She gives a soft, gloating little laugh.*]
Yes, I do not think we have anything to fear, Sara. Between us we
can soon force him to realize how foolish he was to destroy the peace
and harmony of our house. In a very short time, he will feel torn
apart and driven quite insane between us, and he will beg us on his
knees to restore that peace and not punish his wickedness anymore,
but forgive him and take him back into our home again!

SARA [*vindictively*] And won't I laugh to see him beg!

DEBORAH We will both laugh. [*They laugh softly together.*] And this, I think, will be his last rebellion. He has fought for liberty before and was beaten. He must be very tired. After this defeat, I believe, he will scream with fear if anyone ever mentions the word freedom. [*then urgently*] But we must keep on understanding each other! We must never forget our purposes are identical. We must trust each other and remain united in spirit, friends and allies, and never let him make us hate each other! Let us swear that again, Sara!

SARA I swear I won't!

DEBORAH And I swear! [*She smiles contentedly and pats Sara's hand.*] That's settled, then. Now I think we can safely forget him and be as we have been on so many other nights—simple and contented and at peace with each other and with life.

SARA [*smiling*] I'd like nothing better, and it's a help to have him out of the room so we don't have to wonder what he's thinking to himself. [*with a change of tone to that of the doting mother*] Tell me about the children when they were with you in the garden, like you always do.

DEBORAH [*smiling fondly*] Of course I will. [*Then she pauses, trying to remember—finally she admits guiltily*] I can't seem to— I'm afraid I have entirely forgotten, Sara.

SARA [*piqued—resentfully*] You've always remembered before.

DEBORAH [*reproachfully*] Now! I know I have, but— A lot of things have happened since then to disturb my mind.

SARA [*contrite in her turn*] Ah, don't I know. [*then uneasily*] And they're still happening. Even if he is locked in his study. I can still feel his thoughts reaching out—

DEBORAH [*with a little shiver of dread*] Yes, I, too— [*There is a pause during which they both stare straight before them. The expression of each changes swiftly, mirroring what is entering their minds, and becomes sly and evasive and gloatingly calculating. Their clasped hands, without their being aware of it, let go and draw apart. Then each sneaks a suspicious, probing glance at the other. Their eyes meet and at once each looks away and forces a hypocritically affectionate, disarming smile. Deborah speaks quickly and lightly.*] How quiet we are. What are you thinking, Daughter?

SARA [*quickly and lightly*]   Of how foolish men can be, Mother, never content with what we give them, but always wanting more.

DEBORAH [*lightly*]   Yes, they never grow up. They remain greedy little boys demanding the moon.

SARA [*getting up from the sofa*]   I'll get my sewing, to keep myself occupied, and come back to you.

DEBORAH   Yes, do. And I will read my book. [*Sara goes slowly toward her old chair at left-front of table. Deborah's eyes remain fixed on her and abruptly her expression changes to one of arrogant disdainful repulsion and hatred and she thinks.*] You vile degraded slut!— as if I could ever believe your lies again!—as if you needed encouragement from me to become the vulgar grasping harlot you were born to be!—but I am glad I encouraged you because that is the one sure way to make him loathe the sight of you—in the end he will know you for what you are and you will so disgust him that he will drive you out of his life into the gutter where you belong!—you are too stupid to see this—but I see!—and I will see to it he sees!

SARA [*having come to the chair, fiddles around unnecessarily gathering up her sewing things, keeping her back turned to Deborah while she thinks*]   She must think I'm the greatest fool was ever born if she hopes I'd ever trust her again—as if he'd waste his time in her garden every evening humoring her crazy airs and graces if she hadn't begged him to!—but let her look out, what tricks she'll be up to to take him from me—I'll keep what's mine from her if I have to drive her into the asylum itself! [*A pause. She stands motionless, her back to Deborah. Both their expressions change to a triumphant possessive tenderness.*]

DEBORAH [*thinking*]   Then my beloved son will have no one but me!

SARA [*thinking*]   Then my Darling will have only me! [*She turns, making her face smilingly expressionless and goes back toward the sofa.*]

* * * CURTAIN * * *

Act Four, Scene One

―――

SCENE *Same as Scene One of Act Three—Simon's private office. Changes have been made in its appearance. A sofa has been added to the furniture. Placed at front, center, it is too large for the room, too garishly expensive and luxurious, its blatant latest-stylishness in vulgar contrast to the sober, respectable, conservatism of the old office of Simon's father. It offends the eye at once, as an alien presence. It has the quality of a painted loud-mouthed bawd who has forced her way in and defied anyone to put her out.*

Other changes are a mirror in an ornate gilt frame hanging over Sara's high desk at right, rear, and tacked on the right wall beside her desk is a large architect's drawing in perspective of a pretentious, nouveau-riche country estate on the shore of a small private lake with a beach in the foreground and a wharf with small pleasure craft moored to it. A road leads back from the wharf up an elaborately terraced hill to an immense mansion, a conglomerate of various styles of architecture, as if additions had been added at different times to an original structure conceived on the model of a medieval, turreted castle. At rear, on one side of this edifice, are imposing stables. Surrounding these buildings on three sides are woods that have been cleared and made into a park.

It is an early morning in midsummer of the following year, 1841.

Sara is discovered seated on the high stool before her desk, working with a ruler and drafting instruments on a plan. A marked change is noticeable in her appearance. Her body has grown strikingly voluptuous, and provocatively female. She is dressed extravagantly in flamboyant clothes, designed with the purpose of accentuating her large breasts, her slender waist, her heavy rounded thighs and buttocks, and revealing them as nakedly as the fashion will permit. Her face has a bloated, flushed, dissipated, unhealthy look with dark shadows under her eyes. There is something feverishly nervous and morbidly excited about it. Its prettiness has been coarsened and vulgarized. Her mouth seems larger, its full lips redder, its stubborn character become repellently sensual, ruthlessly cruel and greedy. Her eyes have hardened, grown cunning and calculating and unscrupulous. There is a stray suggestion in her face now of a hardened prostitute, particularly in its defiant defensive quality, that of one constantly anticipating attack by a brazen assertiveness which concedes a sense of guilt. Her manner varies between an almost masculine curt abruptness and brutal frankness, plainly an imitation and distortion of Simon's professional manner, and a calculating feminine seductiveness which constantly draws attention to her body.

The door from the bookkeeper's room at right, is opened noiselessly, and Joel Harford enters, closing the door behind him. He is the same in appearance, retains the cold emotionless mask of his handsome face. But there is a startling change in his manner which now seems weak, insecure and furtive, as though he were thrown off balance by some emotion he tries to repress, which fascinates and at the same time humiliates him. For a moment he stands glancing about the room vaguely, his gaze avoiding Sara. She is conscious of his presence but ignores him. Finally his eyes fasten on her and, seeing she is apparently absorbed in her work, he stares up and down the curves of her body with a sly, greedy desire.

SARA [*suddenly explodes angrily in a snapping of nerves, slamming her rule on the desk and turning on him, her voice stridently domineering as though she were rebuking a servant*] Don't stand there gawking! What do you want? Speak up! [*But before he can do so she goes on more angrily.*] How dare you come in here without knocking? You know Simon's orders! And I've ordered you! You better remember, if you want to keep your job! [*then controlling her anger—curtly*] Well? What is it?

JOEL [*has cringed for a second, then immediately has regained his cold poise*] Mr. Tenard, the banker, is in the outer office. I thought, considering his position, I had better announce him myself.

SARA [*with gloating scorn*] His position, is it? His position now is under Simon's feet, and my feet, as he very well knows!

JOEL He states he had a letter from you making an appointment with Simon.

SARA That's true. I wrote him at Simon's dictation. What Simon wants of him I can't see. We've taken his bank from him. He's stripped bare. [*then with a cunning greedy smile*] But he must have something we want, or Simon wouldn't waste time on him. [*curtly*] Well, you see Simon's not here yet. Tell Tenard to wait.

JOEL [*making no move to go—emotionlessly*] My brother seems to be late every day now.

SARA [*betraying an inner uneasiness by forcing a too-careless tone*] Ah, he's taken to paying your old mother a morning visit in her garden as well as in the evening. She's failing rapidly in her mind, poor woman, growing childish and living altogether in her dreams. Simon thinks he ought to humor her all he can so she won't take leave of her senses altogether. [*abruptly, forcing a laugh*] And what if he is late? He knows, the way he's trained me, I can take care of anything here as well as he could.

JOEL [*with an undercurrent of spite*] As long as you don't mind his keeping *you* waiting.

SARA [*stares at him—defensively*] Just what do you mean by that?

JOEL [*betraying an inner jealous excitability, his eyes unconsciously fixed on the sofa—sneeringly*] I—I am not unaware why you are so insistent about my knocking before I—intrude.

SARA [*watching him, her face lighting up with a cunning satisfaction— her expression very like a prostitute's now as she smiles seductively and mockingly*] So that's what's bothering you! Well, that's my business.

JOEL [*his eyes fixed fascinatedly on her now*] Your business! Yes, I quite realize you are—what you are.

SARA [*plainly enjoying this, moves her body seductively—teasingly*] And what am I, Joel Darlin'?

JOEL [*trying to take his eyes from her*] I—I am fully aware of the means you have used in the past year to get my brother to sign over his interests one by one to you.

SARA   You don't think my love is worth it?

JOEL [*stammers*] I would not use the word love—

SARA [*teasingly*] Why wouldn't you? You're a sentimental fool, I'm afraid, Joel. What else is love, I'm asking you? [*Suddenly she looks guilty and repelled—hastily*] No! That's Simon's idea, not mine!

JOEL   I suppose you pride yourself you have cunningly swindled him? [*He laughs gratingly.*] But it's the other way round. It's you who have been swindled!

SARA [*angrily*] That's a lie! [*scornfully*] You fool, you! Do you think, after all he's taught me, I haven't learned to get all I'm worth to him?

JOEL [*ignoring this—sneeringly*] All this imposing edifice of power and greed he has built so unscrupulously—which you have him to put in your name—what is it in fact but a house of cards? You know he has been gambling more and more recklessly in the past year. It was bad enough before you came here, but since he started playing Napoleon to show off his genius to you, he has abandoned all caution! Debt has been piled upon debt! If you had to pay the debts on the properties he has made over to you tomorrow—there would be nothing left! His position, and yours, depends entirely upon the myth he has created of his invincibility, his uncanny luck, that his touch turns everything to gold! But once let the slightest doubt arise, and his enemies see his true position—and their opportunity to revenge themselves—and strip you of everything you possess.

SARA [*with forced defiance*] Let them try! They couldn't! He'll always beat the world! [*then abruptly—frightened and shaken*] Oh, I know, Joel! Sometimes, I go mad worrying! But I can't stop him. And when he's with me, I think what he thinks. I can't help it!

JOEL [*ignores this—with a strange air of being fascinated by the danger*] I tell you there is danger every second. It would take only a rumor. A whisper spoken in the right ear. This banker who is waiting. How he must hate Simon. If he had the slightest inkling—

SARA [*fascinatedly*] I know. [*then frightenedly*] Joel! You sound as though you'd like— [*imploringly*] You wouldn't—!

JOEL [*jerking himself back to his pose—coldly*] I? You insult my life-long loyalty to the Company. Do you believe everyone is like you and Simon, devoid of all probity and honor? [*then with almost a smirk*] Besides, you forget I still own an interest—which is not yet for sale, although I might consider— [*hastily*] I'm merely pointing out that you had been swindled. [*sneeringly*] But you would realize [it] if you spent more time examining the true value of his gifts and less on designing your impossible Irish-Castle-in-Spain. [*He indicates the plan on the wall scornfully.*]

SARA [*furiously*] Impossible, is it? We'll see! That's one debt I'll make him pay—the debt the Harfords owe my father's daughter! [*abruptly changing to a scornful curt tone*] I'm a fool to listen to your silly gab. I ought to know well enough by this to laugh at you, the way Simon does, for an old stick-in-the-mud always prophesying ruin and—! [*harshly*] Get back to your work! You're wasting my time and I'm sick of you! [*She turns back to her desk.*]

JOEL [*stands staring at her, then moves mechanically to the door at right and is about to open it when suddenly he turns—angrily*] I do protest! I own an interest; it is my right. I protest against you and my brother turning this office—my father's office—into a brothel room for your lust! Everyone is getting to know—to smirk and whisper! It is becoming an open scandal—a filthy public disgrace! I— [*He stammers to a halt—his eyes fixed on her in helpless fascination. She has turned to him and again there is the look of a smiling prostitute about her face.*]

SARA [*smiling and moving her body seductively—teasingly*] Now, Joel, Darlin', you shouldn't look at me like that, and me your brother's wife. [*She laughs provokingly.*]

JOEL [*fighting with himself—stammers*] I do not understand you. I do not see why you should laugh—like a common street woman. My brother's wife should have more modesty. I was only looking at your new dress and admiring it. Simon buys you a new dress every week now. Is that part of the bargain? You should not let his greed turn his wife into a low woman whose beauty is for sale! I protest! [*He swallows as if he were strangling and tears his eyes from her teasing gloating ones—he stammers*] No, no! I do not mean—I ask your pardon for saying such things. It is not like me at all. The truth is I have changed in the past year. I do not recognize myself. I disgust myself. It is the atmosphere of disgusting greed here which has become so vilely intensified since you came. I no longer recognize this as my father's office—or myself as my father's son. Something has happened to make me greedy, too. So please forgive and overlook—

SARA [*her prostitute air gone—pitying and frightened*] Oh, don't I know? Haven't I changed, too, so I don't know myself. Don't I disgust myself, at times. But it's not me. It's Simon. It's what he wants. I've got to be what he wants. He makes me want to be what he wants! [*controlling herself—simply*] I forgive you, Joel. And please forgive me.

JOEL [*gently*] I? Of course, Sara. And thank you for your kindness and understanding. [*dully*] I'll go back to my work now. [*He turns to the door but again, with his hand on the knob his eyes fix on her body and grow greedy and he stammers.*] I only wish to say—I've quite decided to sell my interest in the business—that is, to you, if you would care to consider— [*He stops— Again the prostitute leer has been called back to her face. She laughs teasingly. He wrenches open the door and flings himself into the bookkeeper's room, slamming the door behind him.*]

SARA [*looks after him, smiling to herself with a cheap vanity*] Who'd think it of him? So stuck-up and full of don't-touch-me airs! One of the high and mighty Yankee Harfords! And now I've got him under my feet, begging! He'd pay all he's got! I could strip him bare—and cheat him in the bargain—pretend when I'd really give him nothing! [*She chuckles.*] The fools of men! It's too easy for us to cheat them! They want to be cheated so they can cheat themselves! [*She stares in the mirror at herself admiringly—coquettishly in brogue*] Who'd have dreamed it Sara Melody—you in your beauty to have such power over bright and mighty men! By the Eternal, as my father used to swear, I think you could take what you wanted from any one of them! And if he is a poor slave of a bookkeeper, he's a handsome man, and he owns an interest— [*She suddenly shivers with repulsion and tears her eyes from the mirror strickenly—in a guilty whisper*] God forgive me! Me, to have such thoughts! Like a dirty whore smiling at men in the street and showing her leg! What's happened to me. A year ago and I'd never have dreamed such a thought, not even in sleep, but now it seems natural—to be a part of me— [*She stares around her frightenedly.*] It's being here so long, working as his whore, with no life except in his greed—with my children running wild at home as if they had no mother—while I sit here like a miser counting gold, making plans for the grand estate I'll have, or dreaming of my mills and my ships on the sea and my railroad that he's paid me for using my body like a dirty whore's—he's made me think that life means selling yourself, and pride is to get the highest price you can, and that love is lust—it's only lust he wants—and he's made me feel it's all I want and if I didn't have that hold on him, I'd lose him!— she'd take him back with her entirely— [*then with angry defiance*] She'll never! He may forget me when he's with her but once I've got him here, I've only to kiss him and he forgets she's alive! And what if I was having thoughts about Joel? It was only what every woman thinks at times in her heart—was any one of us ever content with one man?—who didn't feel she was worth more—that she'd been swindled by marriage—who didn't want every man to want her to prove her worth to herself, who didn't feel, if she was free, she could get more for herself— [*vindictively*] Let him look out how he comes here late and keeps me waiting his pleasure, like a slave, or I'll show him I can have what I want without him, and get my price for it, too. [*She laughs spitefully—then suddenly tears her eyes from the mirror and shrinks into herself with horrified disgust.*] Ah, you dirty whore, you! Oh, God help me! I must be going daft—as daft as that mad old witch in her garden. [*then with increasing anger*] And who wouldn't be daft, going home every night to that hell with her? Never a moment's peace—hating her and feeling her hate me—watching every move she makes and knowing she's watching me—knowing it's a duel to the death between us—if she'd only leave me alone!—if she'd only be content with what's hers and not try to steal what's mine!—but she's bound she'll get him away from me, and make him drive me out in the street— [*with threatening hatred*] But by God, he can't! And I won't stand much more from her!— She's driving me too far—a little more and my hate will have no pity left! I know her weakness and her fear of going crazy—I'll drive her into the asylum where she belongs, the mad old fool! She's making this life too small for the two of us! One of us must go— and by the Powers it won't be me! [*then hastily*] But let's pray I won't need to, and I can get rid of her the way we planned. Now Simon has the bank I'll make him stop wanting more and let the profit add up. I'll pay off the debts, and we'll sell out and I'll build the estate and I'll pay her a pension to stay alone in her garden. [*trying to reassure herself*] Yes, it won't take long—I'll soon be rid of her. [*then distractedly*] If he'll only let me!— If I'll only let myself not want more and more! [*She jumps from her stool and paces around in a nervous panic.*] Why doesn't he come?— I can't bear life without him with me!— What makes him so late?— That mad old witch keeps him dreaming in her garden to make him late on purpose to torment me! [*in a fury*] And he knows it! He lets her do it!— Well, I won't wait, my fine Simon! Not alone! I've stood enough from you! I'll call in Joel to keep me company!— I'll change entirely to the whore you want me to be, and we'll see how you like that! [*She is moving towards the bookkeeper's room when the door from the rear is opened and Simon comes in. He has changed greatly, grown terribly thin, his countenance is ravaged and pale and haggard, his eyes deep sunken. There is, however, a strange expression of peace and relaxation on his face as he enters, a look of bemused dreaminess in his eyes.*]

SARA [*with a cry of hypocritical happy relief, rushes and throws her arms around him and hugs him passionately*] Oh, Darling! I love you so! [*Then her tension snapping, she bursts into sobs and hides her face against his shoulder.*]

SIMON [*looks startled and bewildered as if only half awakened from a dream—pats her shoulder mechanically—vaguely*] There, there. [*He stares around him, thinking and frowning, as though not quite realizing yet where he is or how he got there.*]

SARA [*stops crying instantly at the tone of his voice—jerks back, holding him by the shoulders, and stares into his face—frightened and pleading*] Simon! You sound—! [*forcing a joking tone*] For the love of heaven, don't you know where you are or who I am?

SIMON [*trying to force himself from his day dream—vaguely placating*] Of course, Sara. Don't be silly. [*Then he relapses and smiles with a bemused pleasure and speaks dreamily.*] Do you know, this morning, talking with Mother, I suddenly remembered something I had never remembered before. Nothing important. Just an incident in her garden long ago. The astonishing thing is that she says I wasn't more than a year old at the time. And yet it appeared as clear as if it were yesterday—or was happening again this very morning. Nothing important, as I've said. Childish and meaningless. But it gave me a feeling of power and happiness to be able to recall the past so distinctly.

SARA [*stares at him—frightened and resentful*] Simon! Wake up! You're here with me! [*She kisses him fiercely.*] Come back to me! To hell with her crazy dreams! I love you! I'm your wife and you're mine! [*She kisses him again.*] Can't you feel how I love you? Tell me you love me.

SIMON [*With a start, awakes completely. His expression changes and becomes tense with desire and he presses her body to his and kisses her passionately.*] Sweetheart! You know I want you more than life!

SARA [*with a sudden revulsion of feeling, pushes back from him—desperately*] No! Please! I want love— [*then forcing a laugh*] But you'll be making fun of me for being a sentimental fool! [*She throws herself in his arms again—passionately*] Oh, I don't care what I am as long as I have you!

SIMON [*passionately*] My dear beautiful mistress! [*He tries to take her to the couch.*]

SARA [*Breaks away from him. The common prostitute calculating look is back in her face now. She laughs tantalizingly.*] Oh, no, you don't! You've a lot of business to attend to. I'll have no laziness. You've got to earn me, you know! You wouldn't want me if I gave myself for nothing, and let you cheat me! Not you! I know you.

You'd think I was a stupid fool not to have learned more from your teaching and example, and your doing your best to train me.

SIMON [*laughs with amused admiration*] You've been a very apt pupil. You'll soon give your master cards and spades. [*teasing derisively*] What do you want me to pay you this time, Beautiful, Insatiable One? You have about all I possess already.

SARA [*greedily*] Well, there's the bank we've just smashed and got control of.

SIMON [*laughingly*] Oh, so that's it! I might have known. In fact, I anticipated and have had the papers drawn. But, of course, I won't sign them until after—

SARA [*mockingly*] Aren't you the cautious one! Are you afraid I'd cheat you? But how do I know you mightn't refuse to sign after—?

SIMON [*laughingly*] Oh, I might like to, but you know I haven't the power anymore. You've taken that from me, too! Your beauty has become more desirable to me than a thousand banks stuffed with gold! [*He tries to draw her to him—passionately*] Darling One! Haven't you learned by this time that my greatest happiness is to prove to you—and to myself—how much you are worth to me? [*He tries to kiss her.*]

SARA [*evading his embrace—coquettishly*] No, I said. Later. [*She kisses him tantalizingly.*] But here's a kiss to bind the bargain.

SIMON But I have to run down to the mill today. As you know there's been some discontent about our lowering wages and the hands are sending a deputation to ask me to reconsider.

SARA [*her face hardening—commandingly*] You put your foot down on that! Fire them! There's plenty to take their place, and starving will teach them a lesson.

SIMON I agree with you. The Company needs every penny of profit from the mill it can possibly extort. [*then smiling*] But about our bargain. You said later, but I can't get back until late afternoon just in time for my evening visit with Mother. So—

SARA [*harshly domineering*] So you'll forget her and only remember me!

SIMON [*struggling to resist—strangely the musing, dreamy expression showing in his face*] But I remember I promised her—

SARA [*harshly*] You'll forget her, I'm saying! [*then moving her body with coarse suggestiveness—with a prostitute's calculating seductive air*] Isn't having me worth that to you? If it isn't, I'll have to find some other man who values me higher.

SIMON [*hungrily*] No, no! Anything you ask!

SARA [*triumphantly, almost sneeringly*] That's better! [*then resentfully and going on with an increasing show of jealous, bitter anger*] And that reminds me, I've a bone to pick with you. You were late again this morning on account of seeing her. I had to sit here alone— waiting and worrying— You let her keep you to make me wait. She did it on purpose to spite me! Ah, don't make excuses for her. Don't I know the hatred and jealousy and the designing greed behind her acting and pretending and her airs and graces of a great lady! It's you she makes a fool of, leading you back to her in the past before you were mine, twisting you around the fingers of her dreams, till you're as mad as she is! But she doesn't fool me! I see through her greedy scheming. And I warn you she'd better watch herself or I'll get to the end of my pity!

SIMON [*his expression has changed during her speech to one of gloating satisfaction. He smiles teasingly.*] What? Don't tell me you're becoming jealous again, Sara?

SARA [*with forced scorn*] Jealous of that ugly old witch, who's old enough to be my mother!

SIMON [*smiling*] Then you mustn't act as if you were. To hear you one would think you feared my poor little old mother as a beautiful dangerous rival.

SARA [*sneeringly*] Her! A skinny wizened hag no man would look at twice!

SIMON [*curtly—in command now*] Very well, then. Why do you talk nonsense? [*sharply matter-of-fact*] We've had this out many times before, Sara. I've explained until I'm tired that I think it advisable, for our own sakes if not for hers, to humor her in any way I can, even if it involves my wasting valuable time—and, if you like, playing the fool myself. You appear to cherish the absurd idea that it is a fascinating happiness for me to sit in a garden with a woman, whose mind is far gone in second childhood, and be forced to watch her greedy spirit, starved by her life-long fear of life, groping in the past and clutching at the dead. [*dryly*] I assure you I can think of many more enjoyable activities— [*He stares at her desirously—with a smile*] Such as being here with you in my arms, Beloved One.

SARA [*gratefully*] Darling!

SIMON [*with a return to his matter-of-fact tone, shrugging his shoulders*] But, after all, I must not complain. Sometimes she amuses me. Sometimes it is restful in her garden. You do not begrudge me a little rest, I hope. Anyway, she is my mother. I owe her some consideration. And someone has to humor her and keep her from being too much alone in her fantastic mind, or we would have a lunatic on our hands.

SARA I've told you before I'm willing to have her have the children for company again, instead of you, and you ought to make her agree—

SIMON [*curtly and resentfully*] Nonsense. I would never permit— She does not want your children now that she has— [*abruptly changing the subject—pleasantly*] But I'll admit, you have reason to complain of me for being late. I have no right to cheat you of time that belongs to you and the Company. I promise in future I'll remember not to humor her into leading my mind so far back that I forget— [*hastily again, going to his desk with his most alert authoritative executive air*] Well, I'll make up for lost time. Tenard is here, isn't he? [*She nods.*] You can tell Joel to have him sent in.

SARA [*Her manner that of an efficient obedient secretary.*] Yes, Sir. [*She opens the door at right, sticks her head in and speaks to Joel— then comes back to the desk opposite Simon and waits for orders.*]

SIMON [*looks at his watch*] I'll have time to dispose of him before I catch my train. You can go back to work on your plans for the estate. [*She turns back toward the desk at right, rear. He glances at the plans—flatteringly, with an undercurrent of mockery*] By the way, my congratulations on the additions you have made since I last examined it.

SARA [*pleased*] I'm glad you like them.

SIMON Now that you'll soon possess a bank, too, you can afford to add still more. [*He smiles—teasingly*] I am sure in your dreams you have already thought of more.

SARA [*with a greedy little laugh*]   Oh, trust me, I can always think of more! [*She stares at the plan—with a strange dreaminess and exultance*] I'll make it the grandest, most beautiful mansion that ever a woman's dream conceived as a house for his pride and her love for her [husband]![1] Ah, won't it be a beautiful life, when I can sit back at my ease there, in the castle of my dreams, in my own house, without a care in the world, with long nights of deep sleep, not turning and twisting in nightmares like I do now, with never a debt, knowing the banks are crammed with my gold, watching my sons grow up handsome rich gentlemen, having my husband and my lover always by me and all of him mine with no will or thought or dream in his heart or brain but the great need to love me!

SIMON [*stares at her back—quietly with a mocking irony tinged with a bitter, tragic sadness*]   There is a poem by Doctor Holmes you should read sometime—for added inspiration. [*He quotes from "The Chambered Nautilus."*][2]

> Build thee more stately mansions, O my soul,
> As the swift seasons roll!
> Leave thy low-vaulted past!
> Let each new temple, nobler than the last,
> Shut thee from heaven with a dome more vast,
> Till thou at length are free,
> Leaving thine outgrown shell—

[*He pauses—then his gaze turned inward, he murmurs aloud to himself, as Sara continues to stare with fascinated, dreamy longing at the plan, not paying any attention to him.*] You must have that engraved over the entrance. And Mother should put it over the magic door to her summerhouse. And I, on the ceiling of this Company's offices—in letters of gold! [*He sneers self-mockingly—then slowly with a sinister determination*] But I will be soon! Oh very

---

1. Carlotta has left a blank here after "her love for her." I inserted "husband" as a logical choice.
2. This poem was written by Oliver Wendell Holmes in 1858, but Simon quotes it in the play in 1841. Holmes' line "Build thee more stately mansions, O my soul" was, of course, O'Neill's inspiration for the title of the play.

soon, now! Either by one way or the other—rid forever of either one or the other—thanks to either Sara or Mother! [*He starts guilt-ily and speaks with a hastily-assumed casualness to Sara.*] I am glad to see, Sara, that you have very properly ignored my stupid muddle-mindedness in remembering childish verses here. I should save such nonsense for my dutiful honoring of my poor old mother.

SARA [*oblivious to him, staring at her plan, her tone becoming more and more coarsely greedy*] Stables full of thoroughbred hunters and fast trotters! Me the great lady, full of airs and graces, riding in my carriage with coachman and footman, through the castle park, or out past the lodge down the road to the city, with the crowds on the street staring, their hearts eaten with envy, and the shopkeepers bowing and scraping, and me gazing down my nose at them, and at the whole pack of the meek, weak, timid, poor poverty-stricken beggars of life! [*vengefully*] No one will ever dare sneer at my origin then, or my poverty! By the Eternal God, I'll spit in their faces and laugh when they thank me kindly for the favor! [*She chuckles viciously—then abruptly her expression changes to one of guilty shame and she exclaims confusedly*] No! I don't mean it! God forgive me, what makes me say such evil, spiteful things? They're not in my dream at all! All I want is a safe home for our love—and peace!

SIMON [*rebukingly gently but firmly*] Now, now! No backsliding into cowardly sentimental remorse, Beautiful Mistress. Remember what I've impressed on you so often in the past year. This office is no garden of dreams. It is a battlefield of reality, where you must face the fact of yourself as you are—and not as you dream you ought to be—where one eats or is eaten. It is silly to be ashamed of the un-desirable fact that the humiliation of the conquered is part of the conqueror's pride in victory.

SARA [*has turned to stare at him fascinatedly—murmurs mechanically*] Yes, I suppose—but— [*There is a knock on the door at rear. At once her attitude becomes that of the efficient secretary.*] That must be Tenard, Sir. Shall I let him in?

SIMON [*A strange, calculating gloating comes into his face.*] No. I've just had an idea, Sara. Let Tenard wait outside the door for awhile

like the ruined beggar he is. It will put him in a more uneasy, recep-
tive frame of mind. [*He gets up from his chair.*] Come and sit in
my place. I want you to handle Tenard, while I watch. You have
learned a great deal in the last year. I am immensely proud of your
rapid progress.

SARA [*uncertainly*] I'm glad, Simon.

SIMON Now I'd like to see you put your knowledge into practice.
Prove that, no matter what happened to me, you are fully competent
to direct the destiny of this Company to a befitting conclusion.

SARA [*uneasily*] What could happen to you?

SIMON [*shrugs his shoulders—carelessly*] Who knows? All men are
mortal. There is always death.

SARA [*frightenedly*] Don't say it, Darling.

SIMON [*in same tone*] Or sickness, accident. Who knows? Life is a
gamble and Fate a master sharper where stacked cards and loaded
dice can cheat the cleverest swindler.

SARA [*frightenedly*] Don't talk like that.

SIMON Or I might simply go away—for a long, much-needed rest.

SARA [*flaring up—with frightened jealous anger*] Ah, I know who
put that in your mind! And I know she'd stop at nothing now to
get you away with her! Not even if she had to drive you as mad as
she is!

SIMON Nonsense! Your jealousy is becoming an insane obsession.
What has that poor childish old woman got to do with it? All I
meant was I might sometime want to leave you in charge. You've
bought the Company, anyway, so—

SARA [*frightenedly*] You'd leave me—? [*then coarsely self-confident,
with her prostitute's seductive smile*] I'd like to see you try to want
to! Don't you know I've bought you, too? [*There is another knock
on the door but neither heeds it.*]

SIMON [*stares at her body—struggling with himself—stammers yearn-
ingly*] Yes, I know—and it's my greatest happiness to belong to
you—to escape myself and be lost in you—I'll pay anything!

SARA [*laughs softly—triumphantly seductive and coarse*] That's my
Simon! That's the way I like you to talk—about life and love—and
not about death, or madness like trying to leave me.

SIMON [*starts toward her—lustfully*] Beloved! [*There is another knock on the door, sharp and impatient. It penetrates and breaks the spell. Simon tears his eyes from her and at once his manner becomes curtly business-like—dryly*] I think our friend is now sufficiently fearful and humiliated. Sit here, Sara. I am confident you can soon show him his place.

SARA [*comes to the desk—smiling gloatingly*] Yes, under my feet, isn't it? [*She laughs softly and sits down in Simon's chair.*] But I don't even know why you had him come, Simon. We've ruined him. He has nothing left we want, has he?

SIMON Yes. A few years of his life. He's past his prime but he's a capable banker and can still be useful to us. Not as he is now, of course. He is too full of old-fashioned ethics and honor. We know that because it made him so open to attack and so easy to ruin. But he can be made to forget all that and become an obedient servant, if you can discover his weakness and then use it without scruple. You will find a couple of notes I made on the pad about his present circumstances. The rest I leave in your capable hands, My Beautiful. Just bear in mind that the end you desire always justifies any means and don't get life confused with sentiment, as you used to. [*He laughs, moving away from her to her desk, at right, rear.*] Pretend to yourself he is I begging for your favors and you cannot fail to swindle him successfully and get what you want. [*There is another, banging knock on the door. He calls curtly.*] Come in!

[*The door is opened and Benjamin Tenard enters. He is a tall, robust, full-chested man in his sixties with a fine-looking Roman face, his clothes expensively conservative. He has the look of success, of financial prosperity still stamped on him from long habit. It is this facade which makes the sense one immediately gets that he is a broken man inside, insecure, bewildered and frightened, all the more pityingly acute. His face as he enters is flushed with humiliated pride.*]

TENARD [*begins to protest insultedly to Simon*] See here, Harford! You made an appointment with me, not I with you! Yet I am allowed to cool my heels in your outer office and then stand outside your door knocking and knocking like someone—!

SARA [*breaks in in a pleasantly indifferent* [*tone*] *without any hint of apology*] Sorry to have kept you waiting, Mr. Tenard. It was necessary. [*He turns to stare at her in surprised confusion not having noticed her at first.*]

TENARD I—I beg your pardon, Mrs. Harford. I did not see—

SARA [*nodding at the chair opposite her*] Won't you sit down?

TENARD [*uncertainly, glancing at Simon*] Thank you.

SIMON [*smiling with cold pleasantness*] It's all right. Your appointment is really with my wife. She has full authority to act for me. So if you will pardon me, I have some important work to do here. [*He nods at the plans on Sara's desk, turns his back on Tenard, sits down, and during the scene between them pretends to be concentrated on the plans. Tenard comes and sits in the chair opposite Sara.*]

SARA [*after a quick glance at the pad—smiling coolly—as she goes on, her tone and manner become more and more an exact mimicry of Simon's executive manner*] I presume you wonder why I wished to see you, Mr. Tenard. Just as I was wondering why you ever consented to come—under the circumstances.

TENARD [*humiliated and guilty*] You mean because your husband is responsible for ruining me?

SARA [*smiling coldly*] Simon does nothing without my consent, Mr. Tenard. I thought that was the cheapest way to take possession of your bank.

TENARD [*unable to keep hate and a look of horror entirely from a glance at her*] Yes, I have heard rumors that you advise him. I could not believe a woman— [*then almost frightenedly as if he is afraid he is prejudicing her against him—avoiding her eye and forcing a smile*] I bear no grudge. All is fair in war. I realize that. Perhaps, I considered the methods used not quite ethical— [*with increasing suppressed bitterness*] —not to say ruthless and unscrupulous. There are some who would describe them in even stronger terms.

SARA [*curtly*] I am not interested in moral attitudes. You owned something I desired. You were too weak to hold it. I was strong enough to take it. I am good because I am strong. You are evil because you are weak. Those are the facts.

TENARD [*gives way for a second to outraged indignation*] An infamous credo, Madam! [*then hastily almost cringingly*] I—I beg your pardon. You may be right. New times, new customs—and methods. [*forcing a laugh*] I suppose I am too old a dog to learn new tricks of a changed era.

SARA [*smiling coldly*]   I hope not—for your sake, Mr. Tenard.

TENARD [*stares at her stupidly*]   Eh? I don't believe I understand— [*hastily forcing a good-natured, good-loser air*] But, as I said, I have no hard feelings. That's why I consented to come here—to show you I bear no grudges.

SARA [*not smiling now—her face hardening into a ruthless merciless-ness*]   Let us be frank and not waste my time. I know your true reason for coming. You are ruined. You have had to sell everything. You haven't a dollar. But you have an old mother, a wife, a widowed daughter with two children, all of whom depend upon [you] for support. You have applied to various banks for a position. None of them want you. You are too old. The evil reputation of recent failure prejudices them against you. One or two have offered you a minor clerk's job—out of contemptuous pity, like a penny of charity tossed to a beggar.

TENARD [*with humiliated anger*]   Yes, damn them! But I—

SARA [*goes on as if he had not interrupted*]   Which your pride refused. Moreover, the wage would have been insufficient to support your family except in a shameful poverty to which they are unaccustomed. You were afraid that, suffering the humiliation of such poverty, your mother, your wife, your daughter, would begin to blame you and to feel a resentful contempt for your weakness.

TENARD [*staring at her fascinatedly—blurts out in anguish*]   And hide it! That would be the worst! To feel them hiding it—out of pity.

SARA   But there was one last desperate hope. You heard I had not yet chosen anyone to manage your old bank for me. You came here hoping against hope that the reason I had sent for you— [*She pauses—then smiles with cold pleasantry*] I am pleased to tell you that is the reason. Mr. Tenard, I do offer you that position.

TENARD [*the strain snapping, he gives way pathetically and brokenly to relief and gratitude*]   I—I don't know how to thank you—I apologize for having misjudged you— [*hastily*] Of course, I accept the position gladly.

SARA [*coldly*] Wait. There are conditions. But before I state them, let me say that any sentiment of gratitude on your part is uncalled for. I am not doing this for your sake or your family's. What happens to you and yours is naturally a matter of entire indifference to me. I am solely concerned with what is mine, or what I wish to make mine.

TENARD [*uneasily—forcing a smile*] You are—brutally frank, at least, Mrs. Harford. [*with growing apprehension*] What are your conditions?

SARA [*smiling pleasantly*] I warn you your pride will probably be impelled to reject them. At first. But I ask you to bear in mind that pride is a virtue only in the strong. In the weak it is a stupid presumption. [*her face and voice hardening*] The conditions are that you agree to obey every order mechanically, instantly, unquestioningly, as though you were the meanest worker at the looms in my mills, or a common sailor in my ships, or a brakeman on my railroad.

TENARD [*humiliated but forcing a reasonable tone*] You can rely on me, I have been the head of a business myself. I know the desirability of prompt obedience.

SARA I can offer you a salary that will enable you very moderate comfort for your family, and so continue to purchase in part, at least, their former love and respect.

TENARD [*stammers confusedly*] I—I thank you—

SARA I am saying these things because, in order to avoid all future misunderstanding, I want you to face the cost of my offer before you accept.

TENARD [*in a panic to get this ordeal over and run away*] I understand. But you need not—I have no choice, I accept.

SARA [*cruelly insistent*] There is still the matter of your old-fashioned ideals of honor in business dealings to consider. I hope you appreciate from your recent experience with my methods that, as my employee, you will have to forget all such scruples. You will be required to conduct my bank business with the entire ruthlessness as to the means used of a general in battle. The end I desire to accomplish must justify any and every means to you. Where it is necessary, you must faithfully do things which may appear to your old conceptions of honor like plain swindling and theft. Are you willing to become a conscious thief and swindler in your own eyes?

TENARD [*at last insulted beyond all prudent submission—stammering with outrage*] I— You must be mad, Madam— You dare— But I cannot answer a woman— I know it must be your husband who— A woman would never— [*He springs to his feet and turns on Simon in a fury.*] Damn you, Sir! You blackguard, do you think I have sunk to your level? I'll see you in hell first! I'd rather be a dog! I'd rather starve in the gutter. [*He strides to the door at rear.*] That's my answer to your infamous offer, Sir. [*Simon has not turned, gives no sign of hearing him. Tenard grabs the handle of the door.*]

SARA [*suddenly bursts out in a strange rage as if he had touched something deep in her and infuriated her—lapsing into broad brogue, forgetting all her office attitudes—glaring at Tenard with savage denunciation*] Arrah, God's curse on you for a man! You and your pride and honor! You're pretending to love your women and children and you're willing to drag them down with you to suffer the bitter shame of poverty, and starve in the gutter, too!

TENARD [*stares at her torturedly*] It's a lie! They would never wish me— [*Then all at once he seems to collapse inside. He nods his head in a numbed acquiescence, forcing a vacant smile.*] Yes, I suppose, entirely selfish—no time to remember self. Thank you, Madam, for reminding me of my duty. I wish to say I see your point about policy of bank—only practical viewpoint—business is business— [*He forces a choked chuckle.*] Must remember the old adage—sticks and stones—and poverty—break—but names don't hurt. Let who will cry thief! I accept the position, Madam—and thank you again—for your—charity! [*He wrenches open the door and flings himself into the hall, slamming the door. Simon gets off his stool and comes to Sara with a smile of approval.*]

SIMON Well done! You disposed of him as well as I could. I'm proud of you.

SARA [*Her expression is changing. There is a look of dawning horror in her eyes. She forces a smile—mechanically*] I'm glad you're proud. But it was you—what you wanted me—

SIMON Oh, no. Don't play modest now. [*He pats her cheek—playfully*]

That last touch finished him, and that was all your own. I had calculated he would leave, indignant and insulted, but be forced to
come back after he'd faced his women again. But your method was
far cleverer. [*He pats her shoulder.*]

SARA [*staring before her—mechanically*] Yes, I didn't leave him one
last shred of his pride, did I? [*She suddenly breaks—with a sob*] Oh,
the poor man! God forgive me! [*Abruptly she turns on Simon—
with rising bitter anger*] It wasn't I! It was you! You— Ah, don't I
know what you're trying to do, make a cruel greedy whore of me,
so you can go back and sneer with her at what a low, common slut
I am in my heart! [*revengefully*] But I won't let you! I'll go to
Tenard! He'll be crazy to revenge himself now! I've only to give
him a hint of the true condition of the Company to turn him loose
to destroy you! And then where would you be, you and your Company? You strutting with pride, playing—you're a little Napoleon!
You'd not have a penny! And I'd be free to take my children and
go to the old farm and live like a decent, honest woman working in
the earth! [*She suddenly collapses, sobbing, hiding her face in her
hands.*] I can't go on with this! I won't!

SIMON [*who has listened, watching her with an impatient frown—pats
her shoulder perfunctorily—curtly*] Come now, Sara. I know you've
just been under a severe strain. But that's no excuse to talk so absurdly. [*He sits down opposite her—curtly*] That nonsense about
your ruining the Company. Don't you realize it's your Company
now?

SARA I realize you've swindled me, paying me with things loaded
down with debts, if that's what you mean.

SIMON [*smiling*] Ah, now you begin to talk like yourself again. [*rebukingly*] Such nonsense, Sara! As if you were a woman who would
deliberately ruin herself for the sake of anything. And there are your
children to be considered. You would hardly ruin them.

SARA [*shakenly*] No.

SIMON [*scornfully*] You go to that old farm, where there's only my
old cabin and a ruin of a farm house. A farm that hasn't been cul-
tivated since God knows when. You would have to work like a
slave for a bare living, with your pride tortured by the shame of

poverty! [*He laughs.*] Don't tell me you can imagine yourself contented living in a potato patch with your bare feet in the earth like a common peasant!

SARA [*with a shiver of repulsion*]   No. I'd hate to sink to that after all my high dreams.

SIMON   Exactly. So don't talk silly. As for your fears about the Company, you sound like Joel playing Jeremiah. [*jokingly*] You are not complaining about the way I manage your properties, I hope. Haven't I reorganized your railroad in two years so that now it is one of the best run small roads in the country?

SARA   Yes. But the debt—?

SIMON   I'm amazed to hear you worrying about debts. It's unworthy of your father's daughter. He never let debts bother him.

SARA [*suddenly smiling, with a proud toss of her head—boastfully*] True for you! He let them whistle for their money and be damned! [*then hastily and guiltily*] But I'm not like him. I—

SIMON [*with a strange tense excitement*]   Of course, you are right in thinking there is constant danger—that a whisper, a hint of the truth, a rumor started among the many defeated enemies who have such good reason to envy and hate you!

SARA [*defensively*]   Reason to hate me?

SIMON [*smiling*]   Well, do you imagine Tenard loves you, for example?

SARA [*confusedly*]   But it was you—

SIMON [*ignoring this, goes on tensely*]   There's no question about the danger. It's like walking a tightrope over an abyss where one false step—

SARA [*frightenedly*]   Oh, I know! It's driving me crazy! I can't sleep, worrying!

SIMON   But you mustn't look down, for then you grow confused and the temptation seizes you to hurl yourself— Don't you think I know by long experience how that impulse fascinates you, how terrible the longing is to make an end of suspense and gain forgetfulness and peace at any cost—the passionate yearning to destroy onself and be free!

SARA [*frightenedly*]   Darling! Don't think of it! Don't make me think—

SIMON I know only too well how tempted you are to whisper and start the rumor of the truth among your enemies—

SARA No! I'd never! I was only talking!

SIMON To throw the burden of responsibility and guilt off one's shoulders, to release oneself from the cursed treadmill of greed! Not to have to go on! To be able to be still, or to turn back to rest! [*He is staring before him with a fascinated yearning.*]

SARA [*frightened, grasping his arm*] Darling! Please don't stare like that! It makes you look so—strange and crazed—you frighten me!

SIMON [*controls himself—with a smile*] Oh, come now, there's nothing crazy about using your enemies' revenge to give you your heart's desire! That seems to me a very cunning, Machiavellian scheme—as ironically amusing as the end of one of Mother's old, fantastic fairy tales. Except, of course, this would be a happy end.

SARA [*flaring up angrily*] Ah, I know it's her puts all this craziness in your head. Wouldn't she laugh with joy to see me ruin myself and lose all I have in the world! But I'll never let her drive me to that! So don't you talk to me of the temptation, when you know I was only joking when I said—

SIMON I? I was only warning you against it. You must not be weak. You must be courageously and ruthlessly what you are! You must go on to more and more!

SARA [*protests miserably*] No. I don't want to. I've enough. [*pleadingly*] Oh, Simon Darling, won't you stop and be content now you've got the bank? Won't you let the profit add up, and not make more debts to buy more, but pay off what you owe? And as soon as the debts are paid and we're safe, we'll pension off your mother, and give her the house to live alone in, where she'll have no one to hurt but herself, and I'll build my estate and have a home of my own for my husband and my children— [*She presses against him with a calculating, wheedling seductiveness.*] and best of all, for my lover I'm madly in love with.

SIMON [*ignoring this last—curtly*] No. You know you cannot do that now. Not unless you wish to ruin yourself. It would be fatal for you to withdraw from the Company the large amount of capital needed to build such a large estate. The battle for this bank has strained your resources to the breaking point. A dollar in cash is worth a hundred to you now. No, you can't stop now. You must go on.

SARA [*distractedly*] No! I won't! I can't! I've come to the end!

SIMON [*as if she hadn't spoken*] You must keep your eyes fixed on the final goal of your ambition. Force yourself not to look down. Keep your whole mind and will concentrated on what must still be accomplished before your Company can be out of danger, safe and absolutely self-contained, not dependent on anything outside itself for anything, needing nothing but itself. Until that is done, how can you enjoy any true security or freedom within yourself—or any peace or happiness. Surely you must see that clearly, Sara?

SARA [*pitifully confused*] I—I don't know—I know I want peace and happiness in your love.

SIMON [*goes on in the same tone*] You still have to have stores to retail your cotton goods. Your own plantations worked by your own nigger slaves. Your own slave ships and your own slave dealers in Africa. That will complete the chain on the end. You see how that will protect you, don't you?

SARA [*impressed in spite of herself and beginning to be greedily fascinated*] Yes, I do see. I'm not such a fool about business after all your training. And, of course, I'd like to feel absolutely safe, and that no one had a chance with what was mine. [*then tensely desperate*] But Darling— I'm so worried—

SIMON [*goes on the same*] On this end, the stores are the last possible link— [*then with a strange laugh*] Of course, it would be the crowning achievement if I could conceive a scheme by which the public could be compelled to buy your cotton goods and only yours—so you would own your own consumer slaves, too. That would complete the circle with a vengeance! You would have life under your feet then, wouldn't you? Beautiful Greedy One—just as you have me! [*He laughs, his eyes glowing with desire, and hugs her.*]

SARA [*her face lighting up with a responsive passion—laughingly*] Yes, I'd like that. I'd be satisfied then. So see that you find a way to do it! [*then with proud admiration*] And leave it to you, I'll wager you will! There's no stopping you, once you want anything! Haven't I always said you've the strength and the power to take anything from life your heart wished for!

SIMON [*teasingly, hugging her*] With such an insatiable mistress to inspire me, how could I dare be weak? It is your heart which has done the wishing, and I could not respect myself unless you were proud of me.

SARA [*passionately*] And I am proud! I've the grandest strongest lover that was ever owned by a woman! [*She kisses him ardently.*] Darling!

SIMON [*passionately*] Sweetheart! [*then with an abrupt return to his strange, obsessed excitement*] So don't let me hear any more of your timid worry about danger. What if there is danger? It lends spice to life! What if it is a tremendous gamble, with the cards stacked by the fate within you, and the dice loaded? Your father's daughter should be proud to be a born gambler and love the risk for its own sake! I'll bet he would have found his greatest happiness in staking his soul with the devil against the world on the turn of a card!

SARA [*excitedly, with a proud toss of her head*] Wouldn't he, though! Didn't he ruin himself gambling, the estate and all he possessed in life, and never blinked an eye or lost the sneer on his lips! He was a great gentleman! And he'd keep that same sneer if he played the devil, for he'd know if the devil won he'd gain only what he owned already, and he'd be laughing up his sleeve how he'd cheated him! [*She laughs with gloating amusement.*]

SIMON [*stares at her—with a strange smile*] Yes, I have come to know that same exultant laughter at myself. [*abruptly, with a complete change to a curt business-like matter-of-fact tone*] Well, that's settled. You will go on. [*He glances at his watch.*] And now I'll have to go and catch my train. [*He starts for the door. She gets in his way.*]

SARA [*seductively*] Leaving me without a kiss? When I'm making myself all you want me to be? [*She suddenly embraces him with a passionate possessiveness.*] Never mind! Be cruel to me! Be anything you like! I'm dirt under your feet and proud to be! For there's no price in life too great to pay to keep you mine! If it's a whore you love me to be, then I am it, body and soul, as long as you're mine! [*She kisses him fiercely.*] I love you so, Darling! I want you! I can't bear you to leave me now! But you'll come back here, won't you? I'll be waiting and longing—

SIMON [*kisses her passionately*]   Yes! I swear to you! Nothing could
keep me from—

SARA [*with uneasiness—pleadingly now*]   You won't forget me like
you did this morning, and go to keep your engagement to visit her?
You'll remember you promised me you'd forget her and let her wait.

SIMON [*vindictively*]   Of course! Let the cowardly old witch wait until
Domesday! It will serve her right to be alone in the twilight she
dreads so with her idiotic superstitious terror of the haunted summerhouse! I am sick and tired of beseeching her to have the courage— [*He stops abruptly and his expression changes to bitter, angry
resentment—harshly accusing*] What are you trying to do, eh? I had
forgotten her! Why do you make me remember? Damnation, can't
I be free of her even here in your arms? Why do you think I pay
such an outlandish price to keep a mistress? You seem compelled to
remind me, to put her back in me! That is the one kind of swindling I refuse to tolerate from you! What trick are you up to? Have
you made a secret bargain with her to play one another's game?
She never lets me forget you long in her garden. She pretends to be
jealous of you, just as you pretend— But, by God, though you may
hate each other, I know you hate me more and have determined to
drive me out and get rid of me! But you had better not go on with
your plot, because I warn you—it will be I who— [*He checks himself, his eyes gleaming with a wild threat.*]

SARA [*staring at him—in a panic of dread*]   Simon! Don't look like
that! What's happened to you? [*suddenly resentful and angry herself*] God pity you for a fool! Have you lost your senses, to say such
crazy blather! Bargain with her, is it? Play her game for her? When
I hate her like hell itself! When my one wish about her is to drive
her away forever where she can never come back to steal what's
mine—

SIMON [*staring at her—with a cold calculating sneer*]   So you boast
here behind her back, but with her you're afraid of her!

SARA   It's a lie! I, afraid of a poor old—

SIMON [*tauntingly*]   Do you think I've stopped watching you together
in the house at night. You're afraid she might prove to be the
stronger if it came to a final decision. So you still pretend to be her

friend. [*slowly*] I will believe your boasting, Sara, when you prove you want me to be yours enough that you have the courage to— [*in a burst of strange deadly hatred*] Are you going to let her come between us forever? Can't you rid our life of that damned greedy evil witch?

SARA [*stares at him with dread—but with a fascinated eagerness too— in a whisper*] You mean you want me to—

SIMON [*with a change to a lover's playful teasing—pats her cheek*] I want you to do anything in life your heart desires to make me yours. You should know that by this time, Beloved. God knows I have paid you enough to prove it to you! [*He laughs and kisses her.*] I must catch my train. Goodbye until this afternoon. [*He goes out, rear. She stands looking after him, the same expression of horrified eagerness on her face.*]

＊ ＊ ＊ CURTAIN ＊ ＊ ＊

Tao House
December, 1938

Act Four, Scene Two

SCENE *Same as Scene Two of Act Three—the corner of Deborah's garden with the summerhouse. It is around nine o'clock the same night. There is a full moon but clouds keep passing across it so that the light in the garden is a dim, pallid, ghostly grey, in which all objects are indistinct and their outlines merge into one another, with intermittent brief periods of moonlight so clear one could read by it, in which the geometrical form of each shrub and its black shadow are sharply defined and separate. Their alternating lights are like intense brooding moods of the garden itself, and under the spell of either it has more compellingly than ever before the atmosphere of a perversely magnified child's toy garden, unnatural and repellently distorted and artificial.*

Deborah is discovered pacing back and forth along the path between the pool in front of the summerhouse and the door to the street in the wall at right. Her manner is pitifully distraught, nervous, tense, frightened and desperate. One feels she is fighting back complete nervous collapse, wild hysterical tears. Yet at the same time she is a prey to a passionate anger and her eyes smoulder with a bitter, jealous fury and hatred. A great physical change is noticeable in her. Her small, immature, girlish figure has grown so terribly emaciated that she gives the impression of being bodiless, a little, skinny, witch-like, old woman, an evil godmother conjured to life from the page of a fairy tale, whom strong sunlight would dissolve, or a breath of reality disperse into thin air. Her small, delicate, oval face is haggard with innumerable wrinkles, and so pale it seems bloodless and corpse-like, a mask of death, the great dark eyes staring from black holes. She is dressed in white, as ever, but with pathetically obvious touches of calculating, coquettish feminine adornment. Her beautiful white hair is piled up on her head in curls so that it resembles an Eighteenth Century mode. Her withered

*lips are rouged and there is a beauty-spot on each rouged cheek. There
is a pitiful aspect about her of an old portrait of a bygone age come
back to haunt the scene of long-past assignation.*

DEBORAH [*distractedly*] God, how long have I waited like this—
hours!—hours since supper even—watching, their prying eyes sneering—mocking, snickering under their breath, exchanging smiles—
but frightened, too—she has told them to beware of me, I am a little
crazy—then after supper out here again—waiting again—waiting,
waiting!—why do I?—what makes me make myself?—why don't I
go in the house?—hide in my room and lock the door—why do I
stay here and hope?— Oh, how can he be so cruel?!—how can he
do this to me? [*She suddenly stops and listens tensely—eagerly*]
There—footsteps—someone coming up the street! It must be he at
last! [*She rushes over and pulls open the door in the wall at right
and looks out in the street—then closes it again—dully*] No one—
[*bitterly*] Except Life, perhaps, who walks away again now—again
forgetful I am still alive— [*She turns away from the door.*] How
many times now have I run to open the door, hoping each time—
[*flaring into sudden anger*] How dare he humiliate me like this! a
common, vulgar, money-grubbing trader like his father!— I made
his father respect my pride—I humiliated him— You had better beware, Simon!—if you think I will bear your insults without retaliat-
ing!— [*then trying pitifully to reassure herself*] No, no, I must not
blame him—he has been detained at the mill by something unfor-
seen— [*with angry scorn*] Ah, how can you make excuses—lie to
yourself when you know the truth—he deliberately forgot you—he
is even now lying in the arms of that slut, laughing with her to
think of the pitiable spectacle you make waiting in vain! [*in a fury*]
Ah, if I were sure of that. I would have no more scruples!— I would
make him go in the summerhouse instead of protecting him from
his insane desire—that would revenge me for all his insults! [*As she
is speaking the moon comes from behind a cloud and shines clearly
on the summerhouse door. She stops and stares at it fascinatedly—
then turns away hastily with a shiver of dread.*] No!—I could not—

he is my beloved son who has returned to me—and he will come here soon—he loves me—he would never deliberately wound—he knows how lonely I am—that his visits here are all of happiness and peace that is left me—all that remains to me of life—if he took them from me, I!— But he will explain it is not his fault, he was unavoidably detained— But if he had been detained at the mills— that does not explain why she has not returned home either—he must be with her!— [*distractedly*] Ah, how can I blind myself—as if I did not know she has turned his office into a brothel bedroom— she is vile and unscrupulous—she uses her one superiority—her body—plays upon the only feeling he has for her—makes herself a whore to keep her hold on him!—anything to keep him from me!— but he shall not!—I can be unscrupulous, too—he thinks I will always be afraid—the fool!—she doesn't realize I have but to take his hand, as he wishes, and lead him from her life forever!— [*She has again stopped by the summerhouse and is staring fascinatedly at the door. Then again she tears her eyes away with a shudder—desperately*] Oh, why can't she leave me alone!—why does she force me to hate her so terribly—I am afraid of what her hate is making me become—I know so well the scheme she has in mind to get rid of me—to drive me insane—she deliberately goads me!—tempts me—it is horrible to be compelled to constantly resist—it exhausts my mind, my will— [*She shudders—then with a sudden change to a scornful gloating*] What a stupid animal—can't she see that in the end her hate will give me the courage[1] I need—that something in me hopes that she will succeed—but, of course, she hopes I would go alone— [*She laughs sneeringly.*] Oh no, my dear Sara, I would take what is mine with me! [*Her eyes are fixed on the summerhouse door again. The moon passes behind a cloud and the light grows dim. She turns away frightenedly.*] No! I could not!— I could not—and there is no need—I have beaten her already—I have taken him from her—as I always knew I could if she gave me the opportunity— [*She laughs with arrogant scorn.*] What a fool she is to imagine she could match me in intrigue—I who have spent years of my life dreaming

---

1. The typescript reads "courage of," followed by a space. I have deleted the word "of."

of power I might wield—I have been too subtle for her—I have used
even her strength against her—encouraged him to make a whore
of her—to feel himself [devoured] and[2] enslaved—until now he sees
her as the filthy slut she is—his one desire is to escape her—soon she
will disgust him so, he will drive her out of my house into the
gutter with her brats—meanwhile, I have led him back, step by
step, into memory, into the past, where he long to be—where he is
my child again—my baby—where my life is his only life—where he
is safe beyond her grasping claws! [*Her face has taken on a soft,
dreamy ecstatic look—exultantly*] My beloved son and I—one
again—happily ever after—safely hidden from life in our old
dreams! [*Her eyes fasten on the summerhouse door—abruptly
frightened—she turns away to stare about the garden uneasily*] If he
would only come!— I am afraid alone in this garden at night—
slowly as night [descends] it becomes strange—somber and threatening—it seems to be evil—it becomes Nature again—a Nature my
arrogant whim had distorted into ridiculous artificial forms—an enslaved Nature, ground under, thwarted and sneered at—in the day
it pretended to be humbly resigned—but as dark comes it strains at
its chains like a black slave and longs for revenge and freedom—I
feel the bitter, poisoned hatred of each amusingly humiliated shrub.
[*She shivers.*] And something in my nature responds—pities—
hates—would help it escape—to possess me—within its evil embrace
I would forget fear and pity—I would have no mercy for those who
sneer and deride— [*She pauses—then with increasing bitterness and
suspicion*] Why do I lie and tell myself it is I who have led Simon
back into the past, when I know it is he who has forced me to carry
out his evil scheme of revenge— [*protesting frightenedly*] No!—
how can I have such a mad suspicion—I should be glad—it proves
how he loves me—how much he needs my love— [*suspiciously
again—sneering at herself*] Love? You know he is incapable of
love—love is a passion of the soul—that greedy trader lost his soul
long ago when he left me—now he is as soulless as his father—lust

2. After "himself" I have replaced a space with the word "devoured," a word often used
by O'Neill in this sense.

is the only passion he feels now—no, do not let him deceive you into
believing it is love for you that impels him—what is it, then?—
hate?—the hate for me she has put in his mind?—a conspiracy with
her to drive me from his life—to imprison me here alone—driving
me back farther and farther within myself—until he finally tricks
me into unlocking the door, taking his hand—and at the last moment he will snatch his hand away, push me inside alone with that
mad woman I locked in there—to be possessed by her again—never
to come out— [*The moon again comes from behind a cloud and
shines on the summerhouse. She gives a dreadful little laugh.*] And
then, of course, it would be so simple to have me locked up in an
asylum— [*furiously*] Yes!—I see through your scheme, Simon!—I
can see you now, lying in her arms, laughing as you gloat together!
But take care! I am not some stupid merchant you swindle!—I am
not impressed by your ridiculous posing as a little Napoleon!—nor
am I that poor dull-witted peasant you cheat and make a whore
of—you will find I will outwit you—I will be the one to snatch away
my hand and leave you alone in there with that old mad Deborah
who will have no scruple—and you beat the walls, screaming for
escape at any cost! [*She suddenly stops, trembling with horror at
herself, and presses her hands to her head torturedly.*] Oh, God have
mercy,— I must stop thinking—if I go on like this, there will be no
need for anyone outside me to—I will drive myself in there! [*She
paces back and forth distractedly, glancing with dread around the
garden.*] This garden has become horrible. I am afraid of myself
here— Oh, if my son would only come!—he is not coming!—why
don't I go in the house?—no, I must wait!—he promised me—he
has been detained—I must be patient—find some way to pass the
time—not think of horrible impossible things—I am still mistress
of my mind—I can still dream, if it pleases me—I remember when
I waited for him at the cabin that afternoon, I passed the time pleasantly in dreaming—and when I opened my eyes he was there—
[*determinedly*] I can do that again. I will! [*She sits on the stone
bench at right-rear of the pool, closing her eyes, her face grows tense
as she concentrates her will, deliberately hypnotizing herself into a
trance. A pause. Then she relaxes slowly and murmurs dreamily.*]

The gardens at Malmaison[3]—the summerhouse—the Emperor—
[*Her dream becomes disturbed and puzzled and uneasy but she only
half awakes.*] No—I do not wish this—it is not the same—not Versailles and the King—the Emperor Napoleon?—how strange—I had
thought I hated him—Father's silly confusing him with God—and
Simon pretending he is like—I always wanted to live in a time before he lived—and now I see that was very cowardly of me—to deny
him—so silly to run and hide like a little bashful girl— [*sinking
happily into dreams*] The Emperor kisses me— "My Throne, it is
your heart, Dear Love, and I—"

[*While she is saying this last, Sara slinks in noiselessly along the path
from the house on the left. She looks worn out and dissipated, with
dark circles under her eyes, her hair dishevelled, her dress wrinkled
and awry, like a prostitute the morning after a debauch. She stands
regarding Deborah with a cruel mocking leer of satisfaction.*]

SARA [*to herself*] Ah, I knew what my keeping him away would do
to her! She's like I hoped she'd be! I'll have only to goad and taunt
and make game of her now to drive her over the edge where she'll
never find the way back! And it's what Simon wants, too, to be rid
of her. It's what he asked me to do!

DEBORAH [*in her dream, her face lighting up with love*] At last you
have come, Sire. My poor heart was terrified you had forgotten I
was waiting.

SARA [*in spite of herself, her eyes grow pitying.*] No. God forgive me.
The poor creature! I couldn't—not yet—not unless it's the only way
to save him from her madness.

DEBORAH [*laughs softly and seductively, rising to her feet*] Yes, give
me your hand and let us go within, Sire, where we will be hidden
from the ugliness of life—in our Temple of Love where there is only
Beauty and forgetfulness! [*She holds out her hand and clasps that
of her royal dream lover and turns toward the door and slowly
begins to ascend the steps.*]

---

3. Malmaison, situated outside of Paris, is the name of one of the royal retreats fre-
quented by Napoleon Bonaparte and the Bourbon kings of France.

SARA [*with a gloating eagerness*] She's going to do it herself! I won't
need to! I've only to let her alone! And that's what Simon wants.

DEBORAH I have the key here, Sire. I have worn it lately over my heart.
[*She reaches down inside her bodice and pulls out a key on a cord
around her neck—hesitates frightenedly—then unlocks but does not
open the door.*]

SARA [*eagerly but at the same time frightenedly*] She's unlocked it!
Nothing will stop her now! I've only to mind my own business.
Why did I come here? I don't like seeing it, when I could prevent
her. But it's what Simon wants—and I want!

DEBORAH [*with a little shiver, holding back, forcing a little smile*] I—I
confess I am a little frightened, Sire. So foolish of me—but— [*pleadingly*] Oh, swear to me again you would not deceive me—that it is
love and forgetfulness!

SARA [*struggling with herself*] She's frightened! She knows even in
her dream! Ah, though I hate her more than hell, I pity her now!
But why should I? It's little pity she'd have for me if she saw her
chance—

DEBORAH [*forcing a determined, exalting tone*] But even if it were hell,
it will be heaven to me with your love! [*She puts her hand on the
knob.*]

SARA [*fiercely*] Yes, go to hell and be damned to you and leave Simon
alone to me! [*Then just as Deborah is turning the knob she springs
toward her.*] Stop! Let go of that door, you damned old fool!
[*Deborah starts and half-awakens with a bewildered cry, pulling her
hand from the door, and stands dazed and trembling. Sara reaches
her side. She is angry at herself for interfering now and takes it out
on Deborah, grabbing her by the shoulders and shaking her roughly.*]
Wake up from your mad dreams, I'm saying! I've no patience to
humor your daftness.

DEBORAH [*whimpering with pain and fright like a child*] Let go! You
are hurting me! It isn't fair! You are so much stronger! Simon!
Make her let me alone! [*Sara has let go of her. Deborah stares at her
fully awake now. She makes a shaken attempt to draw herself up
with her old arrogance.*] You! How dare you touch me!

SARA [*shamefacedly*] I'm sorry if I hurt you, but I had to wake you—

DEBORAH [*with vindictive fury now*]   Oh, I'd like to have you beaten! Lashed till the blood ran down your fat white shoulders!

SARA [*bitterly resentful*]   Divil a doubt you would! And that's the thanks I get for stopping you!

DEBORAH   How dare you come here!

SARA [*angrily*]   To hell with your airs and graces! Whose property is it, I'd like to know? You're the one who has no right here!

DEBORAH   Oh!

SARA   But the only reason I came was because I took pity on you, knowing you'd be kept waiting out here all night, like an old fool, if I didn't tell he'd come home with me and forgotten all about you.

DEBORAH   Then—it is true. He did go back to the office, instead of— He went back to you! You made him, with your filthy—

SARA [*tauntingly*]   Made him? You don't know the strength of his love for me! I couldn't have kept him from me, if I'd wanted!

DEBORAH   You came here to tell me—so you could gloat! You vulgar common slut!

SARA [*goadingly*]   And I've more to tell you. He's paid the last visit here he'll ever pay you. He swore to me on his honor, lying in my arms, he never wanted to see you again, he was sick of wasting time humoring your craziness!

DEBORAH [*in a fury of jealous hatred, making a threatening movement toward her*]   You lie! He would never— He will come! Oh, you despicable filthy harlot!

SARA   He'll never come here again, I'm telling you! So don't be dreaming and hoping! [*then angrily*] A filthy harlot, am I? Well, I'm what he loves me to be! And it's not for you to call names, my high and mighty lady, or to give yourself airs. What were you in your crazy dreams just now—what have you always prided yourself you could be if you had the courage—but the greatest whore in the world!

DEBORAH [*shrinking back to the foot of the steps as if she'd been struck— guiltily*]   No, no! Only in a silly fancy—to amuse my mind—to wile away the time— How dare you insult me by thinking I could ever really wish— It's because you have the vile disgusting mind of a common street woman. You judge everyone by yourself.

SARA [*roughly scornful*]   Arrah, don't be talking! You don't fool me!

[*jeering derisively*] I'll say this for you you have grand tastes! It used to be King Louis of France, no less, you had for your man! But now it's the Emperor Napoleon, God pity you! My, but aren't you the fickle, greedy one! You've never enough! [*She laughs with coarse cruelty.*]

DEBORAH [*shrinking back up the steps as Sara keeps coming nearer to her—distractedly*] Don't! Don't! Oh, how dare you laugh!

SARA [*with cruel mocking insistence*] It'll be the Czar of Russia next! Aren't you the beautiful evil woman with all the kings and rulers of the earth, that are or ever was, down on their knees at your feet!

DEBORAH [*shrinking back to the top step—stammers distractedly*] Don't! Don't! Let me alone!

SARA [*following her*] Begging you to let them sleep with you! [*with savage contempt*] When out of your mad dreams you're only a poor little wizened old woman no common man on the street would turn to look at, and who, in the days when the men did want you, didn't have the blood or the strength to want them but ran and hid in her garden.

DEBORAH [*with a pitiful, stammering, hysterical laugh*] Yes! So ridiculous, isn't it? So pitiful and disgusting and horrible! [*distractedly*] Don't! Don't remind me! Don't make me see! [*wildly*] I can't endure myself! I won't! I'll be free at any cost! I— [*She turns and grabs the knob of the door.*]

SARA [*instinctively makes a grab for her and pulls her away—covering her guilty fear with a rough anger*] Come away from that!

DEBORAH [*struggling*] No! Let me go!

SARA [*angrily*] You will, will you? [*She picks Deborah up in her strong arms, as if she weighed nothing, sets her down before the bench at right and forces her down on it—angrily*] Sit there and be quiet now! I've had enough of your tricks! If you think you'll make me have your madness on my concience, you're mistaken! [*Deborah crumples up and falls sideways face down on the bench and bursts into hysterical sobbing. Sara speaks with a grim satisfaction.*] Ah, thank God, you can cry. Maybe that will bring some sense back in your head, and you won't be calling names that make me lose my temper and force me to do things to you I don't want to do except as a last resort if you keep on. [*Her tone becomes more and more persuasive as Deborah's crying gradually spends itself.*] But I don't think you'll want to keep on now. Not after what happened today—him keeping you waiting here and making an old fool of you! And I've told you the truth, he swore he'd never come to you again. It was part of the price I made him pay for me when he came back from the mills. Well, do you mean to tell me, in the face of that, you'll go begging him to visit you? You've got more pride in you than that, I hope. And anyway, it would do you no good. He'd only refuse you. He'd laugh at you again. He's mine now, I tell you! He's paid me everything he has. He has nothing left but me. He has no life except in my love. And I love him more than ever woman loved a man! I'm mother, wife, and mistress in one.[4] He doesn't need you. You're out in the cold. You're beaten. [*Deborah is still now and listening tensely but she does not raise her head. Sara goes on almost wheedlingly*] Listen to me. The real reason I came here was to have a sensible talk with you, and ask you to face the truth that I've won and you're beaten. You're finished and well you know it! Well you know a moment ago I could have driven you in there where the only door out leads to an asylum! I didn't because I hoped you'd be sensible and not make me do it! I hoped you'd admit you were beaten and give up. [*almost pleadingly*] Won't you own up now that it's no good going on with your mad schemes? If you'll swear to stop, I'll stop too and make peace with you. And I'll give in on my side to make it fair with you. I'll give the children back to you to keep you company and stand between you and your dreams, and you'll be as contented as you were before. And I won't hate you. You know I don't like your forcing me to hate you, don't you? [*She pauses. Deborah remains still. Sara's anger rises.*] Well? Haven't you a tongue in your head? It's you, not me, ought to beg for peace! I've made you a decent offer, and it's your last chance.

DEBORAH [*abruptly straightens up and stares at her with hard revengeful eyes—with a mocking smile*] You are even more stupid than I

---

4. Many of O'Neill's female characters fit this role, and he often expressed his need for the three qualities of mother, wife, and mistress in his wife Carlotta. Indeed, she fulfilled these three roles and more.

thought. Don't you know your begging for peace is a confession of how insecure you are in your fancied victory? I am convinced now that you realize that any time I choose I can take Simon away with me!

SARA [*frightenedly*] You mean, into madness, with you? [*savagely*] I swear by Almighty God I'll murder you if you try that.

DEBORAH [*coldly disdainful*] And get your children's mother hanged?

SARA [*taken aback*] I'll do it a way no one will discover!

DEBORAH [*coldly contemptuous*] Simon would know. Do you think your husband would love a wife who had murdered his mother?

SARA You think he wouldn't? I tell you, he'd thank me for it! If you knew how he hated you now for trying to make him hate me! He begged me today to get rid of you, so he and I could be free!

DEBORAH [*shakenly*] You lie! He loves me! It's you he hates! You have become vile and disgusting to him! He loathes your foul flesh, your filthy, insatiable greeds! He has implored me to drive you out of life into the gutter from which you sprang! Or if that takes too long, he has hinted I might find some subtle way that might never be suspected, to poison you!

SARA [*shakenly*] Ah, it's the evil liar you are! He loves me! He'd never! But I know it's in your mind and I'll take good care what I eat or drink from now on!

DEBORAH [*suddenly gives way to a horrified realization*] Sara! Oh, no! For God's sake, how can you think I—? [*then her face hardening again—defiantly*] I refuse your offer of peace. I do not trust you. How could I trust you? I trusted you once. Besides, even if your begging for peace did not clearly reveal to me how weak you are, your stopping me from opening the door would. You could really have won then but you did not have strength. You are weakly sentimental and pitiful. You cannot be ruthless. You are feeble with guilty scruples. You will always defeat yourself at the last. [*scornfully*] You fool! Do you think, in your place, I would ever have stopped you? I would have laughed with joy! I could watch you lashed to death, with the blood running down your gross white back, and never raise a finger to save you! [*arrogantly*] Pah! What a fool I have been! It is you who are doomed by your weakness to inevitable defeat. I am the stronger as I always knew I would be, if given the opportunity.

SARA [*angrily*] So that's your answer, is it? That's what you think? That's my thanks for— [*vindictively*] You old lunatic, you'll see if I have any pity on you the next time!

DEBORAH [*haughtily—as if addressing a servant*] I see no reason for prolonging this tiresome interview. You have no business in this garden. Will you be good enough to return to the house where you belong and attend to your children. I know my son is waiting for an opportunity to see me alone.

SARA [*angrily, turning toward the path off left*] I'll go, and be damned to you! I've come to the end of pity! [*with cruel vindictiveness*] He's waiting hoping to hear I've found you locked inside there and we can get the asylum to take you away!

DEBORAH [*her will beginning to crumple under this attack—distractedly*] Oh, no! You are lying! Not my beloved son! He couldn't!

SARA [*jeering savagely*] I'll be sorry to disappoint him but I'll promise him you're near the end and it won't be long before we're free! [*She starts to go.*]

DEBORAH [*with a pitiful frightened cry*] Sara! No! [*She runs to her wildly and grabs her arm—stammering with terror*] Don't go! Don't leave me alone, here! I—I'm afraid! Please stay! I—I'll do anything you ask! I'll admit you've won! I'll make peace! I'll prom-ise anything you want! Only—don't leave me here! I need your strength or I'll— [*She throws her arms around Sara and begins to sob hysterically.*] Oh, how can you be so cruel to me?

SARA [*has stared at her at first suspiciously and resentfully—then gloat-ing triumphantly but moved in spite of herself—finally, as Deborah weeps, she is overcome by pity and soothes her as she would a child.*] There, there now. Don't be frightened. I'm here. I'm strong enough for the two of us. And it's all over now. We won't destroy each other anymore. You'll have the children back. You'll be happy and contented. You know I didn't want to be cruel to you.

DEBORAH [*brokenly*] I know. And you know I didn't.

SARA [*gently*] Come in the house with me now. You must go to bed and rest. It's a wonder if you haven't caught your death already, chilled by the night and the dew.

DEBORAH [*exhaustedly—with humble affectionate gratitude*] You are so generous and kind and warm. I know that in my heart so well. How could I have forgotten? How could I have longed so horribly for your death—the one friend I have ever possessed, the one person who has ever understood my pride. I am really so humbly grateful, and yet— How could I be so vile and evil?

SARA [*soothingly*] Ah well, wasn't I just wishing you locked up in an asylum? I'm worse than you. But it's over now. We've made peace. We'll forget. [*urging her*] Let's go in the house now. You're trembling. You've taken a chill. Come.

DEBORAH You are so thoughtful and good. [*Sara begins to lead her off left. Abruptly she stops—with dread*] No. We're forgetting he is there, Sara. We must wait. We can't face him yet. We would be too weak. We must stay here together, trusting each other, until we get back our old strength to defy him as one woman. The strength his evil jealous greed has corrupted and destroyed! [*desperately*] Yes, it is he! He! Not us! We have been driven to this!

SARA [*resentfully*] Ah, don't I know how he's driven me!

DEBORAH [*her desperation angry*] He! He! He! Only he! We saw that so clearly when he first started to goad us into this duel to the death! We swore to each other that we would constantly bear in mind it was he, not us. In him, not in us! We saw our danger if we ever let him make us forget that.

SARA I know! But, in a few days he'd made us forget! He made us deceive each other and hate and scheme—

DEBORAH Yes! Devote our lives to destroying each other! In meek obedience to his whim! Oh, what weak fools we have been! How could we be so blind and stupid!

SARA Because we loved him so much! And didn't he know that, the sly schemer, and use it to have his own way!

DEBORAH We could have defeated him so easily! We would have been so much stronger! He would have had no more strength than a little boy or a baby! We could have kept him absolutely dependent on us, with no life except within our life.

SARA And he'd have been happy and content, not destroyed with hunger and mad with greed like he is now.

DEBORAH Yes! He would have been supremely happy and utterly contented with nothing but our love. But no! It wasn't enough! He had to play the great self-liberator, the conquering Napoleon, of others, with his women, too.

SARA [*with resentful contempt*] Arrah, he's like all the greedy fools of men, never knowing when they're well off.

DEBORAH If we had carried out our determination to remain united we could so easily have curbed his insane rebellion against happiness. He would have had to beg us to restore our peace to him. But instead we let him revive a dead hate of the past to start us clawing and tearing at each other's hearts like two mad female animals he had thrown in a pit to fight for his love—while he stands apart and watches and sneers and laughs with greedy pride and goads each on in turn to murder the other!

SARA [*with bitter anger*] And when only one is left living, he knows she'll be so weakened by the long duel he can easily make a slave of her who'll never have strength to claim her body or soul her own again! [*While she is talking, unnoticed by them both, Simon appears behind them, entering from the path at left. He does not make his presence known but stands staring at them. He is in a state of terrific tension, and there is a wild look in his eyes, cunning, calculating and threatening and at the same time baffled and panic-stricken.*]

DEBORAH Yes, that is what he is trying to accomplish, of course—use one to rid him of the other.

SARA Or both to be rid of both! [*She laughs bitterly.*] Ah, wouldn't he strut and puff out his chest before the mirror then, boasting what a great little independent man he was, if he were free of the two of us!

DEBORAH [*sneering bitterly*] Yes, he would be finally convinced then he was a reincarnation of Napoleon! Yes, I hadn't thought of it before but now I see that must be his most ambitious dream. [*Her face hardens cruelly.*] It would serve him right if we turned the tables on him, Sara. We could have the strength now as we are united again as one woman.

SARA [*fascinatedly*] You mean, throw him in the pit—to fight it out with himself?

DEBORAH For our love—while we watched with gratified womanly pride and laughed and goaded him on!

SARA [*eagerly—but with hesitant dread, too*] Until—

DEBORAH Yes, Sara. Until at last we're finally rid of him. [*with tense hatred and longing*] Oh God, think of how simply contented we could be alone together with our children—grandmother and mother, mother and daughter, sister and sister, one woman and another, with the way so clear before us, the purpose and meaning of life so happily implicit, the feeling of living life so deeply sure of itself, not needing thought, beyond all torturing doubt and sneers and question, the passive "yes" of self-possession welcoming the peaceful procession of demanding days! [*She pauses—then a bit guiltily*] I hope you do not think it evil of me that I can find it in myself to wish he were not here.

SARA [*fascinatedly*] No—there have been times at the office when I—

DEBORAH He has taught us that whatever is in oneself is good—that whatever one desires is good, that the one evil is to deny onself. [*tensely*] Again, it is not us but what he has made us be! So on his head—

SIMON [*speaks with a tense quiet casualness*] You are mistaken, Mother. [*They both whirl on him with startled gasps of terror and cling to one another defensively. Then as he advances, they shrink back to the edge of the bench at the right rear of pool, keeping the pool between them and him. He goes on with the same tense brittle quiet.*] You are hiding from yourself again, Mother. And Sara seems to have caught the cowardly habit from you. It is stupid of you to blame me. It is not on my head but in your hearts. I have merely insisted that you both be what you are—that what you are is good because it is fact and reality—that the true nature of man and woman, to which we have hitherto given the bad name of evil because we were afraid of it, is, in a world of facts dominated by our greed for power and possession, good because it is true. And what is evil, because it is a lie, is the deliberate evasive sentimental misunderstanding of man as he is, proclaimed by the fool, Jean Jacques Rousseau—the stupid theory that he is naturally what we call virtuous and good. Instead of being what he is, a hog. It is that idealistic fallacy which is responsible for all the confusion in our minds, the conflicts within the self, and for all the confusion in our relationships with one another, within the family particularly, for the blundering of our desires which are disciplined to covet what they don't want and be afraid to crave what they wish for in truth. [*He smiles a thin tense smile.*] In a nutshell, if you will pardon the seeming paradox, all one needs to remember is that good is evil, and evil, good. [*As they have listened, the faces of the two women have hardened into a deadly enmity.*]

DEBORAH [*tensely and threateningly*] Do you hear, Sara. We must not forget.

SARA [*in the same tone*] No, we owe it to him to be what he wants.

SIMON [*his tense quiet beginning to snap*] But I did not come out here to discuss my meditations on the true nature of man. [*He pauses— then the strain breaking, his voice trembling, he blurts out in violent accusation*] I—I was trying to concentrate my thoughts on the final solution of the problem. I have been forced to the conclusion lately that in the end, if the conflicting selves within a man are too evenly matched—if neither is strong enough to destroy the other before the man himself, of which they are halves, is exhausted by their struggle and in danger of being torn apart between them—then that man is forced at last, in self-defense, to choose one or the other—

DEBORAH [*starts—staring at him uneasily*] To choose, Simon?

SARA [*echoing her*] To choose, Simon?

SIMON To throw all his remaining strength to one and help it to destroy the other. That appears to me now to be the one possible way he can end the conflict and save his sanity before it is too late.

DEBORAH [*beginning to be cruelly gloating now*] You hear what he's confessing, Sara?

SARA [*echoing her tone*] That we've been too strong for him, and he's near the end.

SIMON [*as if he hadn't heard*] Before my mind is torn and clawed to death between them and devoured!

DEBORAH [*gloatingly*] Yes, he is much nearer the end than I had thought.

SARA [*in same tone*] Yes, we've only to wait and we'll soon be free of him. [*She chuckles.*] Well, I should have known he hadn't much strength left to go on with! If you knew how I've beaten him at the office! I've stripped him clean, Deborah! I got the bank from him

today. He's ruined and finished! He's nothing left to offer me! And
if he hopes, after all he's taught me, that he can cheat me into giving
something for nothing, he's a bigger fool even than I think him!
[*She laughs.*]

DEBORAH [*smiles gloatingly*]   Oh, I have guessed, Sara. I have been with
you in spirit and been proud of you in my imagination! I have
helped you all I could by urging him to encourage your greed. [*then
almost boastfully*] But I should have guessed how near the end he
is through my own experience with him, Sara. If you could see how
I have led him farther and farther away, back into the past, until
now all I have to do is say one word, or even have the thought in
silence, and our great man-conquering Napoleon becomes a stubborn, nagging, begging little boy whose only purpose or ambition
in life is to possess the happy ending of an old silly fairy tale! [*She
laughs and Sara joins in her laughter.*]

SARA [*staring at Simon—mockingly*]   Well, well, you're a great one for
teaching us that everyone is for sale and it should be a woman's
pride to get the highest price she can, but I'm thinking in the end
it will be us who have taught you about high prices!

DEBORAH [*mockingly*]   Yes, I am sure he will have learned that a woman's pride costs more than he could ever afford to pay without going
bankrupt.

SARA [*scornfully resentful*]   So he'll choose, will he, the great man?
Like a master picking which of two slaves he'd like to own! But
suppose they don't choose to let him choose?

DEBORAH [*echoing her tone*]   Yes, it would be very stupid of them,
when all they have to do is to wait together and stand apart and
watch while he destroys himself and sets them free. Encourage him
to do so, even. Goad him on with their laughter. [*She laughs softly
and Sara laughs with her.*]

SIMON [*with an abrupt change to his matter-of-fact tone*]   I don't know
what you're talking about, Mother. I attempt to explain an abstract
problem of the nature of man, and you and Sara begin talking as if
you, personally, were directly concerned in it! [*He chuckles dryly.*]
An amusing example of the insatiable ambition of female possessiveness, don't you think? [*curtly*] Never mind. It is my fault for being

such a fool as to discuss it with you. I know the one problem that interests you. [*He becomes angrily excited.*] God knows I could hardly be unaware of it tonight! I heard you from my study quarreling out here, clawing and tearing at each other like two drunken drabs fighting over a dollar bill! God, it becomes disgusting! You might at least have the decency to confine your revolting greedy brawls to the house! Do you want to create a public scandal, screaming where all the neighbors can hear, cursing and threatening to murder each other!

DEBORAH [*quietly*] We were not screaming. You could not possibly have heard us in your study. I am afraid what you heard were the voices of your own mind. You were dreaming your old dream of liberty for men, perhaps, and listening to your hopes.

SIMON [*with angry excitement*] That's a lie! I heard you as clearly as if I were here! I could not concentrate my thoughts on the final solution of the problem, listening to your screaming hatred! It seemed there would never be a moment's peace in my life again—that you would go on with your horrible duel, clawing and tearing each other, until my mind would be ripped apart! [*He checks himself uneasily—quickly, trying to adopt a tone of confident scorn*] I heard you, I tell you. So don't attempt to evade your guilt by saying I imagined it. Are you trying to insinuate I am going insane? Ridiculous! You will find you were talking louder than you realized. Hatred seldom remembers to keep its voice decently lowered. And then when you finally did become quiet, there was no peace—It was the stillness that follows a shriek of terror, waiting to become aware—I was afraid one of you had killed the other. I thought when I came here I would find only one—

DEBORAH [*staring at him—cannot control a shrinking shudder*] We know—you have been hoping—

SARA [*with a shudder*] Ah, God forgive me!

SIMON [*wildly*] Well, I might have been hoping. Suppose I was? Do you think I can endure living with your murderous duel forever—always between you—a defenseless object for your hatred of each other—rent in twain by your tearing greedy claws? No! I tell you there comes a point where the tortured mind will pay any price for peace! [*He suddenly breaks and sinks on the bench at left of pool, his head clutched convulsively in his hands—brokenly*] Why can't you stop? Why won't you make peace between you? I will do anything you wish! Is there no love or pity left in your hearts? Can't you see you are driving me insane? [*He begins to sob exhaustedly— the two women sit together, as one, on the other bench, staring at him. Their first reaction is one of victory. But there is no satisfaction or triumph. They are exhausted and without feeling.*]

DEBORAH [*dully*] We have won, Sara.

SARA [*dully*] Yes, Deborah. He admits he's beaten. [*They stare at him. He remains still, his head in his hands. Suddenly, their faces, as one face, are convulsed by pitying, forgiving maternal love.*]

DEBORAH Our poor boy! How could we be so cruel!

SARA Our poor darling! How could we feel as we were feeling about you! [*Then, as one, they spring to their feet and go to him, separating, one coming round one side of the pool, the other round the other. They kneel at each side of him, putting an arm around him, hastening to tenderly console and comfort him.*]

DEBORAH There, there! Our beloved son!

SARA Our husband! Our lover!

DEBORAH You mustn't cry, Dear. You break our hearts when you cry.

SARA There's nothing need frighten you now. We've forgiven you.

DEBORAH We love you again.

SARA You'll be hidden safe and sound in our love, where no one can hurt you.

DEBORAH Yes, it's so silly of you to be frightened, Dear. Couldn't you see as soon as we came here we had made peace between us?

SARA And now you're at peace in our peace, don't you feel that, Darling?

SIMON [*raises his head, a confused, dreamy wondering peace in his face—dazedly*] Yes. It is very restful here. I am very grateful to you for life. [*He turns to Sara.*] I love you, my mother. [*He turns to Deborah.*] I love you, my— [*He stops guiltily—then springs from their arms to his feet, stammering distractedly.*] No, no! I could not live in such confusion! [*Keeping his back to them, as they remain kneeling, he adds with a sneering mockery.*] As for this peace of yours, if you think I can be taken in by such an obvious sham— [*The two women spring to their feet. Both cry as one with anguished despair: "Simon! Don't!" and each grabs one of his arms*

and clings to it. Simon trembles with his effort to control himself.
He speaks with a hurried acquiescence.] I ask your pardon. My
mind is still extremely confused. It is such an unexpected shock—to
find Sara here where she never intrudes—and then to hear of your
confusing reconcilement— But it was very evil of me to doubt and
sneer—particularly as I love you both so deeply and it is my dearest
wish for my women to live in harmony and I may enjoy love and
peace in my home!

SARA [*with happy relief*] Darling! [*She hugs his arm.*]

DEBORAH Dear! [*then teasingly*] And here's the kiss you cheated me
of a moment ago. [*She kisses his cheek.*]

SIMON [*smiles pleasantly*] Thank you, Mother. [*then with a too-
pleasant, natural affectionate air*] Well, all is forgotten and forgiven then, and I start a new happy life within your united love, is
that it?

DEBORAH [*gaily tender*] Oh yes, Dear! And we will make you so
happy! Won't we, Sara?

SARA [*gaily tender*] Indeed we will! He won't know himself!

SIMON [*pleasantly*] I am sure I will not. Let us sit down and rest for
a moment together then, shall we, in this garden so hidden from
the ugliness of reality, where it is always so restful— [*Then, as they
are about to sit, he suddenly exclaims.*] Ah, what a fool I am. I had
entirely forgotten the object of my coming here. It had nothing to
do with your quarrel, which, as you say, must have been merely my
imagination. I came to remind you, Sara, it's the children's bedtime
and they are waiting for your goodnight kiss. They were a bit hurt,
I might add. It isn't like their mother to forget.

SARA [*guilty—rebuking herself*] Ah, the poor darlings. Bad cess[5] to
me, how could I forget—

SIMON [*with a calculating insistence*] You'd better take a good look at
Honey. Unless I'm mistaken, he's getting a cold. It seemed to me he
was a bit feverish.

SARA [*worriedly*] Ah, the poor lamb, and me out here gabbing— [*She
starts off the path at left, then hesitates.*] You're coming in?

DEBORAH [*quickly*] Yes, of course—

---

5. "Cess" is an Irish expression that means, in this case, "bad luck." It is also a short
form of the word "assess."

SIMON [*quickly*] Yes, it's too damp and chilly. We'll go in, Mother. But you better run ahead, Sara, and see Honey.

SARA [*worriedly*] Ah, I hope he's not going to be sick. I'll— [*She hurries off, left. Simon turns and stares at his mother.*]

SIMON [*with a sneering chuckle*] Well, you must admit I got rid of her very successfully, Mother.

DEBORAH [*staring at him—smiles gloatingly*] Yes, I felt that was what you were doing. She is such a stupid, trustful— [*then tensely*] No! You are making me say that! I—

SIMON [*ignoring this*] She will be occupied fussing over Honey and getting them all to bed. She will not notice we have remained out here.

DEBORAH [*stiffening—coldly*] I am not remaining here.

SIMON [*ignoring this*] It will give us an opportunity to be alone.

DEBORAH [*tensely*] I do not wish to be alone with you. I am going in and help her with the children. I am going in! At once! [*She takes a step towards left, stiffly, as if by a determined effort of will staring at him with a fascinated uneasiness. He reaches out and takes one of her hands and she stops, trembling, rooted to the spot. She stammers.*] You—you may do as you please. It is not my affair— [*Her tone becomes taunting.*] if you choose to stay out here alone in the darkness—and make an idiot of yourself—dreaming childish make-believe—like a silly little boy—you, a grown man!—if you could only see yourself!—what a ridiculous comic figure!—a Napoleon who believes in fairy tales and marches to Moscow in search of a magic door—the Emperor whose greatest ambition is to invade and capture a summerhouse in his mother's garden and conquer spider webs and the dirt and mould of old dreams and the forgotten ghost of an absurdly vain and selfish and cowardly woman who longed to escape— [*She forces a sneering laugh.*] But I—I am sick and tired of humoring you, as one would a half-witted child. I am finished with your romantic nonsense. I have talked it over sensibly with your wife and she agrees with me that my permitting you to come here was a great mistake. It has benefitted neither of us. It only encourages you in your most cowardly weakness of character—your ignoble fear of a man's responsibilities in life—your streak of sickly-mindedness and unbalanced fantasy. And, for my part, your visits have bored me to exhaustion! Furthermore, my grandchildren will keep me company again now, and I shall have no time to spare for you. [*with a sneering smile*] Of course, perhaps they might consent to humor you by letting you take part in their games, but I think it would be bad for you to encourage your morbid childishness. No, on second thought, I will not permit that either. I forbid you to ever come to this garden again! Do you hear me, Simon?

SIMON [*frowning—with a touch of impatience*] I have heard you talking, yes. But I know you were not really addressing me, but attempting to cheat your own mind. So I paid no attention—

DEBORAH [*uneasily*] Ah. [*tensely*] Will you kindly let go my hand? I wish to go in and join Sara.

SIMON [*quietly*] You know you do not, Mother. What has your rare and fastidious, dreaming poet's soul in common with that mating and begetting female animal who is all material greed?

DEBORAH [*stares at him, her eyes lighting up with satisfaction*] Ah! You see what she really is at least, do you? Haven't I always told you she was nothing more than a common, vulgar— [*abruptly*] No! no! She is a finer woman than I! She is sweet and generous and kind! Why do I let you twist my mind! And you—it is despicable of you to speak like that about a woman who has been such a good wife to you and who loves you so deeply and unselfishly.

SIMON [*sneeringly*] You are speaking of my mistress, I think. But I owe her nothing. She made me pay two-fold the value of every pound of flesh—

DEBORAH [*disdainfully*] What did you expect? She is a natural born— [*then catching herself—jeeringly*] It serves you right! I am very glad she—I told her to make you realize, in the only terms you could understand, what a woman's love is worth!

SIMON [*taunting in his turn*] Oh, I am not grudging her her price. She is very beautiful. No one could have a more desirable mistress!

DEBORAH [*tensely—tugging to pull her hand away*] Let me go! You have become gross and filthy! The touch of your hand disgusts me! [*with an abrupt change of tone—sneering jealously*] And you are a blind, besotted fool to call her beautiful! She has youth and health and a certain peasant prettiness, but that is all. She has thick ankles and fat hips and rough dish-washing hands. She— [*violently*] No!

You cannot make me think ill of her and enviously criticize her beauty—

SIMON You are quite right about her repellent fleshiness. I have been so conscious of it lately I have almost screamed with repulsion each time I touched her.

DEBORAH [*her eyes lighting up with vindictive triumph*] Ah, so at last— Oh, I knew it in the end— [*fighting with herself*] No! How dare you disdain the wife who loves you, as if she were a low prostitute you had bought and then grown tired of and were planning to discard—

SIMON Yes, I have grown tired of her. I have had enough of her. All I want now is to get rid of her forever.

DEBORAH [*eagerly*] Simon! Do you really mean— [*struggling with herself again*] No! You are lying to save your face! You do not fool me! It is she who is tired of you. Good heavens, what woman wouldn't be disgusted with the greedy, soulless trader in the slave market of life you have become—the vulgar tasteless lustful owner of goods— the cotton mill Napoleon! It is Sara who had had enough and now is planning to get rid of you! Planning with me! I shall help to find the most effective means—I shall advise her never to go to your office again. Why should she waste her youth and beauty now you have nothing left to offer her! [*vindictively*] We will give you the freedom you used to dream about! We will laugh when we find you begging on the street of every woman who passes a little pitying love to save your soul from starvation! And finally, the solitary soul you used to be so proud of in yourself as a mark of unique, superior distinction will come cringing and whining and pleading to our door and implore us to open and take you back in to our love again—at any price! [*She laughs jeeringly—then with an abrupt change to a strange remorseful pity*] No—forgive me—I do not mean to be cruel and laugh—But you— [*then eagerly*] Simon! Is it true you are really planning to get rid of her now? [*savagely*] Ah! Haven't I prophesied to your office that the time would come when you would feel so devoured and degraded and enslaved by vice that you would loathe her and drive her out in the gutter where she belongs!

SIMON No. Driving her out in the streets to ply her trade is not the way to escape her, Mother. She would stand before the door soliciting—begging for love. It would be her revenge to never allow me to forget the past. She would still live in my life, greedily possessing it.

DEBORAH [*furiously*]   Ah! What a contemptible confession of weakness and cowardice! Have you no pride nor shame that you can admit yourself such a weak, will-less slave?

SIMON   She would still be beautiful and desirable.

DEBORAH   A base slave to a vulgar common trollop! And you call yourself my son!

SIMON   I cannot tell you how sick I am of being a fool who keeps a whore in luxury and power and watches helplessly while she swindles and ruins him. But what can I do when her beauty [arouses] my desire? [*tensely*] Oh, if you knew how desperately I long to escape her and become again only your son!

DEBORAH [*deeply moved—stammers*]   I—I know. Dear—I know that must be true because—I have longed so desperately myself— [*then abruptly with a distracted suspicion and resentment*] Oh, how can you lie like that? How can you be such a hypocrite? Do you think I can believe—you have any feeling for me whatever—except scorn and hatred—when you deliberately kept me waiting here hour after hour—deliberately ignored and humiliated—spat in the face of my pride—my love—while you lay in the arms of that low slut and laughed with her to think of me here listening to each footstep on the street, thinking each time—excusing you, and lying to myself— hoping against hope, like a swindled, defrauded fool! [*She glares at him with hatred.*] Ah, how I hated you! How I cursed the night you were conceived, the morning you were born![6] How I prayed that you would die and set me free from the intolerable degrading slavery— [*She stops, appalled—stammers*] No! I don't mean—I couldn't mean— [*brokenly*] Forgive me—but— Oh Simon, how could you be so horrible and cruel to me! [*then ashamed of her abjectness—her pride forcing a pitiful attempt at a belittling tone*] But

---

6. This speech of Deborha's is one of many that reflect the character of Mary Tyrone in *LDJ*. Among several bitter comments Mary addresses to her son, Edmund, are the lines: "I was so healthy before Edmund was born" (Yale edn., p. 87), "I never should have borne Edmund" (p. 88), and "I never knew what rheumatism was before you were born" (p. 116).

how ridiculously emotional and dramatic I sound! So absurd! I fear there must be a great deal of truth in the accusation you always make that I am always acting an unreal part! The truth is I did not much mind your not coming. I was annoyed. Naturally, I do not like absent-minded people who forget appointments. But I was also very glad to be alone for a change, and be relieved of the strain of humoring your fantastic childish whims and morbid yearning with the past. I was free to be myself. It was a pleasure to sit here in my own mind and dream— [*She checks herself—sharply*] I would like to go in the house now and join Sara. Will you kindly let go of my hand?

SIMON [*staring into her eyes—slowly and compellingly*] I wish you to sit here beside me, Mother, and let me explain—

DEBORAH [*stares back fascinatedly—with confused eagerness*] Yes, I knew you'd explain when you came. I kept telling myself, he will explain and I will see it was not his fault and forgive him. [*She sits on the bench beside him as if his will drove her down.*]

SIMON [*quietly*] I realize how hurt you must have been, but I thought you would understand it was not I. It was she who insisted I must deliberately forget and return to her instead.

DEBORAH [*tensely*] I know! I knew that must be true! I know my Simon would never— [*then bitterly*] But that doesn't excuse you! You deliberately consented!

SIMON [*with tense quiet*] What could I do? She is so beautiful and she demanded it as part of her price. And you must remember that there with her, my life lives in her life, and hers in mine, and I am her Simon, not yours. So how could I wish to remember you?

DEBORAH [*tensely—making a futile movement to rise*] And you think that excuses—I will not listen!

SIMON [*ignoring this*] Just as here with you now, as always in the past before she intruded, my life lies in your life, and yours in mine, and I am your Simon and my one longing is to forget she is alive.

DEBORAH [*immediately eagerly tender*] Yes, Dear, I want you to forget.

SIMON [*goes on in the same tone of tense quiet*] You know her true nature well enough to realize it was she who made me laugh with her in her arms to think of you waiting here like an old fool—

DEBORAH [*in a deadly fury*] Yes! I could hear her! The infamous harlot! And to think I just let her deceive me into making peace! But there will be no peace as long as we both remain alive! I will make her pay! Oh, how terribly I hate her! How terribly I wish that she would die! That someone would murder— [*She stops frightenedly.*]

SIMON [*in same tone of tense quiet*]   I am glad you see there is no possibility of getting rid of her as long as she is alive. [*He pauses.*] If she were dead, of course— [*insinuatingly*] If someone stumbled and fell against her when she was starting to descend the steep front stairs, it would be obviously an accident if—

DEBORAH [*in a shuddering whisper*]   Simon!

SIMON   Yes, I agree that is too uncertain.

DEBORAH [*stammers in confused horror*]   Agree? But I never—!

SIMON   Poison would be certain. And no one would ever suspect anything but natural illness in an eminent, wealthy family like ours.

DEBORAH   Simon! Good God in heaven, have you gone mad?

SIMON [*with a cold impatience*]   No. Quite the contrary. I am being extremely sane. I am alive as it is behind our hypocritical pretences and our weak sentimental moral evasions of our natural selves. I am facing the truth. I am dealing with the facts of things as they are. I am not frightened by the bad names we have called certain acts, which in themselves, are perfectly natural and logical—the killing of one's enemies, for example. Our whole cowardly moral code about murder is but another example of the stupid insane impulsion of man's petty vanity to swindle himself into believing human lives are valuable, and related to some God-inspired meaning. But the obvious fact is that their lives are without any meaning whatever— that human life is a silly disappointment, a liar's promise, a perpetual in bankruptcy for debts we never contracted, a daily appointment with peace and happiness in which we wait day after day, hoping against hope, listening to each footstep, and when finally the bride or the bridegroom cometh, we discover we are kissing Death.[7]

---

7. This is another speech reflecting O'Neill's late plays. Louis Sheaffer (*O'Neill Son and Artist*, pp. 495ff.) has suggested that O'Neill's notion for this line and the bridegroom as death, and later the "Iceman" as death, derived from the novel *The Bridegroom Cometh* by Waldo Frank. Sheaffer also notes that O'Neill was well versed in the Scriptures and must have been familiar with the passage from Matthew (25:506): "While the bride-

DEBORAH No! Stop!

SIMON Or, obsessed by a fairy tale, we spend our lives searching for a magic door and a lost kingdom of peace from which we have been dispossessed by a greedy swindler.

DEBORAH [*suddenly taunting*] Ah, if you are going to start harping on that childish nonsense—

SIMON And when we find it we stand and beg before it. But the door is never opened. And at last we die and the starving scavenger hogs of life devour our carrion! [*with sudden strange fury*] No, by God, it shall not happen to me! What has been taken from me, I take back!

DEBORAH [*terrified*] Simon! Don't look like that! You frighten me!

SIMON [*quietly again*] So, let us not be sentimental and vain about the value of others' lives to us, Mother. Or of our own lives to ourselves. Regarded sensibly, we should all have clauses in our wills expressing gratitude to, and suitably rewarding anyone who should murder us. The murderer, I think, possesses the true quality of mercy. [*He chuckles sardonically.*] So, although I know how you have always, at any cost, escaped confronting facts—

DEBORAH [*with strange scorn*] You are a fool! As if I did not once think exactly as you have been thinking. I used to sit alone in there in disdainful self-contemplation [*She looks at the summerhouse.*] and make my mind face every fact until my thoughts beat with broken bleeding hands at the walls of my brain and I longed to escape by any door— [*stops abruptly—staring frightenedly at the door*] But I do not wish to remember that dead woman!

SIMON [*as if she hadn't spoken*] You must at least admit it—your right in self-defense to kill the enemy who plots to destroy. Surely you cannot be blind to the fact that Sara's jealous hatred has reached a pitch now where she will use any means whatsoever to get rid of you.

---

groom tarried, they all slumbered and slept. And at midnight there was a cry made, Behold, the bridegroom cometh." Larry Slade says in *The Iceman Cometh,* "for Death was the Iceman Hickey called to his home" ([New York: Random House, 1954], p. 680). See also the first chapter of Judith Barlow's *Final Acts* ([Athens: Univ. of Georgia Press, 1985]) for a thorough analysis of the analogues of *Iceman.*

DEBORAH [*eagerly*] Yes! I know! [*struggling with herself*] No! It's a lie! She would never—

SIMON   And you must acknowledge that in your mind you have murdered her countless times. So I cannot see why the thought should make you shudder now.

DEBORAH [*confusedly*] Yes, I confess I have dreamed— But those were dreams. Now it becomes real—when you put it in my mind. It begins to live in my will. It is born. It begins to me, to direct itself toward a consummation, like a destiny! [*struggling with herself*] No! I will not let you put it in my mind! [*with wild desperation*] But you have! It is there now! It will go on! I cannot stop it! And one day soon I will be hating her young body and her pretty face, and I will follow her to the top of the stairs—! Or I will remember the gardener keeps arsenic in the cellar for killing vermin—! [*deliberately jumping to her feet*] No! I couldn't—I couldn't! It is your thought, not mine! How can you think your mother— You are horrible! How could I have born such a cruel, evil monster into the world! You terrify me! You are insane! I am afraid to be alone with you! [*pulling at her hand*] Let me go! I will call Sara! [*She calls.*] Sara! Sara!

SIMON [*keeps hold of her hand—quietly*] She cannot hear. She is too busy devouring her children. [*He pulls her gently back—quietly*] Come. Sit down, Mother. What have you and I to do with her— except to plan together how we may be free of her? [*persuasively*] I am sorry if I frightened you by forcing you to confront your desire to murder her.

DEBORAH [*weakly letting herself be pulled down beside him*] No! Not my wish! Yours!

SIMON   I did it to make you realize what must inevitably happen soon. That the hate between you has reached a crisis—that one life can no longer contain you both without being torn apart and destroyed! [*He suddenly bursts out with a terrible intensity.*] I tell you I have reached the end of the tether! I cannot go on! One of you must cease to live in me! It is you or she! Can't you see I am trying to make clear to you that I have chosen you?

DEBORAH [*her face lighting up with a passionate joy*] You mean—you really mean— Oh, I know! I knew in the end I could not fail! Oh, my son! My beloved son! [*then frightened*] But not murder— You must not murder—promise me you will not—

SIMON   No. There is another way for us to be free.

DEBORAH   Ah! Oh, I will do anything, if you will not compel me to murder! What—?

SIMON   We will leave her here. We will go together so far away from the reality that not even the memory of her can follow to haunt my mind. We will go back where she never existed. You have only to open that door— [*His eyes fasten on the summerhouse door with a fascinated longing.*]

DEBORAH   [*stares at it with dread and longing herself—forcing a belittling tone*] Now, Dear, you mustn't start harping on that fantastic childish nonsense again!

SIMON   [*ignoring this—gets to his feet—holding her hand, his eyes on the door—eagerly*] But we must hurry, Mother. She will come back before long. She will try to keep me within her greed. She will open her arms to me. She is very beautiful. She will make me believe her lust is love.

DEBORAH   [*her face hardening—gets to her feet*] No! I am willing to pay any price to save you from her, and if this is the one possible way, so be it! [*She takes a step toward the door—then her eyes fixed on it, she recoils, shuddering, stammers*] No! Wait!

SIMON   [*his eyes on the door—fascinated*] I have waited ever since I was a little boy. All my life since then I have stood outside that door in my mind, begging you to let me re-enter that lost life of peace and trustful faith and happiness! I cannot wait any longer, Mother. And you cannot wait. You must choose between me and yourself. You once chose yourself and drove me out, and that has happened since [then].[8] Now you must either choose to repudiate that old choice, and give me back the faith you stole from me, or I will choose her!

DEBORAH   No!

---

8. The typescript reads "since began." I have substituted "since then" to retain the logic of the thought.

SIMON   I will choose her! And then there will be no choice left to you but to run and hide within yourself in there again, and dream yourself into the madhouse to escape yourself!

DEBORAH   [*horrified*]   Simon! For God's sake, how can you say such things to your mother who loves you more than life! As if you wished—

SIMON   I wish to be free, Mother!

DEBORAH   [*anguished*]   Oh! You can admit that to me!

SIMON   Free of one of my two selves, of one of the enemies within my mind, before their duel for possession destroys it. I have no longer any choice but to choose. Either you and all the life of dreams, in which love is spirit, of which you are the living symbol in my mind—or her and all the world of reality in which flesh is fact, and love is the body's lust. To belong wholly to either is my one possible escape now. [*He adds grimly.*] Or would you prefer I should go insane—and so be rid of me again?

DEBORAH   [*shuddering*]   No! Oh, how can you say—! You must be insane already or you wouldn't—

SIMON   I am waiting, Mother—for you to open that door, and give me back what was mine—my kingdom of the spirit's faith in life and love that your greed for yourself dispossessed me from!

DEBORAH   [*bitterly*]   So it was all my doing, was it? You have changed your tune! You have always boasted your love of liberty and the natural rights of man left of its own free will! [*She sneers tauntingly.*]

SIMON   You are speaking of something my pride was forced to choose long after I had been driven out in spirit. Naturally, to keep my self-respect—to go on living at all—I had to pretend I had found more worthy objects for my dreams—and, to the outside world to which you exiled me, a more unselfish object for my love, someone who would be mine, and not I, hers!

DEBORAH   [*her eyes gleaming with satisfaction—tauntingly*]   And how Sara has turned the tables and cheated you, poor boy! How common prettiness has but to smile and pretend desire for your desire and you begin begging on your knees! [*She laughs.*] I must warn you to take care, Dear. Your pride is making the most humiliating confessions for a Napoleon among men! Why, I begin to think now you were to have no life at all that did not hide within a woman's life—that you have never loved liberty at all but hated and dreaded it! [*She laughs mockingly.*]

SIMON [*coldly*] You are compelling me to choose her. [*He lets go her hand.*] Very well. I shall go to her. Do not attempt to follow me in the house. I shall lock you out as you once did me. You will stay here alone until you do what you must do to escape. I have no doubt you will find happiness in a foolish dream as a King's courtesan! And I shall be free to be Sara's—body and soul. Goodbye, Mother. [*He turns to go.*]

DEBORAH [*grabs his hand—pleading frantically*] No! For God's sake, don't leave me alone here! I will do anything you ask! [*She leads him a step towards the door—then falters again and begins to argue desperately as if she were trying to convince a child.*] But—it is all so silly and childish—so absurd and perverse—and revolting—for you, a grown man—a great man of worldly affairs—to remember— to make into a literal fact—an old fairy story—a passing fantasy of my brain—I made up in an idle moment to amuse you and make you laugh.

SIMON [*with bitter hatred*] You know that is a lie, Mother! To make me realize you hated your love for me because it possessed you and you wanted to be free! To hurt me, to taunt me, to laugh at my love, to force me from you back into myself! That's why you told it!

DEBORAH [*weakly*] No! How can you think I could be so cruel to my beloved little boy? [*then defensively*] But even if what you accuse me of is true, surely I had a right to own my own life!

SIMON [*ignoring this*] You know I knew who you meant by the evil enchantress and that I was the exiled Prince!

DEBORAH [*defensively*] You are being ridiculous. That was your old selfish demand that I might not even dream of myself without including you! [*trying to argue again—desperately*] But surely you see how idiotic it is to connect the door and that silly tale, which has no existence except in your fanciful imagination, with the actual wooden door of a common old summerhouse—the one we see so clearly in the moonlight now! Why that—that really is insane, Simon.

SIMON [*tensely*] I know very well it is a wooden door to an actual summerhouse—in the reality outside us— But I know, too, as you know, that in the deeper reality inside us, it has the meaning our minds have given it.

DEBORAH   Your mind has given it one meaning, but in mine it has an opposite—you think it is the door to some fantastic dream of Heaven, but I remember the hell—

SIMON   [*ignoring this—obsessedly*]   It exists in our minds as a symbol of our destiny, a door through which you drove me out of your love when you became evil and greedy for a false freedom. Surely you see that is what you meant in your symbolic fairy tale?

DEBORAH   No! No! It was merely a humorous fantasy—a capricious whim! I meant nothing!

SIMON   [*in same tone*]   The actual door there is a necessary concrete symbol. Your opening it and leading me inside will be the necessary physical act by which your mind wills to take me back into your love, to repudiate your treachery in driving me out of your heart, to deny the evil ruthless woman your dreams of freedom made you and become again your old true self, the mother who loved me alone, whom alone I loved! [*He smiles at her with a sudden awkward tenderness.*] So you see it is all perfectly rational and logical in my mind, and there is nothing insane about it, Mother. The kingdom of peace and happiness in your story is love. You dispossessed yourself when you dispossessed me. Since then we have both been condemned to an insatiable, unscrupulous greed for substitutes to fill the emptiness, the loss of love we had left within us. [*He stares obsessedly at the door again.*] But you have only to open that door, Mother—which is really a door on your own mind—

DEBORAH   [*with a shudder*]   I know!—and I know only too well the escape it leads to!

SIMON   [*pats her hand—tenderly persuasive, but his eyes are fixed on the door*]   Forget those silly fears, Mother. They came after. We have gone back before they existed, or the woman who dreamed them existed. Just as we are now back in a life before Sara existed in me and I in her. We have got rid of her.

DEBORAH   [*eagerly*]   Yes! I will pay anything to do that to her!

SIMON   We are back here in your garden on the day you told me that story. [*He pauses—then turns on her with a bitter vindictive condemnation*] You knew I knew what you meant me to know! I have never forgotten the anguished sense of being suddenly betrayed, of being wounded and deserted and left alone in a life in which there was no security or faith or love but only danger and suspicion and devouring greed! [*harshly*] By God, I hated you then! I wished you dead! I wished I had never been born!

DEBORAH [*with an obviously fake air of contrition thinly masking a strange, cruel satisfaction*] Did you, Dear? I am sorry if I hurt you. It is true I hoped you would guess what I meant. You were such a stubborn greedy little boy, so inquisitive and pryishly possessive. I could feel your grasping fingers groping toward every secret, private corner of my soul. I had come to the point when I even preferred Joel because I was utterly indifferent to him, where at times I hated you and wished you had never been born. So I had to do something to warn you, and I thought a fairy tale would be the most tactful way— [*Abruptly her expression changes to one of horror for herself—distractedly*] No! I never meant—! You put it in my mind! It's insane of you to make me confess such horrible things! And how can you admit you hated your mother and wished her dead!

SIMON [*contritely stammers*] I—Forgive me, Mother!—I did only because you— [*then passionately*] All I ask is that you go back and change that—change the ending—open the door and take me back— and all that has happened since, which you began that day, will be out of memory, forgotten! There will be only love and faith and trust in life—the old greedless security and content with what we have! There will be only you and I! There will be peace and happiness to the end of our days! Can't you believe me, Mother? I tell you I know!

DEBORAH [*shakingly—staring at the door fascinatedly*] Oh, if I could, Dear! If I only could believe, how willingly I would go! If you knew how I have loved you, how desperately I have longed to have you back, to take you from her, to know you were mine alone, to be nothing but your mother, to live and forget myself, to live solely in your life, to make any sacrifice of self with happiness, exultantly in self-fulfillment, to dream no dream except to love you more and more! [*passionately*] Yes! I think I believe now—believe that if the mind wills anything with enough intensity of love it can force life to its desire, create a heaven, if need be, out of hell! [*with a strange triumphant laugh*] Yes, taking you with me, I would have no fear of insanity, for all is fair in love, and love would make it sane.

SIMON [*strangely*] Yes, we need not concern ourselves with the bad names men have given to things they fear or do not understand. [*He laughs harshly.*] Good God, if the reality of hoggish greed and dog eat dog and lust devour love is sane, then what man of honorable mind would not prefer to be considered lunatic! [*with sudden urgency*] Come, Mother! Let us leave this vile sty of lust and hatred and the wish to murder! Let us escape back into peace—while there is still time!

DEBORAH [*with forced eagerness, mounts the first step*] Yes, let us hurry, Dear—before I can think— [*then she stops—desperately*] But I must warn you—I could never forgive myself if I did not warn you once more of the danger—

SIMON [*scornfully proud*] Danger? Don't you know Sara has made me a greedy gambler who loves danger and the greatest possible risk? What do I care if the fate in there has stacked the cards and loaded the dice? I promise you I will outswindle it and steal our happiness and love from under its nose! [*boastfully*] What I want I have the power to take, and will always take! You forget they do not call me a Napoleon of trade without my having proven my right to the title!

DEBORAH [*hangs back resentfully now—almost jeeringly*] You had better not boast of your power to enslave, for I warn you you may bitterly regret your daring if you find it is, in truth, the evil enchantress of my fairy tale who waits there to enslave you in her arms! If I remember the mad woman I locked in there, she must have chosen madness long ago, because she was entirely ruthless and unscrupulous, a daring courtesan who takes what she wants by any means she can, even madness. She will not recognize you as her son! She never had a child. Her pride would have made her kill herself before she would ever have shared herself, or seen her beauty grow bloated and misshapen, with an alien's possession! Her arrogance would never put her life in bondage to another's life, or create another she would be forced to love as she loved herself! She has loved herself alone! She has remained free! You will be no more than another man to her—that is, no more than a slave to her every whim and caprice—like the King before she discarded him to make a fool of Napoleon whom her poor weakling of a father confused with God and himself! [*She stops abruptly—guiltily confused—and stammers stupidly.*] I—please do not mind me—I do not think I know what I was saying—

SIMON [*has turned on her sneeringly*] I should hope not! You remember how I had to laugh at you the time you boasted to me of that preposterous romantic evil dream about yourself! You, my poor little, old mother! [*He gives a taunting, sneering chuckle.*]

DEBORAH [*stung—with furious hatred*] How dare you—! [*then with a sudden change to an ominous gentleness*] But I see. You are so cunning to get your own way by any means, aren't you, Dear—like Napoleon? You were clever enough to see that while love might make me hesitate, for your sake, hate would give me the necessary courage to be quite ruthless in thinking only of winning a final victory over her. [*She laughs softly, turns abruptly and goes up the remaining steps—tenderly*] Come, Dear. Mother is only too glad to do anything you ask her to now.

SIMON [*strangely*] We will go far back before that laughter existed, Mother. You will not know you ever heard it, then, or that I ever laughed. There will be peace and unity. We shall have gone back beyond separations. We shall be one again. [*suddenly in a panic*] But hurry, Mother! Hurry! I hear someone coming! It must be she! But I will run away from her now and hide in my mind back there in our past together. She will be a stranger!

DEBORAH [*begins to assume an air of a cruel ruthless gratification*] Let her come! It will add strength to my hatred! And it will be a pleasure to have her witness my final victory! Now I have decided, I am stronger than she ever dared to be! [*She moves so that she stands protectingly before Simon, her right hand on the knob of the door. Sara comes hurrying in from the left. She is in a panic of apprehensive dread. When she sees them both still outside the summerhouse, this changes to rage against Deborah.*]

SARA [*to Deborah*] You liar! You thief! You black-hearted traitor! I should have known better than to leave you— But God be praised I'm back in time!

DEBORAH [*jeering quietly*]   Yes. You are just in time—to bid us farewell!

SARA [*frightened—forcing a commanding tone*]   Simon! Come here to me away from that door! Do you want to lose what little wits you've left, playing her crazy games with her? [*But Simon appears not to have heard her, or to have noticed her coming. He keeps behind his mother turned sideways to Sara, his eyes fixed fascinatedly on the door.*]

DEBORAH [*addressing him over her shoulder, her eyes on Sara*]   My love, you no longer remember this woman, do you? You will not permit a vulgar, common slut to intrude and delay our departure.

SIMON [*starts and turns his head to stare at Sara without recognition over his mother's shoulder. His face has a strange, mad, trance-like look. He murmurs obediently.*]   No, Mother. [*He addresses Sara with a sharp arrogance.*]   Who are you? What do you want? How dare you trespass here and start making a disgusting scene? Do you think my mother's garden is the parlor of a brothel?

SARA [*shrinks as if she'd been struck—strickenly*]   Simon! Don't speak like—

SIMON   By what right do you presume to call me by my first name? I do not know you. [*strangely*]   It is true you remind me of a mistress I once bought to amuse myself observing her greedy attempt to swindle me of myself. But it was I who swindled her by paying her with counterfeit appearances. Then when her lust began to bore me, I deserted her and went off with another woman, an old lover in my childhood. [*He adds hastily.*]   Whom I loved with a great pure love, a spiritual love of the mind and the soul, rare and beautiful, her ethereal passion, a love belonging to fantasy and dreams!

SARA [*trembling*]   Simon! It is mad you are!

SIMON [*disdainfully—as if he were addressing a servant*]   Begone! Before I summon the police! [*pointing to a door in wall at right*]   That door leads to the street where you belong. Go back and ply your trade there. Your body defiles the pure atmosphere of my mother's garden.

SARA [*pitifully*]   Darling! It's I! Your Sara!

DEBORAH [*gloating—haughtily*] You have my son's orders! [*then to Simon*] But I think, Dear, it might be simpler for us to leave her now.

SIMON [*eagerly*] Yes, Mother. Let us go!

DEBORAH [*exultantly*] Yes! I can now! I am as strong as I ever wished to be in any dream! I will take what my whim desires from life, and laugh at the cost! [*She laughs and with an abrupt movement jerks open the door behind her so it stands back against the wall. Simon gives a gasping eager cry and leans forward, staring into the darkness inside. But Deborah does not turn to it but remains confronting Sara.*]

SARA [*wildly*] No! [*rushes up and grabs Deborah's skirt and falls on her knees before her.*] For the love of God have pity, Deborah!

DEBORAH [*starts*] Pity? [*then angrily*] Would you remind me of pity now, you scheming slut?

SARA [*pleadingly*] Remember I had pity on you!

DEBORAH You lie! I will not remember! I have forgotten pity. [*She kicks at Sara viciously.*] How dare you hold me! Let me free!

SARA [*pleadingly*] I'm asking your pity for him, not for me! You love him! You can't do this!

DEBORAH [*scornful*] You weak sentimental fool! Love is proud, not pitiful! It takes what it desires! [*hastily*] You dare to speak of pity! You, the harlot whose greed is devouring him and driving him insane! It's because I love him that I must save him from your destroying lust! So let go! [*She kicks her skirt from Sara's hand and half turns to the door, grabbing Simon's arm.*] Come, Dear! Quick! Let us go where we cannot hear her lies about love and pity!

SIMON [*with a crazy eagerness*] Yes! The door is open! I feel our old peace and happiness waiting to welcome us! Take my hand, Mother!

SARA [*wildly, grabbing Deborah's skirt again*] No! Wait! Listen! Deborah! I give up! I admit I'm beaten now! I'll pay you any price you ask, if only—

DEBORAH [*triumphantly*] Ah! So you admit—I always knew that in the end— [*then with arrogant disdain*] You have the impertinence to believe there is anything you possess that I could be so low as to desire? You flatter yourself!

SIMON [*turns his head a little from staring inside the summerhouse—*

dazedly and uneasily] Sara? Sara? Who? Who are you talking to, Mother? What is she trying to make me remember? How could I? This is long before any other woman. There is only your love. I do not need her. Make her leave us alone, Mother!—so we can go back to peace.

DEBORAH [*cruelly scornful and at the same time uneasy*] Yes, I will not listen to her pleading lies! We will go—

SARA [*in anguish*] Simon! Darling! It's her madness in there! It's the asylum!

DEBORAH [*shakenly—fighting back fiercely*] You lie! Our minds will compel it to be our dream! Our love can make a heaven even in hell if we are together—if we are one again! [*She half turns to Simon but keeps her eyes averted from the doorway.*] Do not listen to this low, vulgar harlot, Dear! What could she know of the transfiguring power of the mind, or the miraculous power of the spirit, she whose soul is a pound of greedy flesh! [*She reaches out her hand which he clasps eagerly.*] Here is my hand, Dear! Come! [*She tries to [   ] determinedly—to rush in with her eyes shut, leading him.*]

SARA [*distractedly—throws herself forward and flings her arms around Deborah's legs—pleading wildly*] For the love of God! For the love of your son, Deborah! You can't! And don't you see there's no need now! You can have him back without—I'm telling you I'll give him up to you! I'll go away! I'll leave him to you! I'll never trouble you again! You'll be rid of me! And that's all you've wanted, isn't it? So, for the love of God, stop—!

DEBORAH [*stares at her, her face lighting up eagerly, but unable to believe her ears*] You really mean—you will give up—go away—never again intrude or trespass—on what is mine?

SARA I will—for love of him—to save him. You can have him all to yourself again. I know I can trust your love for him, once I'm out of the way, to protect him from himself—and from your own mad dreams. And I know, when he has only you to love, he'll forget me, and he won't be destroyed and torn between us within himself.

DEBORAH [*eagerly*] Yes! I swear to you I will protect and make him contented and at peace with life. [*complacently*] After all, I am his mother, and I would give my life for him. [*relaxing with a smile of triumph*] Ah! [*then immediately with suspicious anger*] You're lying! This is all another of your cunning tricks! Do you still think I trust you?

SARA [*dully*]   No, Deborah. I'm beyond tricks now. I'm finished.

DEBORAH [*smiles down at her with contemptuous gloating*]   You must be utterly beaten, then—more beaten than I ever hoped you could be! Evidently, I gave you credit for more strength and pride than you possess! [*sneeringly*] But I think I see! You've swindled him out of everything he owns, except what you find you cannot steal—what is mine—himself! So now, having got all you can, he's useless to you and you'll discard him like the unscrupulous slut you are, and go soliciting a new victim! Is that it? [*She sneers insultingly. A strange angry hostility is creeping into her attitude as if, now she had won a complete victory, she was beginning to feel it was a defeat.*]

SARA [*dully*]   No. I'll sign all that over to you. I don't want it. All I'll keep is the old farm, so I'll have a home for my children, and can make a living with them. I'll take them there tomorrow. [*She gets to her feet slowly and exhaustedly.*]

SIMON [*who has remained tense and motionless, staring fascinatedly into the darkness inside the summerhouse—in a boyish uneasy whisper, tugging at her hand*]   Why are you waiting, Mother? We mustn't wait—or it may be too late! You will get afraid again. [*But neither woman seems to hear him.*]

DEBORAH [*sneering more insultingly*]   You are welcome to the farm. I am glad you at last realize what you are and where you belong. A stupid peasant tilling the soil, her bare feet in the earth, her gross body stinking of sweat, a dumb brainless, begetting female animal with her dirty brats around her! [*jeeringly*] But what becomes of your grand estate, and the ridiculous Irish dream castle in Spain?

SARA [*resignedly—without resentment*]   That was foolishness. I'm done with that, too.

DEBORAH [*sneeringly*]   What virtuous Christian resignation! How shamelessly abject and humble you are!

SARA [*quietly*]   If I'm humbled, it's by myself and my love, not by you. [*with a flash of pride*] And I'm proud of that. For, if I'll never rise to owning a grand estate now, I've risen in life now in the only way that counts, above myself, which is more than you'll ever do! I can wish him happiness without me, and mean it! Yes, and I can even wish you to be happy so you can make him happy, and mean that, too!

DEBORAH [*for an instant moved in spite of herself—stammers gratefully*] I—thank you, Sara—you are generous and fine— [*then in a burst of sneering hostility*] You lie! You cannot fool me! This is all cheap acting, and the role of sacrificed, unselfish love is absolutely fake to your true nature! [*jeeringly*] The truth is what I have always known! You are incapable of love! I alone really love him because I would rather see him dead—or kill him myself!—than give him up to another woman!

SARA [*quietly*] You don't believe that. You know no woman could love a man more than when she gives him up to save him!

DEBORAH [*with strange repressed fury*] I know—I begin to see your scheme—the trick behind—with your superior self-sacrificial airs— you want to show me you—to make me feel vile and contemptible—

SARA [*quietly and exhaustedly*] No. I've told you I'm beyond scheming. I'm too—dead. [*dully*] I'll leave you now, Deborah. I'll get the children up now and take them to a hotel where he can't find us. You keep him out here until I'm gone. That's the best way, to get it over and done now. You can explain in any way you think it best for you and him. But make it strong that I'm sick of him, and I'm getting another man and I never want to see him again. Give him a good excuse to give himself to forget me. That's all he needs to bring him peace with you alone. [*then giving Simon a worried look*] And look out you bring him back to his senses right away now. It isn't good for him to stay long—so far away in the past as you've taken him. [*She turns to go off left—brokenly, without looking at him*] Go bless you, Simon, Darling, for all the joy and love you gave me, and give you peace and happiness!

SIMON [*with a sort of bewildered anguish*] Mother! Someone is calling me! I'll have to go! I cannot remain back here much longer! Hurry, Mother! Hurry!

SARA   Goodbye, Deborah. [*She starts to walk away.*]

DEBORAH [*stammers weakly*] No—Sara— [*then fiercely*] Goodbye and
good riddance! Get out! Go! Leave me alone! I hate the sight of
you! [*then brokenly*] No, Sara—forgive—wait—I want to say—my
gratitude—want to tell you—you are beautiful and fine—so much
more beautiful—fine—than I— [*then bursting into a jealous fury,
glaring at her with hatred*] Ah, God damn you. You low, scheming
trollop! Do you think I don't see through you? All this hypocritical
sentimental posing! Your false self-sacrificial airs! You the noble
loving woman! I am the evil one who desires her son's life! Whose
greed does not scruple to use any means—base and utterly ignoble—
cruel and insatiable. You dare insult me so!—humiliate and put me
to shame before my son!—my beloved son— You dare to boast before him you love him more than I, his mother, who, ever since the
day I bore him, would gladly give my life for his happiness! As if
a low lustful creature like you could even imagine the depth of the
love I have for him, let alone feel it! And yet you have the vulgar
effrontery to pretend— [*in a fresh burst of savage passion*] You liar!
But I'll prove to you who is the final victor between us, who is the
one who loves him most! [*She turns to face the darkness within the
doorway.*]
SIMON [*with an eager cry*] Mother! At last! Hurry! She is coming to
take me!
SARA [*frightenedly*] Simon!
DEBORAH [*pulls her hand violently from his*] No! Alone!
SIMON [*despairingly—grabbing at her hand*] Mother!
DEBORAH [*flings his hand away—with a strange boastful arrogance*]
Alone, I said! As I have always been. As my pride and disdain have
always willed I be!—hating the vile sordid ugliness of life—choosing
to keep my spirit pure and untouched and unpossessed!—my soul
my own!—at any cost—at any sacrifice— [*looking at him now with
repulsion*] Go away! Do not dare to touch me! What are you to me!
I am my own! Ah, how could I have ever been so weak as to allow
you to intrude on my dream and involve me in a filthy sordid intrigue with a greedy, money-grabbing merchant and his peasant slut
of a wife! I, if I had been born in a nobler time, could have had the
love of a King or an Emperor! [*to Simon with hatred*] You—get

back to the greasy arms of your wife where you belong! [*With extraordinary strength she gives him a push in the chest that drives him off balance and sends him spinning down the steps to fall heavily and lie still by the stone bench at left of pool.*]

SARA [*flings herself on her knees beside him and raises his head*] Simon! [*He stirs and moans feebly.*]

DEBORAH [*turns and stops on the threshold, confronting the darkness—with a self-contemptuous laugh*] To think you were afraid, Deborah! Why, what is waiting to welcome you is merely your last disdain! [*She goes in quietly and shuts the door.*]

SARA [*oblivious to her going*] Darling! Are you hurt bad? [*She feels his body.*] I can't find anything broken—but I heard his head hit—

SIMON [*suddenly raises his head and stares at the door and mutters stupidly the unhappy end of the fairy story*] So the Prince waited before the door and begged for love from all who passed by. [*He falls back in her arms in a faint.*]

SARA [*frightenedly*] Simon! Merciful God! Speak to me, Darling! [*In a panic she puts her hand over his heart—relieved*] No, he's only fainted. [*She chafes his wrists.*] Maybe it's best. He'd be trying to get in there. [*She stops rubbing his wrists and turns to stare at the summerhouse—in an awed horrified whisper.*] God help me, she's done it. [*with admiration*] Ah, it's a great noble lady you couldn't help proving yourself in the end, and it's you that beat me, for your pride paid a price for love my pride would never dare to pay! [*She shudders—then with growing intensity*] But I swear to you now, Deborah, I'll try to keep up my end of the bargain and pay back all I can. I see now the part my greed and my father's crazy dreams in me had in leading Simon away from himself until he lost his way and began destroying all that was best in him! To make me proud of him! [*brokenly*] Ah, forgive me, Darling! But I'll give my life now to setting you free to be again the man you were when I first met you—the man I loved best!—the dreamer with a touch of the poet in his soul, and the heart of a boy! [*with a strange almost masochistic satisfaction*] Don't I know, Darling, the longing in your heart that I'd smash the Company into smithereens to prove my love for you and set you free from the greed of it! Well, by the Eternal, I'll smash it so there'll be nothing left to tempt me! It's easy. It needs only a whisper of the true condition to Tenard, pretending I'm a fool woman who takes him into her confidence, now he's in the Company. [*with a gloating smile*] I can hear the revenge in his heart laughing, rushing out to tell all our enemies and combine with them to pounce down and ruin us! Well, they can't take the old farm anyway, and we'll live there, and the boys will work with me, and you'll never have to lift your hand again, but you can spend your days in your old cabin where you first were mine, and write poetry again of your love for me, and plan your book that will save the world and free men from the curse of greed in them! [*She pauses guiltily.*] God forgive me, I'm happy at the mere thought of it, and it's no price at all I'll be paying to match yours, Deborah, if I'm happy! [*then with an abrupt change to practical calculation*] That reminds me, before I start the whisper, I'll get all the Company's cash from the banks and put it in her name, along with this house, with Joel to take care of it, so she'll have enough and plenty to keep her here, with her garden, and the comfort and riches and luxury that's due the great Princess on her grand estate she'll be on in her dream till the day she dies! [*While she has been saying this last, the door of the summerhouse has slowly opened and Deborah has appeared. She now stands on the top of the steps. Her eyes have a still, fixed, sightless, trance-like look, but her face is proud, self-assured, arrogant and happy, and she looks beautiful and serene, and many years younger.*]

DEBORAH [*in a tone of haughty command*]   Be quiet! Who is talking? How dare you come here? Who are you?

SARA [*starts and stares at her—in an awed whisper*]   Ah, God pity her, the poor woman!

DEBORAH [*coming down the steps— As she does so, Sara gets to her feet, letting Simon's head rest back on the grass.*]   Answer me! [*A look of recognition comes over her face—with a regal gracious condescension.*] Ah, you are the Irish kitchen maid, are you not? I remember you—

SARA [*An impulse of angry insult flashes in her eyes—but immediately she controls this, whispering pityingly to herself.*]   Poor creature! She's hidden herself in her dream forever!

DEBORAH [*approaching her, erect and arrogant and graceful, her head *held high*] What are you doing in the Palace grounds at this hour, poor peasant? Do you not know there is a terrible punishment for trespassing in my domain?

SARA [*humoring her—bobs her an awkward servant-girl curtsy and speaks humbly*] I know I have no right here, My Lady. If you'll be kind enough to forgive me, I'll never intrude again.

DEBORAH   This garden is the Emperor's gift to me. He is very jealous of my privacy. [*then with a cautious backward glance at the summerhouse*] Sush, we must not wake him. [*with a soft gloating little laugh*] But he sleeps soundly. My love is too great for him. It devours him. In my arms, he is so weak—so like a little boy, the Great Napoleon! So small, compared to my great love! He will give me the world, and still it will be too little! [*then suddenly—sharply and suspiciously*] Why are you silent? Do you dare to doubt me?

SARA [*humbly*]   Indeed I don't, Your Majesty.

DEBORAH [*reassured and pleasant*]   I am not Majesty, my poor woman. Of course, if it were my whim— He would gladly divorce his wife, who is a stupid, common woman, quite unworthy. But I tell him marriage is a trader's bargain. It corrupts love which shall be always beautiful and free. [*then with a condescending kindliness*] But you would not understand that. You have not told me why you are here, poor peasant. You came to keep an assignation with your lover, I suppose. Doubtless some groom from my stables. You peasants are such animals. But never mind. I am disposed tonight to be lenient toward all lovers, for love's sake. I forgive you.

SARA [*with another curtsy*]   Thank you, My Lady. [*then impulsively*] I wanted to ask you to forgive me, Deborah.

DEBORAH [*wonderingly*]   Deborah? Who is Deborah? [*Her eyes fall on Simon. She starts—then indifferently.*] Who is that lying at your feet? Your lover? Is he dead? Did you murder him for love of him? Oh, do not be afraid. I understand everything a woman's love could possibly compel her to desire. I know she can even kill herself to prove her love, so proud can she be of it.

SARA [*quietly*]   I am sure you know that, My Lady. [*She stares at Deborah and suddenly her face is convulsed with a look of horrified suspicion and she grabs her by the arm and stammers*] For the love of God, Deborah, tell me you're not just pretending now—for love of him, to save him and set him free! That would be too great a price—I couldn't let you—!

DEBORAH [*trembles and seems about to collapse—avoiding Sara's eyes, falteringly*] I—I do not understand you—You must not—! [*Suddenly she is the arrogant grand dame again—with haughty anger—snatching Sara's hand off her arm*] You forget yourself. Do not presume to touch me. Your presence wearies me. I must go back to the Emperor. See that you take your lover away at once and never return here.

SARA [*stammers*] Yes, My Lady. [*confusedly to herself*] No, no—I'm a fool. She's really gone forever in her dreams! But— Tell me this, are you happy now? Ah,—My Lady?

DEBORAH [*smiles condescendingly*] You are impertinent. But I forgive it, because I *am* happy. And I wish you may be happy with your lover, too. [*haughtily*] But now farewell, good woman. [*She holds out her hand arrogantly.*] You may kneel and kiss my hand.

SARA [*A flash of insulted pride comes to her eyes and for a second she seems about to retreat angrily—then impulsively she kneels and kisses her hand.*] Thank you for your great kindness, My Lady. [*Deborah turns from her to ascend the steps. Sara adds huskily.*] And God bless you.

DEBORAH [*ascending the steps, looks back, with a smile of gracious understanding amusement*] Why, thank you, good woman. I think that I may say that He has blessed me. [*She goes in the summerhouse and closes the door behind her.*]

SARA [*stares after her—miserably*] I wonder—I wonder— Oh, God help me, I'll never be sure of the truth of it now! [*Simon groans and stirs and looks up at her.*]

SIMON [*murmurs stupidly*] Mother. Hurry. Let us go. Peace and happiness.

SARA [*at once forgetting everything but him*] Yes, Darling. We'll go. Come on. Raise yourself. [*She bends and puts her arm around his shoulder to help him.*] That's it.

SIMON [*dazedly—like a little boy*] I fell and hit my head, Mother. It hurts.

SARA   I'll bathe it for you when we get in the house. Come along now. [*She turns him into the path leading off left and urges him along it.*]
SIMON [*dazedly*]   Yes, Mother.
SARA [*with a fierce, passionate possessive tenderness*]   Yes, I'll be your mother, too, now, and your peace and happiness and all you'll ever need in life! [*They disappear off left.*]

* * * CURTAIN * * *

Tao House
Dec. 30, '38

Epilogue

———

SCENE *Same as Act One, Scene Two, Simon's old cabin by the lake on the farm. It is a late afternoon of a fine day in early June of the following year, 1842.*

There is a great change in the cabin and little clearing from the abandoned, neglected appearance it had in the first act scene of 1832. The grass, a fresh green, has been cut and the paths across it from the woods at left to the door of the cabin, and from the door down to the shore of the lake, off right, are clearly defined. The windows of the cabin are washed and clean, with their frames a newly painted white. The chinks in the logs have been caulked, the chimney patched up with fresh mortar. The bench against the wall of the cabin has been painted green.

Sara's and Simon's youngest son, Owen Roe "Honey" Harford, is discovered, squatting on his heels on the grass before the bench, playing a game with a jackknife, flipping it from his fingers to make it stick in the ground. He wears only an old shirt and a pair of short pants. Both are dirty. So are his sunburned, freckled face, his hands and bare legs and feet. He is going on nine and a half now, is big for his age, stout and healthy. His face is typically Irish with blue eyes, dark curly hair, and he has a marked resemblance to his mother. His expression is happy and good-natured. He has a charming ingratiating grin and a sparkle of sly, droll humor in his inquisitive eyes. As he plays he sings softly Thomas Moore's[1] "Believe me if all those endearing young charms." He has a fine voice, clear and pure.

His brother, Jonathan, next to him in age, a year and a half older, comes in from the path at left. Although older he is smaller than

———

1. Thomas Moore, an Irish poet, lived from 1779 to 1852.

Honey, undersized, thin and wiry, with a large head out of proportion with his body. His face is long, with a big nose, and sharp intelligent grey eyes, and straight mouse-colored hair. He is dressed much the same as Honey but his clothes are clean, as are his face and hands and legs. He gives one the impression of being older than his years, full of a tense nervous vitality, but remarkably self-disciplined and sure of his own capabilities. Between these two younger brothers the relationship is one of close affection with Jonathan the leader, a bit bullyingly superior and condescending, and Honey an admiring satellite, but not so admiring he does not poke constant fun at him.

JONATHAN [*stops just inside the clearing and attracts his brother's attention*] Ssstt! [*Honey looks up. Jonathan beckons and Honey goes to him without stopping his song. Jonathan asks in a low voice.*] Is he still there?

HONEY   What d'you think? I'd have gone after him, wouldn't I if he'd left. [*He starts singing again.*]

JONATHAN [*scornfully*] He could sneak out and you'd be too lazy to catch him. [*scowling*] Shut up that music, can't you?

HONEY [*derisively*] Now? I sing good. You're jealous because you can't keep a tune! Anyway, Father likes it. Once when I stopped he called out to keep on. [*He glances back at the cabin.*] I think he's asleep now. I peeked in the window and he's lying down.

JONATHAN [*anxiously*] Did he know you all right? I mean, really know he was your father?

HONEY [*eagerly*] Sure! He talked like he used to—before he got sick. And the way he was talking to himself he remembers this place, and when he used to live here, and everything.

JONATHAN [*relieved*] That's fine. Gosh, I hope he'll be all right now, for keeps! [*with a trace of bitterness*] It's been no fun having him out of his head for so long, acting like a kid, and us having to pretend to him he was our brother.

HONEY   Yes. It's been crazy. [*then guiltily—loyally*] But he couldn't help it. It was brain fever. Mother says brain fever always does that to people.

JONATHAN [*guiltily*] Who's blaming him? He's my father, too. [*abruptly changing the subject*] Mother just got back from the funeral. Ethan told her how Father seemed to wake up all of a sudden and knew all of us in the potato field this morning, and asked for her, and how we'd lied and told him she'd gone to the city shopping. She burst out and started to cry she was so happy. She sent me down to tell you to keep him here. She'll be down as soon as she's changed her clothes. She doesn't want him to see her in mourning. She doesn't want him to know Granny's dead yet.

HONEY I'm glad Granny's dead. Aren't you? She was a crazy old fool. I got to hate her.

JONATHAN [*frowning*] So did I. But we ought to forget that now.

HONEY [*stubbornly*] I won't. She hated Mother. I don't see why Mother had to go to her funeral, or why she never let us say a word against her.

JONATHAN [*sharply*] That's Mother's business. [*then practically*] Anyway, what's the use of thinking about it now.

HONEY [*grinning*] I won't anymore. [*in brogue*] The divil take her! [*He turns away, carefree, and begins to sing again—then stops abruptly, looking around him*] Let's go for a swim, as soon as Mother comes. Gosh, I like it out here. I don't mind being poor, do you?

JONATHAN [*scornfully*] You like it? Yes, you do! When you don't have to work!

HONEY Well, who wants to be a farmer? You don't. Neither does Ethan. Nor Wolfe either, even if he pretends not to care.

JONATHAN [*seriously*] No, I don't want to be a farmer. And I won't be any longer than I have to. There's no money in farming. You can't get ahead. [*determinedly*] And I'm going to get ahead.

HONEY I'm going to own an hotel and run a livery stable. I love horses. And renting rooms and hiring out carriages, that's easy.

JONATHAN [*scornfully*] Something easy! That's what you always want!

HONEY [*grins*] Sure! I'll get mine! [*then after a glance up the path*] Here comes Mother. [*He dashes over and sits on the bench as if he were dutifully keeping guard. A moment later Sara enters. She wears a cheap calico working dress and is barefooted. Her fair com-*

plexion is tanned and her fine figure is strong, firm and healthy. She looks younger and at the same time older. Younger in that her face is no longer haggard, lined and tense. Older because of the look of resigned sadness in her eyes and the streaks of white in her black hair. Just now, however, her face is lighted up by an excited hope that is afraid that it is too good to be true.]

SARA [*in a whisper to Jonathan as she enters*]   He's in the cabin?

JONATHAN [*nods*]   He's asleep.

HONEY [*comes over toward her—virtuously*]   I never stopped keeping guard over him one moment, Mother.

SARA [*mechanically*]   That's a good boy. [*then a bit disappointedly*] Asleep, is he? I'd best let him sleep then. He's so weak. I was hoping he'd— It's hard to wait, wondering if he'll know me.

HONEY   Can I go swimming now—me and Jonathan?

SARA [*welcoming his interruption, surveys him critically*]   You can. But you'll go up to the house first and get soap to take with you, and you'll use it! Look at you! You can get more dirt on you in an hour than two pigs could in a week! Look at your clothes, too! And to think I ever dreamed of making you a gentleman! [*She gives him an affectionate pat and push.*] Get along with you. Go up to the field first, and you and Johnny help Ethan and Wolfe finish the row they're doing. Tell them they can stop work after that and come swimming. We all have a right to take a bit of a holiday and give thanks to God, if your father is getting well— [*She gives a longing look toward the cabin, but uneasy, afraid her hope may not be true. The two boys start eagerly off left. Suddenly she has a thought— guiltily*] Wait. Did you remember, like I asked you, to say a prayer for your grandmother's soul at the time of the funeral? [*They hang their heads and avoid her eyes. She says sadly.*] I see you didn't. [*to herself*] Poor woman! I was the only one really to mourn her. I kept my distance at the cemetery, with my veil on my face so none would know me. Ah, if she ever knew in her dreams what I've suffered, with him all mixed up and lost in his mind, calling me Mother, as if I was her, and forgetting he'd ever had a wife, she'd feel she was the one who'd won in the end after all.

HONEY [*fidgeting impatiently*]   Can we go now, Mother?

SARA [*starts—then sharply*]   You can't till you've said the prayer. You
  had no right to forget. Get down on your knees, now! [*as they
  hesitate sheepishly—peremptorily*] You hear me! [*They flop down
  self-consciously. She goes on argumentatively.*] Just because we have
  no faith in it doesn't mean it mightn't be true. No one knows. And
  it does no harm. It's a mark of respect. Say a prayer now. [*The two
  boys exchange looks. They feel silly and giggly.*]

JONATHAN   We've forgotten. What'll we say, Mother? [*She starts and
  hesitates, looking confused.*]

HONEY [*with an impish grin*]   You don't remember any either, Mother.

SARA [*hastily*]   Say God rest her in peace, and that'll do.

JONATHAN AND HONEY [*burst out in mechanical chorus*]   God rest her
  in peace.

[*They bound to their feet with relief that the absurd business is over.
As they do so the door from the cabin is opened and Simon appears.
He is terribly emaciated, pale and hollow-eyed, as though he had
passed through a long and devouring fever. His eyes have a groping
and bewildered stare. His clothes, the same as he wore in Act Four, are
clean and well kept, but wrinkled now as though he had slept in them.
He stands in the doorway, fixing his eyes on Sara, clinging weakly to
the door frame for support. The boys see him at once and start. Sara
guesses from their faces and whirls around. She tries to speak but is
terrified to risk it, and only her lips move soundlessly.*]

SIMON [*with a great gasp of relief and longing*]   Sara! [*He takes a
  weak, faltering step toward her.*]

SARA [*with a happy cry*]   Simon! [*She rushes to him.*] Darling! Oh,
  thank God you know me! [*She throws her arms around him and
  hugs him to her. The two boys give them an embarrassed, and yet
  happy look and then dart away up the path.*]

SIMON [*stammers brokenly*]   My love! I was so afraid I had lost you!

SARA [*tenderly—with a trembling smile*]   Lost me, is it? You couldn't.
  I'd never let you—not in this life—nor in death, neither! But you
  know I love you! [*protestingly*] Sit down. Here like we used when
  we first knew love—me on the bench and you on the grass with

your head on my lap. [*She sits on the bench and he obeys mechanically, sitting on the grass, his arms around her hungrily and clingingly, his head on her lap. She goes on in a blissful, tender, emotional croon.*] There now. Don't talk for a while. Just rest and be happy, Darling.

SIMON [*lets himself relax for a second, closing his eyes*]   Yes, Sweetheart. [*Then he jerks awake—pleading almost hysterically.*] No! You must tell me. At once! I want to know! I've been lying in there trying to remember—how I got here—why?—when?—what happened?

SARA [*bullying him soothingly*]   Now, now. Be quiet, and I'll tell you. There's nothing to be worried about. You've been sick with brain fever you got from working too hard and worrying too much about the Company—and I brought you here to get well. And now you are well, Darling.

SIMON [*dazedly*]   Brain fever? Yes—that would explain— [*frightenedly*] But—

SARA [*pulling his head back*]   Sush now, I tell you. Everything is all right. All the doctors said it was the most natural thing for you to lose your memory for a while. It's the way the sickness takes everyone that gets it.

SIMON [*beginning to be relieved*]   Is it? [*forcing a smile*] Well, I've come out all right, haven't I? [*pleading again*] But please tell me everything, Sara. I feel, so strange—as if part of me were lost—or had died. [*He shudders.*] It's a horrible feeling.

SARA   Sush, be quiet and I'll tell you every bit of it. [*Then she hesitates and casts a worried look at him—calculatingly*] But maybe it would be simpler if you told me first the last thing you remember.

SIMON [*with frowning concentration*]   The last? I have one clear memory. It came to me when I was lying in the cabin. The last thing I can remember was one day at the office I had an appointment with the directors of the bankrupt railroad to sign a final agreement forcing them out and taking it over. [*A look of bitter self-disgust comes to his face.*] Damned hog and fool that I was!

SARA [*with a deep breath of relief*]   So that's the last you remember! [*then quickly*] Ah, don't be blamin' yourself, Darlin'. That was all my fault. I was always egging you on. I was never content. Nothing would do me but you must become a Napoleon of business. It was me was the greedy fool, Darlin'. With my dream I got from my father's boasting lies that I ought to rise above myself and own a great estate. But that's dead and gone and I'm cured of it, so don't worry.

SIMON [*obviously comforted by this—protests weakly*] No, you're not to blame. I had the same greedy streak in me. [*then almost accusingly*] But it was true you were the inspiration. I was so afraid you couldn't be proud of me unless I kept on—

SARA Ah, don't talk. I'm prouder of you now you're all mine again than ever I've been since the day I first met you. [*She kisses him tenderly.*] But now tell me what else you remember of that day.

SIMON [*frowning*] I remember you came in. I was surprised because you hadn't been there for a long time.

SARA [*stares at him*] Ah.

SIMON [*forcing a smile*] You had seemed to become entirely wrapped up in the children and to have forgotten me. I confess I felt a bit jealous. So what was my delight to have you tell me you felt guilty for neglecting me, and lonely, too, and you wanted us to be again as close as we were in the old days, and you asked if I'd give you the job of my confidential secretary.

SARA [*gives him a strange look—slowly*] Ah, you remember I asked you that, do you?

SIMON [*with a smile*] Yes, I remember it distinctly, and how happy it made me.

SARA [*forcing a laugh*] Well, God be praised. You're well again when you can remember that so clearly.

SIMON [*uneasily again*] But—I can't remember a thing after that. How long ago was that Sara?

SARA [*hesitating apprehensively*] Well, maybe longer than you'd think. Only bear in mind it's only natural, the doctors say, that with brain fever you forget not only the time you're sick but a long time before it—sometimes years. [*She hesitates—then blurts out.*] That day at the office was five years ago.

SIMON [*frightenedly*] Five years! Good God!

SARA [*hastily*] Now, now! Don't be worried! I'm telling you the truth when I say there's nothing in those years you'd miss remembering if you knew.

SIMON [*excitedly*] I must know everything, Sara. All that happened!

SARA [*with an evasive teasing tone*] You're a great one for asking to know everything and have all, aren't you? But my memory's not that good. I've forgotten a lot since I brought you here on the farm to get well—here where the spell of the sun and the earth is in me and life is clear and simple. And right now with you in your right senses and me in mine, it's hard to remember it ever happened, except as a dream in my mind, a nightmare. [*As he stirs uneasily, she forces a joking tone.*] But what I remember clear as day is the one important thing, that you and I kept as much in love as ever, and more than ever! You're glad to hear that, I hope.

SIMON [*smiling tenderly*] I know that without remembering, Dear. Nothing could ever change that.

SARA No, it couldn't. And nothing ever will. Another thing worth remembering is that your sons grew into the fine lads they are now, that you can be proud of.

SIMON I am, Sara. I was so proud of them today in the field when I first—awakened from my nightmare—and saw them. [*then excitedly*] But what else? Tell me! The Company? Do I have to go back?

SARA [*with a certain savage satisfaction and at the same time bitterness*] Ah, don't let the damned old Company bother you. It went bankrupt and the creditors stripped us clean. We've not a thing in the world except this farm. We're as poor as Job's turkey. You're free as you always wanted to be in your heart. We're back where we started with only our love for riches! [*hastily*] And it's more than enough! It's the greatest treasure in the world!

SIMON [*stares before him—with a dreamy exultance*] Yes, it is, Sara. Love! Freedom from greed! This is a happy awakening for me, Sara. I confess I always hoped something would turn up to release me from the soul-destroying compulsion to keep on enslaving myself with more and more power and possessions.

SARA [*smiling tenderly—but with an undercurrent of pitying scorn for his weakness*] Don't I know it? I could almost hear your heart dreaming it at times.

SIMON That's why I gambled as I did. But my cursed luck kept me winning when I wanted to lose. Many a time I was tempted to deliberately ruin the Company. But I was afraid you would think me a coward and never forgive me.

SARA [*roughly tender*] Then get that idea out of your head right now. Don't have it in our new life that's beginning. It shows how little you know me. If you'd read my heart, as I'd read yours, you'd seen I wanted to be free as much as you.

SIMON [*gratefully—kissing her hand*] Sweetheart! Forgive me! What a fool I was! If I'd known—

SARA [*proudly*] And I proved it! It was I who smashed it! Oh, it couldn't have gone on long after you took sick. But I didn't wait. I used old Tenard to do it for me. You'd have laughed to see the crafty way I fooled him. I'd learned a lot about men from you, working in your office, and watching the fools come in and try to hide their greed and fear and the price tag of their souls hanging in their eyes!

SIMON [*bewilderedly*] Tenard? The banker? What had he to do?

SARA You took his bank from him.

SIMON I? But what did I want with his bank? Good God, wasn't I burdened enough already?

SARA You wanted to give it to me because I wanted it. You don't know how greedy I get. Haven't I told you I egged you on? I alone was to blame. You did everything for love of me.

SIMON [*eagerly*] Yes, now that you've said it yourself, that is the real truth of it, Sara.

SARA [*a bit mockingly*] It is. It's the best excuse in the world for you. So forgive yourself, do you hear? And I'll make up to you by doing everything I can for the rest of life to keep you free and happy.

SIMON Oh, I know I'll be happy now, Sara. I never really wanted to leave here, you know. It was a great mistake your insisting I go into business. Because I was bound to fail in the end. It really isn't in me to succeed. It's a damned sordid hog's game.

SARA I know, Darling. You're a gentleman and a poet at heart, and a lost child in a world of strangers. I'll never ask you to succeed again. With the boys helping me you'll have a living here, at least, and you needn't ever lift your hand. You can be in your dream of a world free of greed where men are good, and write the books you planned here in the old days. And maybe write a poem of your love for me once in a while, as you used. And there will be a song of happiness in my heart, knowing you're happy, even when I'm digging praties in the field, with my bare feet in the earth like a poor ignorant bog-trotter. [*She starts—then adds proudly.*] I mean, like the common woman I am, and my mother was, whose one pride is love.

SIMON [*pats her hand tenderly*] You're the finest woman on earth. [*then weakly, even reluctantly assertive*] But don't think I will spend all my time on my back writing poetry. I can do my share of work in the fields. Of course, I'm too weak now. But later I'll be strong—

SARA [*bullying him*] You won't. You've done enough. You'll do as I say! You're mine, now!

SIMON [*gratefully—resting his head on her breast*] Yes, yours, Sweetheart. Everything in and of me yours! That is my heart's whole desire now! [*again weakly assertive*] But don't think I'll let you and the boys support me. I'll at least do enough work on the farm to earn—

SARA Oh, an hour now and again, for the exercise, like a gentleman's hobby. I'll let you do that. But it will be a long time before you're strong enough. So rest now and don't think of it, but be at peace. [*She cuddles his head against her. He closes his eyes.*]

SIMON [*vaguely and drowsily*] I seem to remember I tried to find relaxation from the grinding daily slavery to the Company by engaging my mind in some study of the duality of man's nature. Did I, Sara, or is that just a dream?

SARA [*uneasily*] Just a dream, Darling. You were too worried about business to have time. Anyway, you've got too much sense to waste thought trying to solve the old puzzle of life that there's no answer to, except an answer of death that's no comfort except to those who have lost love.

SIMON [*vaguely*] No, it's silly. There's no duality in me, I know. At least, not now.

SARA [*after a pause—unwillingly as though her conscience forced her to speak*] There's something you haven't asked me—about your mother.

SIMON [*vaguely and drowsily—and indifferently*] That's true, I had forgotten. But I think the reason is I have a feeling that Mother is dead. She is, isn't she?

SARA [*blurts out*] Yes. She's dead.

SIMON [*indifferently*] I think I can picture what the rest of her life was without your telling me. I remember what a doting, contented old grandmother she had become. I imagine she grew more and more wrapped up in the children, and more at peace with herself, and was quite happy and reconciled to life—and to death—by the time she died. Isn't that true?

SARA [*tensely*] Yes. That's what happened to her. Exactly.

SIMON [*indifferently*] I'm glad. All that Mother ever needed was some unselfish interest that would take her away from her childish daydreaming and give her the courage to live in reality. It was fortunate for her you were generous enough to give her the opportunity by sharing the children with her and becoming her close friend—I remember how grateful she was to you. I hope she remained so to the end.

SARA [*tensely*] I—I'm grateful to her.

SIMON [*drowsily*] I remember it was such a pleasure to me to find you two get on together so well. I had been afraid— But why speak of that now, when it all worked out so happily. [*Sara smiles a twisted bitter smile over his head.*] I was glad for her own sake, particularly. Your friendship meant so much to her. Poor Mother, she was always such a lonely, isolated woman.

SARA She was, and she was proud to be, no matter what it cost her. She was a great lady.

SIMON [*as if something in her voice frightened him—uneasily*] She—Mother *was* happy when she died, wasn't she? Wasn't she, Sara?

SARA [*tensely*] No woman could be happier. She had all the love her heart dreamed of. [*then hastily*] But don't think of the dead, Darling. It's bad luck with our new life starting. Think only of me, and my love for you, and that you're safe and at peace in it, at last!

SIMON [*drowsily smiling*] I am only too glad to, Sweetheart. That's all—I ever want to remember. [*a pause—more drowsily*] I feel so sleepy. Your breast is so soft and warm—forgive if I— [*He falls asleep.*]

SARA [*stares down at his face with a fierce, brooding tenderness—then speaks to herself with a strange intermixture of maternal admiration and pride, and a bitter resentment*] Ah, sleep, my Darlin'. Sleep on my breast. It's yours like the heart beating inside it! Rest in peace. You're home at last where you've always wanted to be. I'm your mother now, too. You've everything you need from life in me! [*She chuckles to herself bitterly and admiring.*] But ain't you the craftiest, greediest man that ever walked the earth, God forgive you, to keep on and never let anybody beat you, not even yourself, but make life give you your own stubborn way in the end! But don't think I'm complaining, for your way is my way! Yes, I've made even that mine, now! [*She laughs softly with a strange gaiety. The four boys enter from the path at left, on their way to the lake, led by Ethan and Wolfe. The two latter look the same as in Act Three, Scene Two, except that Ethan is taller and heavier, and Wolfe taller and still slender. As their eyes fall on their father and mother, they are all embarrassed, look away, and quicken their pace to hurry past them down the path to the lake off right. Sara speaks.*] SuSSH! Quiet now. He's asleep. [*They disappear off right. Her eyes follow them. She speaks aloud to herself dreamily, her thoughts with her sons now—proudly*] Fine boys, each of them! No woman on earth has finer sons! Strong in body and with brains, too! Each with a stubborn will of his own! Leave it to them to take what they want from life, once they're men! This little scrub of a farm won't hold them long! Ethan, now, he'll own his fleet of ships! And Wolfe will have his banks! And Johnny his railroads! And Honey be in the White House before he stops, maybe! And each of them will have wealth and power and a grand estate— [*She stops abruptly and guiltily—self-defiantly*] No! To hell with your mad dreams, Sara Melody! That's dead and done! You'll keep your hands off them if you have to cut them off to do it! You'll let them be what they want to be, if it's a tramp in rags without a penny, with no estate but a ditch by the road, so long as they're happy! You'll leave them free, do you hear, and yourself free of them! [*She looks down at Simon's sleeping face on her breast—with a brooding, possessive, tender smile*] After all, one slave is enough for any woman to be owned by! Isn't it true, my Darling? [*She laughs with a gloating, loving, proud, self-mockery—then bends and kisses him softly so as not to awaken him.*]

* * * CURTAIN * * *

Tao House
Sept. 8th '38

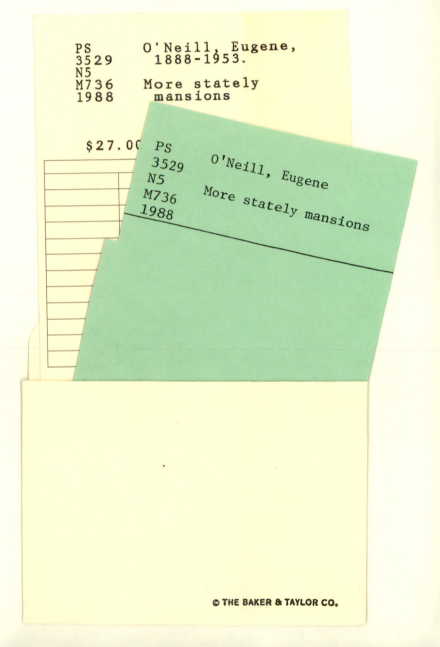

PS
3529
N5
M736
1988

O'Neill, Eugene,
  1888-1953.

More stately
  mansions

$27.00

PS
3529
N5
M736
1988

O'Neill, Eugene

More stately mansions